ORDINARY PEOPLE WHO AREN'T

AN ANTHOLOGY

By CHARLES A. WELLS, JR.

Also by Charles A. Wells, Jr.
Nude Nuns and Other Peculiar People

ORDINARY PEOPLE WHO AREN'T
AN ANTHOLOGY

CHARLES A. WELLS, JR.

Periwinkle Princess Press
First Edition
Sanibel, FL

Printed in the U.S.A.

PHOTOS:
Various by the author, Cory Bettinger, Colonel Robert 'Carrot' Foltyn, Howard Haynes, Art Ditto, and Richard Hoener, Nevin Waters

Design by Frank M. Addington

ISBN: 978-0-9975331-0-1

DEDICATION

To Wylie Bettinger

1986 - 2015

He lived a beautiful life

"Hardship prepares ordinary people for an extraordinary destiny."

Maya Angelou

PROLOGUE

The town of Winfield, Kansas doubles in population for four days each September as bluegrass enthusiasts assemble in the tree-lined fairgrounds nestled in the oxbow of the Walnut River. Tractors collect day-trippers from the parking lots, where the sounds of fiddles, banjos, and mandolins resonate. Four stages at the Cowley County Fairgrounds offer nonstop performances from 9 am until after midnight. Thirty-four acts are staggered throughout the weekend along with amateurs vying for top honors in one of seven contests. Dozens of campground jam sessions proffer opportunities for players of all abilities. The abundance of unheralded, but gifted musicians, amazed and entertained. The crowd was festive, and, apparently in tribute to recent World Series appearances, those wearing Kansas City Royal's attire outnumbered those with tee-shirts proclaiming, "Paddle Faster I Hear Banjo."

While rushing from one venue to another, I noticed a pretty young woman in a wheel chair with canted wheels like those used by athletes. I didn't want to stare, but I did steal a glance. She had a little girl, about three, sitting in her lap, but she didn't have a lap. She had no legs and only a vestige of stubs. Whatever the origins of her misfortune, she carried herself with a quiet dignity, and one couldn't help but admire her grit. And Judy and I continued on our way to the mountain dulcimer contest.

Later, we were sitting in the Stage III bleachers awaiting the performance of a Scottish band, The Tannahill Weavers, as they were setting up. My mind wandered aimlessly wherein I pondered that the Winfield High School teams should have been named the Wipers. What a missed opportunity! Then I saw something that touched me to my core. The young lady who earlier caught my attention was wheeling our way, once again with the little girl sitting in front of her.

It had rained hard earlier in the afternoon. As the young woman's wheelchair reached a grassy surface, the wheels slipped and began to sink into the soft earth. Then the little girl hopped off and started running forward but immediately circled around, gaining momentum, and crashed into the back of her Mother's wheelchair. She was consciously building up speed to insure she would be of the greatest assistance. It appeared the little tyke had done this before. Together they managed to reach drier ground and settled in for the rousing performance featuring pipes, fife, fiddle, and four strong voices.

A second woman, also legless and wheel chair bound, presumably her identical twin, then joined the two.

And I was reminded of the ancient proverb, "I cried because I had no shoes, and then I met a man who had no feet."

I collect stories. With few exceptions, I conduct my daily affairs disguised as an old white guy wearing khaki trousers with pleats and a non-descript blue oxford cloth shirt. This renders me virtually invisible, a useful trait for one predisposed to observation and listening. It's a given that most people would rather talk than listen, creating an unbalance not unlike the phenomena experienced by aspiring writers: too many writers, not enough readers. This does however provide a terrific opportunity for learning and entertainment for those with a modicum of patience.

I recently encountered a lady whose occupation/avocation is ghostwriting memoirs for people. She explained, "I believe that everyone has interesting stories. Not everyone is inclined to write them down. So I assist." I hope the reader will agree that the stories that follow are a testament to her premise.

If you were to encounter those portrayed herein in everyday life, you'd most likely look past them with nary a glance. You may or may not notice an older man slightly overweight with glasses and a hearing aid, or a thin young man with red hair and jaundiced skin, or a waiter who greets you in a friendly manner, or a small town doctor, a gas station attendant, and so on. I regret not learning more about the legless twins. I've thought of them often, and in my imagination I want to believe that they are living their difficult lives with grace and dignity. But there are others about whom, I've learned more. This anthology attempts to introduce the reader to just a few amongst the millions of ordinary people who aren't.

Thanks to all the people who shared their stories with me including: Benjamin Anderson, Peg Armstrong, Cory Bettinger, Friends of Wylie Bettinger, Fred and Philip Coulson, Art Ditto, Bob Fay, Bob Foltyn, John Fontenot, Bill Harris, Howard Haynes,

Richard Hoener, Paul Hopkins, Mark Johnson, Steve Lacey, Phil Love, Mark and David Martin, Randy Miller, Jane Priest, Johnny Roney, Jim Sneed, Patrick Van Hoorebeek, Tom Ward, Judy Wells, Mike Williams, and many others. A special thanks to my volunteer editors: June Padgett, Scott Giffen, Judy Wells, and Bill Wells. Thanks to the many excellent teachers from whom I have learned, both in school and in life.

In assembling these stories my travels have taken me to Arizona, Washington, Tennessee, Alabama, Florida, Mexico, Colorado, New Orleans, Missouri, and Kansas. My work with community hospitals around the country has proven fruitful in introducing me to many of the characters in this book. I like people, the quirkier the better, and I find them interesting. I can only hope that readers enjoy meeting the characters in this book as much as I have.

All errors of omission or commission are mine alone. Some of the stories involve people behaving poorly. In those instances, I've used pseudonyms with the convention of placing an asterisk following the first use of a name or place.

CONTENTS

CHAPTER 1

Wylie

1986 - 2015

"The flame that burns twice as bright
burns half as long."

Lao Tzu, *Te Tao Ching*

Wylie's illness made it impossible for him to sit quietly for any period of time, making school difficult. Many of his teachers lacked even a molecule of empathy making matters worse, but he didn't take it passively. It could truthfully be said, in teacher-speak, he 'acted out' often. In fifth grade he organized a strike against the teacher that would not allow him to run for class office. In junior high art class he was assigned a project to draw a cartoon. He drew an Al Hirschfeld-like (New Yorker fame) caricature that was impressively sophisticated. But in tiny, almost imperceptibly small, letters he wrote 'eat shit' in the eyes. His teacher first displayed the remarkable piece in a place of prominence. An alert classmate pointed out the epithet causing riotous guffaws amongst the adolescents and anger from the teacher. She destroyed his work of art and banished Wylie to the furnace room to spend the rest of the day with the janitor. This turned out well for both Wylie and the custodian, as they became fast friends. John Cougar Mellencamp sang it, but Wylie lived it, "I fight authority, authority always wins."

Wylie's Honey Brews, headquartered in Ashland, Oregon grew out of his quest to benefit himself and others with a tasty, healthy, Jun honey drink. Wylie invented and tested his recipes, perfected his fermenting and production techniques, obtained necessary state and local approvals and licenses, developed artistic and imaginative marketing materials, hired workers, and quickly built a loyal following. It was unusual for a young man who had chosen an alternative life style, but he was a gifted entrepreneur.

Shortly before his death he signed a three-year lease for expanded space, bought a new labeling machine, upgraded the printing for his labels, added three new flavors (Tulsi, Rose-Lavender, and Birch), and engaged a distributor expanding his reach to stores from Portland to Northern California, including New Seasons Markets, the regional equivalent to Whole Foods. Bottles of Wylie's Turmeric, Ginger, and Root Beer had some how found their way into a Whole Foods store in NYC. His next major project was the installation of an automated bottling line. It was clear from recent business decisions that his plans didn't include dying. Wylie's Honey Brews was poised to take off like a rocket.

One of Wylie's closest friends, Michael, is a Native American man in his 40's, ruggedly handsome with a wispy beard and moustache. They shared many common interests as members of the Red Earth Descendants, and they sang and drummed in the same longhouse group, an eclectic group of native and non-native Americans who once performed before the Dalai Lama. At Wylie's memorial service in Ashland, Michael told how they met shortly after Wylie arrived in Ashland. "A group of Native Americans were playing stick ball, a form of lacrosse, in the park. It's a pretty rough game, and this small red haired boy was sitting nearby watching. I would later learn he had recently recovered from a bicycle accident where he suffered a spiral compound fracture in his leg. He asked if he could play, we said 'sure', and he's been part of the Red Earth Descendants ever since."

Michael, continued, "I've known several tough Native American men who were terribly racist. They hate whites passionately, but they loved Wylie. They learned so much from him, and he learned from them. He had the ability to relate to a wide range of people. I've never met anyone who better bridged the gap between natives and non-natives. He would approach a homeless man the same way he would a rich man. He would be respectful and listen with sincere empathy.

"Wylie is a minor celebrity in Ashland. People in Eugene also know of him. He has an almost mystic quality that enables him to connect to people from all walks of life. He greeted every new person in his life as a friend. Perhaps because he didn't have a wife or children, it made him approachable to everyone, almost like a shaman."

THE CELEBRATION

Ashland is a town of about 20,000 located in the Rogue River Valley about 10 miles north of the California border. It is home to Oregon Southern University, the Oregon Shakespeare Festival, and a large, but transient, community of people once known as hippies. Wylie loved Ashland, and Ashland loved Wylie. Over 300 souls packed the Ashland community center adjacent to Lithia Park to celebrate his life. For one who trod the earth so lightly, he left large footprints.

Michael served as the informal master of ceremonies. Wylie had been warmly welcomed into the Native American community, and his celebration was conducted in a manner respectful of their traditions. Six singers sat around a large drum and opened with several Indian burial songs. Their leader spoke of how the next journey can take up to a year as the spirit winds its way to a new home by way of the Milky

Way. He explained that they wouldn't mention the departed by name, so as to not confuse the spirit world.

Two elders, both significant personages, spoke of their love for Wylie, Roy, the great grandson of Chief Joseph of the Nez Perce tribe and Eddie, the great grandson of Sitting Bull of the Lakota tribe. Family members were pleased but puzzled when Roy privately referred to Wylie as an elder. Roy explained that Wylie was wise beyond his years, and his departing spirit was now worthy of that tribute. Roy loved Wylie deeply, and Wylie often spoke of 'Uncle' with reverence. Michael explained that had Roy been in charge of the ceremony, there would have been 3-4 hours of songs not 3-4 songs. Michael told me, "After you meet Roy, go online and look at a picture of Chief Joseph. The resemblance is startling." He was spot on.

The room was built for 100 and there were chairs for 100, but the overflow crowd filled every inch of space. All listened intently and politely as friends of Wylie came forward to share stories. The Native singers / drummers finished with a few more songs, followed by a potluck dinner and sampling of Wylie Honey Brew beverages. Eighteen cases, three of each of his six flavors, were quickly devoured. Most of Wylie's worldly possessions were spread out on tables for attendees to take what they might need.

It was instructive to mix, listen and learn how people knew Wylie:

STELLA JANE

Stella was one of the people who spoke lovingly of Wylie during the celebration. She also spoke passionately of corn and how Wylie helped her plant and harvest the ornamental varieties that are important to Native Americans. She urged young people to take up the task as she is 70, and her knowledge must be passed on.

One doesn't really chat with Stella; one gets cornered. She holds some pretty radical views, but as long as the listener nods appreciatively, no one gets hurt. I asked her how she met Wylie.

"I live in a yellow school bus that I park near the Wellsprings Center. I farm a few rented acres nearby. It was a Christmas morning, and I heard a knock on my door, and it was Wylie and his sister Cory. I'd never seen him before in my life. He said, 'I don't know if you celebrate Christmas or not, but could we come in and share some of our tea?' We spent the rest of the afternoon together, and I've loved him ever since."

INFINITY

While waiting for the celebration to begin, I sat next to a tall, thin young man with crutches. He said his name was Infinity. When he stood up, I noticed he was missing a leg, and I would later learn that resulted from a motorcycle accident ten years earlier. His face, neck, and all visible parts of his body were covered in tattoos. We talked for some time giving me the chance to look at him carefully, but I could find no perceptible design or pattern for the markings. He had matching rings stuck in his lower lip, and his hair was cropped on the sides with a Mohawk-like band of long hair running across the top of his head. His manner of speaking reminded me of the Beau Bridges character, Dude, in the movie The Big Lebowski. Oddly, I looked more out of place at the gathering than did Infinity. He had just returned from the 'give away' table proudly displaying Wylie's former backpack, explaining how much he needed such an item. We introduced ourselves and chatted.

"Wylie and I were kindred spirits. I'd see him around town, and we'd visit and maybe share some of our possessions. He would always be interested in what and how I was doing. We were brothers."

When I asked him how he came to be known as Infinity he explained, "My name used to be Rex, but about a year ago I used that word in response to a question, and it didn't feel right. I believed that was a sign from God, or whatever moniker you choose for your spiritual father, and He told me to change my name. I looked at the tattoo of the infinity symbol on my left wrist, and I had just started a drug rehab service I dubbed Infinity, so I decided to call myself Infinity. My full name is now Infinity Ra El."

"Is that on your driver's license?"

"I don't have a driver's license."

JEANINE

"I visited Wylie when he first went into the hospital in Ashland. He took his briefcase and some work with him. In typical Wylie fashion, he insisted that we not tell anyone he was in the hospital. He called the day before he died to tell me that he loved me. The night after he passed I dreamt of Wylie dressed in a bright blue shirt with polka dots accompanied by an unrecognizable friend. He was skipping and happy. It was totally out of character for cynical Wylie. He was a friend to everyone, but he only let a few people get close to him."

HAWAII GUY

"I owned and operated a perma-culture organic farm in the Pangaia Region on the island of Hawaii, when I met Wylie. He was only about 15 or 16 at the time. He came as part of a Willing Workers on Organic Farms (WWOOF) group, and we became acquainted. I introduced him to the healing benefits of turmeric and ginger, my two primary crops. These ingredients would later form the basis of his two best selling sodas. Wylie was a sponge for information. He was willing to do whatever was necessary to learn more about everything.

"I moved to the Ashland area in 2004 continuing to farm turmeric and ginger. Serendipitously, Wylie came to the area, started Wylie Honey Brews and became one of my best customers."

BANJO MAN

An older man was sitting in the back of the hall holding a Deering Good Time banjo in his lap. He was wearing a Tyrolean style hat, a loose fitting, nearly ragged, wool sports coat, and dirty khaki shorts. A meaningful portion of his teeth were missing, and his fingernails were nearly one inch long, unusual for a banjo player. After the formal celebration, people were gathered on a nearby patio eating their potluck delights and drinking Wylie's beverages. Banjo guy was playing and singing accompanied by a pretty young girl with a percussion instrument. He had a raspy, but pleasing, voice. In between songs we chatted, and he explained the long fingernails noting he played only chords that could be fretted with the flat of his finger. Then he asked if I'd like to hear his version of Wylie's Honey Brews done to the tune of Bascom Lamar Lunford's Good Old Mountain Dew? It was pretty darn clever, and he boldly emphasized the critical phrase, 'Them that refuses are few.' It would have been the perfect theme for Wylie's ads.

OLDER WOMAN WITH
BERNIE SANDERS BUTTON

"Did Wylie dye his hair?"

After laughing, I replied, "No. Why do you ask?"

"I don't really know Wylie. I would see him around town, and he would greet me with a warm smile. I would see him leaving Tai Chi when I was going in, and he just seemed like a wonderful young man. When I read about his death in the paper, I thought I would just come and learn more about this wonderful spirit. But his bright red hair seemed to be a slightly different shade each time I'd see him."

I explained about his illness and how it affected his skin color and perhaps his hair coloring as well.

CULT BOY

A handsome young man laughed as he told the following story: "I was at a party and was apparently pontificating about some bull shit with a bevy of beauties hanging on every word. Afterwards, Wylie came up and chastised me for exhibiting cult-like behavior. I shrugged it off. Later that evening I encountered Wylie sitting cross-legged in the middle of a circle surrounded by chicks. He was speaking rapturously about acorns or some such shit. I pointed my finger at him and gave him the 'gotcha' look, and it was his turn to shrug."

A BUSINESS ASSOCIATE

"I was walking in Lithia Park when a commotion caught my eye. There was a grouping of deer surrounding something that I couldn't see. I was intrigued so I moved closer and saw Wylie in their midst performing meditative Tai Chi exercises. The deer were mesmerized."

A PRETTY YOUNG WOMAN

"I met Wylie ten years ago. I was having a bad day, so I walked down to Lithia Park. I saw Wylie sitting alone on a park bench. I didn't know him, but I felt comfortable joining him. I sat down, and we chatted, I felt better instantly, and we've been friends ever since."

ANOTHER PRETTY YOUNG WOMAN

"A group of us were living communally in a large house on Ohio Street. One day, Wylie showed up in his blue truck filled with 1,000 lbs of pears and a fruit press. He needed help juicing the load before he had to return the borrowed tool, and we all pitched in. It was hard work, but we've laughed about it forever and that's how we met Wylie. I also remember his fig phase. He planted over 100 fig trees along the area highways."

AND ANOTHER PRETTY YOUNG WOMAN

"He wanted his sodas to be perfect. I remember helping him in the early stages of fermenting and brewing his sodas. He'd bring them to my house to test taste, but they would mostly blow up when you'd twist off the cap. Everything was a huge mess, but he kept experimenting until he perfected his products. Later, Wylie would contribute sodas to every event we organized. I'd offer to pay, but he'd always decline."

A YOUNG MAN

"I didn't really know Wylie, but I knew of him. I figured there'd be a lot of hot chicks here."

WYLIE'S HOUSE

On Sunday morning family and friends again gathered at Wylie's house to help clean up and dispose of his remaining possessions. A 10-point buck stood in the midst of beehives situated in the apple orchard in Wylie's front yard. His back yard is shaded by large Douglas firs and pines and is bordered by Lithia Creek, a tributary of the Rogue River. Two bucks, a half dozen does, and an abundance of squirrels appear to have made the place their home. As we were about to leave, a large gray owl watched over us from a perch high in one of the trees. The owl waited until everyone came out from the house for a suitable viewing, and then it flew off. Wylie's rented property was a veritable Snow White scene, lacking only bluebirds holding a cape and singing *Hi Ho*.

Wylie loved bees. He once observed a swarm balled together at the top of a Douglas fir in his yard. He climbed to it, swatted it down to the ground and managed to get the swarm safely in a hive. He later found a queen and introduced it to his hive, repeated the process, and started producing his own honey, the principal ingredient for his honey brews. It was a sad moment when a knowledgeable beekeeper came to take Wylie's beloved hives.

Wylie's illness caused constant itching making rest difficult, and he rarely slept for more than a few hours at a time. He made the best of this bad situation by never allowing his mind to be idle. Wylie's possessions spoke volumes of his interests. He did not own a television or electronic games. He did own several guitars, mandolins, ukeleles, fifes, ceremonial drums, and thumb pianos. He played them all well, and he had a beautiful singing voice. His books were about oaks, acorns, plants, bees, herbs, spices, Native American culture, and philosophy. He had boxes of exotic spices and herbs with which he experimented seeking to continually improve Wylie Honey Brews. He left a collection of his beautiful fabric art creations and clever promotional items he designed to market his brews. His music assemblage consisted of artists totally unknown to his un-hip 70-year-old uncle. Most pronounced was the presence of baskets of acorns in varying states of processing to become flour. His outbuilding contained unique tools designed specifically for acorn processing.

A common theme was sincerely expressed, "He was always there for us. He was kind and gentle. We loved him so. He was an inspiration." But those were his acquaintances. There was also a very small group who really knew him and knew of his suffering. They knew he couldn't sleep and was in near constant pain. They knew he had forestalled death on several occasions, yet he still kept fighting. He used his limited energies to build a remarkable business, pursued his artistic and musical inclinations, was supremely curious, and stayed active in causes about which he was passionate. His inner circle saw him and knew him at his low points, when the steroids made him crazy, when the healthcare system attempted to rob him of his dignity, when the pain made him want to withdraw and quit, and when he felt all alone. And like his family, they loved him deeply.

But there is more to the story than the end.

Wylie was my sister Sally's son, and he had been seriously ill since he was 10 years old. He contracted ulcerative colitis making digestion difficult and was later diagnosed with primary sclerosing cholangitis, a chronic liver disease, presumably a consequence of the colitis. Progressive inflammation and scarring of the bile ducts prevents them from functioning properly causing constant itching as the waste seeks an outlet through the skin. Famed football player Walter Payton died of PSC at the age of 45. Living past the age of 30 is rare for anyone suffering from this ailment.

Wylie was handsome, and some might say he resembled a leprechaun. He had striking red hair as does his older sister Cory. When they were little, people would stop to stare and seek to touch their heads. Sally, a natural brunette, once dyed her hair a matching color in order to forestall the inevitable and annoying queries, "Where did those children get that red hair?"

Wylie was never able to enjoy a "normal" childhood, whatever that might conjure in peoples' minds. Even as a little kid it was apparent he was quick witted and spiritually gifted. He possessed a Siddhartha-like stoicism and calmness, as well as a dry and sharp sense of humor. He read people well and found goodness even in those who tormented him. More than a few knuckleheads posing as teachers mistook his inability to sit for long periods of time as a deficiency they could remedy through mockery and punishment. He tolerated this ordeal with uncommon grace, bearing them no lasting ill will.

He had a knack for making the best of a bad situation. Wylie's troubles at school eventually got him placed in an 'alternative academy' that essentially served as a warehouse for adolescents. The good news was they let the kids leave early most days. Wylie used his abundant free time to ride his bike the short distance to visit his maternal grandmother at her independent living community. Helen was then in her 80's, she had once been an auburn haired beauty, and, aided by weekly trips to the beauty parlor, maintained her coiffure in a reddish tint not seen anywhere else in nature. Her status within her small community was enhanced immeasurably by the frequent visits from her adorable and uncommonly charming, when he wanted to be, 13-year-old, red haired grandson.

But Wylie's body could not tolerate the extreme weather of his hometown, Kansas City, so at age 15 he joined his sister Cory, then a sophomore in college in Santa Cruz, California. He lived in a garden shed behind Cory's dorm and worked at the university farms, and Cory introduced him to her college community.

From there Wylie moved to the island of Hawaii and worked in a communal farming compound. He experimented with varying diets and lifestyles in search of relief from pain and enjoyed some commercial success in Hawaii, buying and selling undeveloped land. Wylie next moved to the north coast of the south island of New Zealand, spent a year, but eventually tired of the isolation.

Then he learned of Ashland from friends. This reunited him with his sister Cory, who was living in Portland, four-hours drive away. Ashland's climate was moderate, and Wylie found a welcoming environment of likeminded individuals. He rented a small A-frame house situated on a wooded lot adjacent to a bubbling brook in which he immersed himself seeking temporary respite from his itching.

He was often jaundiced, and as one of his friends eloquently remembered, "He wore a yellow suit put on by an unworthy liver." He managed his disease through an extreme diet consisting primarily of raw foods. He chuckled as he recalled attending a potluck dinner with vegans who had to expand their guest list to include raw-foodists in order to attract sufficient numbers.

Conventional western medicine maintains that a liver transplant is the only treatment for PSC. For years Wylie resisted this course of action. He studied the pros and cons thoroughly, as anyone in his shoes might. His early years of being probed and prodded, with little benefit, by an array of 'ologists' made him skeptical of conventional medicine. He once shared that he didn't feel comfortable with the general idea of organ transplantation or with the specific idea of being tethered to anti-rejection drugs for the remainder of his life. He believed he could contain the disease through a natural diet and stress avoidance techniques. He was justifiably confident that he possessed the internal discipline to manage a unique and difficult lifestyle.

He tolerated the well meaning, but unsolicited, advice from numerous family and friends about a transplant, "Get a transplant as soon as possible. Waiting increases the chance of the introduction of cancer into your body at which time a transplant is no longer possible." During one of Wylie's visits to Kansas City, family members were introduced to the concept of the MELD (model for end stage liver disease) score. MELD scores calibrate the probability of death in the next ninety days: 40+ = 72% mortality; 30-39 = 52% mortality; and 20-29 = 20% mortality. During that visit Wylie underwent testing at the Kansas University Hospital, the primary liver transplant center in the Kansas City region, and his score was 23, then the minimum to qualify for a transplant.

Wylie continued to resist the idea of a transplant until the spring of 2012 when he made the agonizing decision that it was time. The transplant started on Monday night August 13, 2012 and was completed the following day.

WYLIE'S HONEY BREWS

In the months that followed his transplant, Wylie devoted much of his new 'lease on life' to Wylie's Honey Brews. This story is best told in Wylie's own words, when he subsequently assembled a prospectus for a community public offering to raise $100,000 to expand his business.

"I started working with live probiotic cultures at the age of 15.

I have been highly motivated by agriculture and natural foods after receiving a life changing diagnosis of an autoimmune illness called Primary Scherosing Cholangitis. This has required me to be extremely diligent with food and lifestyle but also allowed me the clarity to pursue my true passions instead of continuing my high school education.

"Throughout the past twelve years, I have been lucky to live on countless farms, cooperatives, and international communities. Many of these were hotspots for alternative diets and accommodated others recovering from serious 'incurable' illness. I eventually landed in Ashland, finding a great community that shares many of the same values of sustainability, natural healing, and environmental advocacy.

"Ten years ago I was an apprentice at a perma-culture farm in Hawaii. While working hard under the hot sun, I often enjoyed a beverage that was made purely from fresh pressed ginger juice, honey, and water. My friend, the brewer, was able to make a brew that was overwhelmingly pungent and would burn your throat, yet it had a unique grab and natural sweetness that kept me drinking more. I compared this drink to the high-fructose-corn-syrup-infused beverages that fill the shelves of grocery stores and concluded that the beneficial properties of ginger could be the basis for a drink I could create. I wanted a root beer that would be sweetened with raw quality honey, flavored with whole spices and herbs, while also preserving the enzymatic benefits of honey.

"Through countless trials of home brewing, with me as the insatiable critic, I came upon the 'Jun Culture' as the best probiotic to ferment and carbonate the honey sodas. Jun is a lesser known relative of Kombucha that thrives off of honey rather than sugar. Its origins lie in the complex fermented food cultures of central Asia. Jun had a positive effect on the flavor profile while also increasing the stability and consistency of the ferment. I wasn't getting the lag associated with disaccharide sweeteners, and the herbs in each brew were viscerally tangible. Thus I was getting closer to having the functional beverages I desired."

"Wylie's Honey Brews incorporated in November 2012 and hit the shelves a month later starting with two flavors, Turmeric and Ginger. The sodas were immediately received with enthusiasm. The growing loyalty of our customer base enabled incremental up-scaling with increased internal cash flow. Within three months, and with the help of a distributor, our product reach extended north to Eugene and south to Mount Shasta, California. We received positive press and were highlighted by our local channel ten news for their 'Sustainable Table' segment. Within our first year, we were able to easily sell our entire production capacity.

"Our mission is to create the highest quality beverages that result in an appreciation of the beauty of food and flavor, as well as create awareness of the issues that threaten our environment and the food supply system. To do this, we've created a line of six high quality artisan honey sodas with the finest ingredients.

"We believe we can nourish and promote a healthy human and bee population by sourcing high quality honey from beekeepers that use non-synthetic pesticides. By supporting beekeepers that consider the environment, we are effectively improving the quality of our food systems all while creating delicious beverages that people love.

"Wylie's Artisan Honey Sodas use the finest quality ingredients and brewing techniques to create a genuinely wholesome soda. Sweetened with unheated raw honey, our sodas are delicious while harnessing the benefits of herbs and live enzyme cultures.

Author's note: Wylie's prospectus and business plan would have done justice to the work of any Harvard MBA. Mighty impressive for a 28-year-old whose formal education ended in ninth grade, living with a borrowed liver and on borrowed time.

RETURN OF HEALTH PROBLEMS

Lamentably Wylie's health problems returned a year after the transplant. He had a hard life, but he never expressed resentment for the things he couldn't enjoy, i.e. a pain free day, a long-term relationship, or the dream of a brighter future. His life force was spent at 9:34 am PST Saturday November 28, 2015.

Wylie was a spiritual man, but not religious. I believe he would forgive the use of the following Bible verse from the Old Testament that aptly describes his approach to life.

"Do justice, love kindness, walk humbly with your God"
Micah 6:8.

POSTSCRIPT

Chaucer gave his highest praise among the assembled pilgrims to the Oxford clerk, who was a student of philosophy. Chaucer described that thin, serious young man as one who "would gladly learn and gladly teach", traits that are rarely found in tandem. Wylie would gladly learn and gladly teach the mysteries of our natural world that interested him so greatly, perhaps explaining his harmony with the native Indian community and the animal kingdom.

To gain a further appreciation of Wylie's short but remarkable life, peruse the following sampling of excerpted comments placed on Facebook by those whose lives he touched.

BEN TOSCHER

I remember the man as one of the bees he loved and cared for so much: fastidious, industrious, strong, and a seeker of truth and beauty. What's more true to life than the syncopated invitation of pollen? I was reciting poems on the corner in the summer of 2011. Wylie used to come by frequently. "How about a poem about oaks," he'd ask, "or how about rhubarb," or "got a rhyme about reason?" He'd sneak in, displaying a subtle and brilliant wit that I'd come to appreciate over the years. Whether the afternoon heat was oppressive, whether his body was suffering, and he wore a yellow suit put on by an unworthy liver, Wylie was always present. Attentive. He saw me. And I tried to see him. Without fail, his generosity was always marked. I was living poem to mouth, and he'd donate an Abraham Lincoln, a green cinco, for a string of fleeting rhyming words.

In a funny way, humility might be one of the truest mirrors in the world. Through observation of his humble dedication to his work and product, I was humbled. He frequently spoke to the privileged position he was in as a business owner, and through that channel being a proponent of food justice, quality ingredients, and the elegant simplicity of brewing. I see the outpouring of love, reflection, kind words, and can't help but view Wylie Bettinger as one of those bees he revered, pollinating the minds, hearts, and mouths of those he met in this life, leaving us this big sweet pot of honey we call memory.

KENNY CHADBOURNE

Oh Wylie, my little acorn brother. My heart is sad and I am crying, not for you because I know you are in a truly wonderful place, but for me. I am going to really miss you. It seems to me that you were one of only a few who truly understood the songs of the acorn, her magic and her true purpose. I will miss our little moments talking about acorns and how magnificent they are. From this day forward, I will honor your life and your true and loving heart by seeing your spirit in the Oak Tree and her little children the acorns. You will live on in her seeds and her food. You were an Angel here, and you are an Angel there. Your life here was a blessing to all who were touched by your presence. Dance on little brother.

Somehow I knew that a soul as brilliant and unique as Wylie's was not meant to last for long in this world. His wise, old soul burned brightly and shone light upon so many. He was often cynical but, nevertheless, lived the best life he could educating himself and others, nourishing the land and his community. I count myself lucky to learn from him and loved him.

Some memories that I hope will never fade:

- Cracking acorns next to the fire during potlucks on Ohio St, in the back of his truck, wherever... such a meditative practice using two stones and bare hands... the gift of a skill that is centuries old.

- Fasting on Thanksgiving Day 2010 (after a feast the night before) with Benji & Carys and walking to Wylie's house to have tea. It was such a peaceful day spent in good company.

- Working with Wylie in Phoenix (Oregon) stirring honey, brewing, bottling, labeling, and packaging honey brews. His integrity for providing nourishing drinks, with no room for shortcuts, could never be surpassed. Selling them at the Tuesday Ashland market was a privilege and a joy. I'll never forget the loyal customers and the 3 year olds who loved the turmeric sodas!

- Hearing Wylie chant in the sauna at the Wellsprings.

- The gift of a ukulele to "borrow" for years if I promised to play it. I used to walk around Ashland strumming on it, not playing anything in particular. I will keep strumming in his memory.

- A hand-drawn feather that he gifted me on my birthday. It has been the cover of my poetry journal for years; his spirit was definitely as inspiration for some of my writing.

- Finding Wylie at Mix drinking tea and working on his business. I could always sit down and chat with him, no matter how much he had to do at the moment. Time didn't matter with friends.

TYE AUSTIN

We often went hiking, biking, or rock-hopping through the fairy ponds in Lithia Creek. We always inspired each other to reach our highest potential. We started off as hippie kids with a dream and turned into entrepreneurial businessmen who seized fate by the throat, recharted the stars, and manifested our own destiny and legacy. When I visited home last summer, Wylie was one of my only friends who seemed genuinely excited to see me again. He had such a kind heart and we shared a deep respect for each other. I'll always have fond memories of us attending potlucks, playing music, chillin' in the hot springs and imitating the weird hippie chants in the sauna, or hanging out at his soda shop where he brewed herbal and sugar-free sodas. Wylie was well-researched and well-informed about most important things in life. He was always identifying edible plants, researching Native-American and other cultural traditions, and harvesting more acorns than squirrels every autumn. His house always had boxes upon boxes of acorns! His passing still feels incredibly surreal and the weight of depression seems to be momentarily suspended between denial and reality. It will be tough to return to Ashland without his strong and engaging community presence. He will be sorely missed and I hope the Ashland community can heal from this tragic loss. I love you, Wylie Bettinger! I wish I would have told you in person when I had the chance, but something tells me I didn't have to. Rest well, my friend.

COREY EYMANN

This morning I learned that the world just lost the most brilliant mind and soul I have ever had the pleasure of knowing. One of the fondest memories I have of my time with him growing up was the great ice storm of 2002, schools were closed, everyone's power was out, I went to his house to stay the night, where he taught me how to make a portable stove out of candle wax, cardboard and a coffee tin. We then used it to make scrambled eggs in his backyard while tree branches were snapping and falling to the ground around us. You will be missed but never forgotten. Be with mother earth friend.

MITRA STICKLEN

I feel mighty oak-textured gratitude love for Wylie, our brother. I met Wylie at the farmer's market just weeks after moving to Southern Oregon. I was working at Wagon Trail Gardens selling plants, and he came over and asked me about the white sage. We spoke for a while about magical healing plants, and he told me about his magical healing sodas. Week after week, we would talk fermentation and plants and foraging and cultivation and humanity and poetry and politics and pain. After months of farmer's market friendship, we started hanging out 'in real life', walking in Lithia park and stopping to touch and discuss his favorite trees (I think now that he was introducing me to his plant family here in town). He was so brilliant and had such a sharp, dry sense of humor that he often went over peoples' heads. Cracked me up like an acorn! Wylie was a fire keeper, and we talked about fire and water often. I thought of him while lighting the first fires this autumn, and thought of his passion for fire and slow care. We shared a love for the mighty oak. He asked me for stories of oaks I grew up with in Michigan, and he told me ancient stories of oak lore, so many interesting beautiful stories, that he had gathered from friends and so many books from all over the world. He inspired me, and everyone lucky enough to know him, and he nourished thousands more people than he ever met in person with his healing beverages. I will always hold a fire for Wylie. Thanks for the lessons and the joy and the sharing of sweet life

NICOLE BRADY

What a light in our sweet little Ashland community. I love you Wylie. You will always hold a special place in my Heart. I was blessed to get to be roomies with you twice, immersed in your pure sweetness, and unique creativity and passions in the forms of sewing, hearing your original songs on guitar, singing your Native American pow-wow sounds with wild abandon, community action gatherings, and grating acorns for flour. You taught me how to make my first lavender bundles in a meditative state of brother and sisterhood camaraderie on the front steps. And you loved my dog, Hayley, like she was your very own. I felt peaceful around you and happy.

I am inspired to fill my life with more amazing Souls like you. May your next adventures, in your new life in the other world, be filled with the most abundant and prosperous blessings beyond your wildest dreams!!!!!!

LUMIN EGRESS

Damn I miss Wylie so much that my whole body is on fire and I got a constant stream of tears and snot running down my face. But I'm happy because I know he had an amazing life. Our Ohio Street house was a place Wylie really loved. While he didn't technically live there he was around every day, sleeping in the hammock or messing around with acorns in the living room. On summer days he would pull up in his truck in a cloud of dust as we whooped and hollered at him from the porch.

The days we lived were long and full. We built greenhouses and huts in the backyard, we gardened all day and listened to cassette tapes. We raised chickens and built coops and all other kinds of weird things that disturbed our well-to-do neighbors. When it got dark we would have potlucks and play music late into the night.

Wylie was always there, and eventually he moved across the street. He had an interesting way of being everywhere at once. I remember saying to him one night, "I don't know about you but each day here feels like a whole life time." He agreed. Each day somehow felt eternal and complete. The Tidings should have written a front-page article titled, "A group of kids living in a dilapidated farm house on Ohio St. have found nirvana."

Some days Wylie would come by and I would be back in the garden planting seeds or whatever. And we would hang out in the grass, strumming guitars and talking about whatever was happening in town. That's one thing I really liked about Wylie. He was an intense activist, but then he could also just hang out in the garden and pluck guitars all afternoon and be totally at peace. Wylie was an incredible mixture of things. Stubborn, outspoken, fierce, gentle, super loving, always concerned for his friends and community. He truly walked his own path.

KATY LEIFER

Until we meet again, Wylie, as those playful children chasing all of those critters around the pond, in another universe.

CHAPTER 2

Benjamin Anderson

PROLOGUE

Over the past few years I have enjoyed periodic 'catching up' lunches with long-time friend, Lowell Kruse, the retired CEO of Heartland Health System in St. Joseph, Missouri. During one of these encounters, he told me about his new, young friend.

"One day, out of the blue, I received a call from a total stranger. Somehow, he managed to get through Edie (Lowell's gatekeeper). The young caller introduced himself as Benjamin Anderson, the newly appointed CEO of a small, critical access hospital in Ashland, Kansas. He said, he needed help, and asked if I would be his mentor. I inquired, how on earth did you choose me? And Benjamin explained, 'I did a Google search and identified the hospitals who have earned the Malcolm Baldrige National Quality Award, and I started there. You were the first on my list.'" And that's how their mentor/mentee relationship, now going on six years, began.

I told Lowell that I would like to meet this guy and introductions were made. A few months later, while en route to Colorado, Judy and

I stopped by Lakin, Kansas to have dinner with Ben and his lovely wife Kaila.

Benjamin grew up in Hayward, California. His parents divorced when he started high school, and Ben's Mom found herself in dire financial straits after her now ex-husband ceased providing any financial support. She moved in with her sister's family in Springfield, Missouri along with her two sons. The transition from modest financial security to abject poverty, combined with the move to a new town, contributed to a lackluster sophomore year, and Ben received all F's. Things improved over the next two years, thanks largely to the generosity of his extended family, but Ben aspired to go to college, although he had no money and an abysmal transcript.

A few weeks before the start of the school year, and having received rejection letters from every college to which he applied, Ben knocked on the door of the admissions director at Drury University in Springfield. Ben told the man, "I know my application is weak, but if you admit me and provide financial aid, I will promise you that I will succeed and be a credit to the school." And they did. And he has.

He graduated from Drury four years later with a degree in English. When I asked why he selected English, he explained, "I couldn't afford the books required for most majors, but with English I could borrow most of what I needed from the library." He then started a non-profit organization with the mission of helping promising, but poor, kids in circumstances similar to his own, get a college education. After six years and helping over 70 young people start their college careers, he met Kaila. They married, and Ben decided they could no longer live on $13,000 per year. He then took a position as a physician recruiter for rural hospitals.

An epiphany occurred at a hospital meeting in Bend, Oregon during a conversation with three senior rural hospital CEO's with whom he had worked. Benjamin told them, "What I'm doing isn't helping anyone. We basically charge $30,000 to move a physician from one town to another. As a hospital CEO you have the opportunity to make a positive impact on a small community. I want to do what you do."

After a three-hour conversation, one of the CEO's said, "I'm retiring within the year. Would you consider replacing me?"

"Why would your board take a risk on a 29-year-old who has never worked in a hospital?"

"Their choices are to pick someone promising on the way up, or a journeyman on the way down. It's not a tough decision. You look teachable. I'll mentor you, and perhaps you'll stick around."

Unfortunately, the opening was in rural Oregon and Benjamin's new bride sought to be closer to her family in Sabetha, Kansas. So he began a cold calling campaign and eventually contacted the board chair of the hospital in Ashland, a local veterinarian. Benjamin learned that the hospital was near closing, had been without a CEO for over six months, was losing money, had no cash reserves, and their only doctor left the community eight months earlier.

So, at the young age of 29, Benjamin Anderson was hired as the new CEO for Ashland Health Center, in Ashland, Kansas.

THE GAME

The idea originated during a drive from Ashland to the Oklahoma City airport. Benjamin was several months into his new position. Kaila was still teaching in Dallas and periodically commuted to their new home located in the southwest corner of Kansas. Ben had been making the weekly drive and initiated the practice of inviting one of his 72 employees to accompany him, affording an opportunity to get acquainted and to get a 'lay of the land'. On this particular trip, his companion was Joe Labelle, a 21-year-old dishwasher. And the conversation went like this:

"How is life treating you?"

"Not so well, my Grandmother just passed away from breast cancer."

"That's very sad. I'm sorry for your loss."

"The worst part is that it was preventable. If she would have had a mammogram it could have been diagnosed and treated."

"Did she have some reason for not getting a mammogram?"

The young man looked at Ben like he was incomprehensively dense and replied, "She didn't get a mammogram because she would have to take a day off work to drive 160 miles to Wichita, and she would have spent money that she thought would have been better used buying new shoes for grandkids. We need to make mammograms available here."

"Any thoughts on how we make that happen?"

"Basketball. A girl's basketball tournament."

"Why basketball?"

After again looking at the newbie CEO with a mixture of pity and bewilderment, he emphasized, "This is Kansas! Basketball was invented in Kansas! Basketball is important to people here." *Author's note: James Naismith came to Kansas six years after drafting the first rules for the game of Basket Ball. He would go on to coach the KU men's basketball team from 1898 - 1907 and would be the only coach of that program to have a losing record (55-60). Forrest 'Phog' Allen, Dean Smith, Adolph Rupp, and Wilt Chamberlain were among the many hoops hall of famers with ties to Naismith and KU basketball.*

And that is how it began.

The first obstacle occurred when they learned that high school girls' teams wouldn't be able to participate. No more than three girls from any team could appear together in an unsanctioned event. When informed of this setback, the young dishwasher was undeterred and suggested, "We'll form teams with three high school girls, three alumnae, and nine celebrity players from colleges or the pros."

Ben, not knowing the first thing about girl's basketball said, "Like who?"

"We could start with Jackie Stiles! She was an All-American at Missouri State who holds the NCAA scoring record and who later went on to play in the WNBA. She grew up in Claflin, KS, a few hours east of here. Her Dad still lives there. He's the track coach. I'll get you his number."

So Ben called Jackie's Dad who had him call her, and he told her of the plans for the celebrity game in Ashland.

She said, "I can't play, because my body is beat up, but I'll come, and I'll coach."

And that started the ball rolling. Within a matter of weeks, college players were recruited to attend the event, some from the some of the most elite women's basketball programs in the country: Connecticut, Tennessee, Notre Dame, and USC, Kansas, and K-State. The game was on.

A group of nurses working at the hospital formed a committee representing each of the small towns in the area (Wilmore, Englewood, Protection, Ashland, and Coldwater) and quickly dubbed themselves WEPAC (aka We Pack The House), and they took charge.

The high school gymnasium in Ashland seats 1,000, a considerable number for a town of 912 souls. Ticket prices were set at $30 apiece to keep it affordable for area residents. A couple of wealthy ranchers purchased one hundred of the tickets to give to kids who otherwise couldn't attend.

Benjamin, using cold-calling talents refined during his days as a physician recruiter, called Fox Sports Midwest in St. Louis. He told them of the upcoming event, and asked if they would consider broadcasting it. After they realized he wasn't joking, they agreed, but the audience would be limited to Kansas, Missouri, Iowa, and Nebraska. And there was a catch.

"They told us it would cost $30,000 to set up the cameras, sound equipment, and broadcasters in the tiny gym. If we would guarantee $30,000 in ad revenue, they'd do it. That equaled our entire ticket revenues, but we agreed and set out to sell ads."

Then Benjamin contacted the cheerleading coach at K-State. She said they loved the idea and would send their entire squad. Not to be outdone, the KU cheerleading squad heard of the game, and said they would come to cheer for one of the teams. K-State responded offering to send their pep band. Ashland was set to enjoy a big day.

Benjamin contacted ESPN, and they assured him they would send a reporter and camera crew. Sports Illustrated got wind of the remarkable gathering of stars from the world of women's basketball and joined the bandwagon. Two aspiring opera singers in NYC who were friends of Ben's brother, called to say they would appear to sing the national anthem.

Marion Jones was famous for winning three gold and two bronze medals in track and field at the 2000 Sydney Olympics. And she played basketball, first for University of North Carolina and later with the Tulsa Shock in the WNBA. She also spent six months in a federal prison and was stripped of her medals for steroid use and for lying to federal investigators. She learned of the event in tiny Ashland and said to Ben, "I'd be honored to come and play. I'll come a day early and speak to kids in the area about drug use." Fortuitously, the Clark County sheriff confiscated drug monies in excess of $1 million in a random drug stop the previous year. The sheriff generously offered a portion of those funds to cover the travel expenses of the athletes whose visits to Ashland could be linked to drug prevention efforts.

Chamique Holdsclaw, University of Tennessee All-American, Olympic Gold Medalist, and WNBA star, called to say she would come play and also speak to girls and women in the community about her experience with depression. The out-of-town speakers would eventually reach 1,500 kids from twelve school systems in southwest Kansas.

One local resident built his new home extra large in anticipation of future family reunions, and he housed and fed the entire 30-member pep band. Virtually every home in the county hosted the multitude of out-of-town visitors.

And so on the last Friday night in October 2009, the most heralded event in the history of Clark County, Kansas was held before a packed house and a live television audience, with coverage by the national media. Joe Labelle, the 21-year-old dishwasher whose idea started it all, was interviewed on Fox Sports wearing a cowboy hat and a pink shirt, in honor of Breast Cancer Awareness month, and tearfully told the story of how it happened.

POSTSCRIPT

Fox Sports Midwest won an Emmy for their coverage of the WEPAC Hoops for Hope. More importantly, the event brought in $70,000. By 2013, Ben's last year in Ashland, the total amount raised exceeded $250,000. The funds were used to bring a mobile mammography unit from Wichita monthly to provide free annual mammograms for every woman in the county.

The hospital in Ashland continues to survive, but not without difficulty. Joe Labelle has been promoted to the maintenance staff.

Benjamin accepted a new position as CEO of Kearny County Hospital, a more stable situation in the larger community of Lakin, Kansas. He has been successful in recruiting doctors through the innovative practice of targeting family practitioners with a zeal for missionary work. The hospital provides ten weeks of paid vacation enabling the recruits to provide missionary medicine in third world countries. He has also been successful in appealing to the same sense of mission in serving underserved communities in western Kansas.

Benjamin and Kaila's family life has become exponentially more complicated. They became the parents of four children under the age of three. This happened first through the adoption of a baby from a local unwed mother, followed by the birth of their twins, followed by the adoption of a second child from the mother of their first, almost as complicated as the lyrics to "I Am My Own Grandpa."

Building on this experience, Benjamin and Kaila were instrumental in building and supporting an adoption agency in Lakin, the Circle of Love. Benjamin explained, "When a woman is seeking an adoption plan for her child, we work to connect her with a loving adoptive family who will commit not only to loving her unborn child, but also to supporting and caring for the birthmother. The child is born at Kearney County Hospital and the adoption is facilitated by the local social services agency. The mothers are supported as long as they are open to receiving help. Some stay in southwest Kansas, and some don't."

And, if things weren't sufficiently busy, Benjamin began and is now completing his Masters Degree in Health Care Delivery Science from Dartmouth College, one of the most prestigious programs in the nation attracting executives from a veritable 'who's who' of the health care world. Benjamin has used these contacts to directly benefit his community, most prominently by hosting two Dartmouth faculty members in Lakin to provide a continuing medical education program for area health leaders.

Lowell continues to mentor Benjamin and makes the 800-mile roundtrip when called upon. He reports, "Early on I'd make some suggestions, and I would later hear back about what worked and what didn't. He'd then grill me for more ideas and seek feedback on his. After I told Lowell of our meeting he replied, "You can tell from meeting Benjamin and Kaila, some people really can make a difference. The world needs many more Benjamin Andersons, and people like you and me need to do everything we can to provide support and encouragement."

CHAPTER 3

Sally, Howard and Bill

PROLOGUE

An 84-year-old friend, Bob Fay, shared tales of two gentlemen he has come to know over the last sixteen winters spent in San Miguel de Allende, Mexico. The story that most caught my attention was of the time Howard and Bill hosted Sally Rand, the 1930's burlesque fan dancer, in their home. And she stayed for five years. By 8:30 the next morning, Bob, perhaps the best advance man in the world, had wrangled an invitation to be their guests and to listen and record some of their remarkable adventures. As Bob accurately foretold, the Sally Rand tale was but one layer of the onion.

Our flight into Queretaro arrived two hours behind schedule, but Howard was gracious and waited even though we were responsible for his being late for the fundraising luncheon he and Bill were hosting for 70 guests.

The highway from the airport in Queretaro to SMA follows a valley bracketed by distant mountain ranges. The natural terrain features scrub trees, grasses, and cactus of varying kinds. Large swaths of land reminiscent of U.S. corporate farms lie in stark contrast to smaller fields still harvested manually featuring hand-made cornshock teepees and haystacks. Ancient stone fences border many of the properties, especially the vineyards. It's not England-like tidy, but still surprisingly pleasing.

Arriving in SMA, we drove down a narrow, cobblestoned street surrounded by centuries old stone walls and entered the handsome gate leading to Howard and Bill's one-acre estate. We walked into a courtyard packed with well-dressed people. Howard made introductions and began working the crowd. Liveried waiters offered margaritas and hors d'oeuvres.

We were seated at a table set for eight on the lawn and began the first of a five-course dinner. A 10-piece Mariachi band serenaded the crowd. Howard took me aside to comment on the piece being played, "Lost Child." One of the trumpets played a wailing lament from somewhere distant in the house. A second answered boldly from the gardens. This continued as the trumpeters moved about, finally coming together, all to the accompaniment of four violins and four guitars.

Bob introduced me to our dining companions, and several said, "Oh you're, the Nude Nuns guy", and they would recite a portion from my first book. Bob informed them I had come to write about Howard's stories, and they assured me I wouldn't be disappointed. I would later be introduced as Howard's biographer.

We rested after lunch in preparation for a 6:30 dinner party. Our guests arrived, both attractive 50ish women, neither of whom knew the other. The first just moved to San Miguel from Palm Beach having just sold her orchid growing business. She knew all of the characters in the book, The Orchid Thief, and proclaimed that she, too, was an orchid thief. She told of a trip to the Peruvian Amazon basin searching for orchids. Her companion, the chief botanist for a large Midwestern botanical garden, was arrested, but she escaped. She also spoke of a trip to Burma in search of exotic orchids. She is athletic, tall, and slender and told of once losing to Chris Evert in a national level junior tennis tournament. She is an heiress of a family whose name you'd recognize, and she despises Chilangos, nouveau-riche Mexicans who apparently treat everyone shabbily.

The second dinner guest hailed from Toronto's aristocracy and was uncommonly gracious. She seemed genuinely interested in the stories that brought us to Howard and Bill's. We learned that her godfather was Edward Brooke, the late senator from Massachusetts, and her cousin is Ruth Bader Ginsberg. I told them that I know the owner of the now defunct Prairie Village Standard station. At one point in the conversation, I mentioned 'my wife', and she seemed mildly disappointed saying, "Oh! I thought that you and Bob were partners."

Howard kept us on a busy schedule throughout our seven-day stay, attending cocktail parties, lengthy comidas (lunches), dinners, impromptu gatherings and house calls in and around San Miguel. We made side trips to nearby Queretaro and Celaya, traveling by car and bus. The premo bus from Queretaro to San Miguel offered luxurious accommodations, for the modest sum of 115 pesos ($7 U.S.). My expectations upon arriving in central Mexico had sadly and erroneously been formed from exposure to border towns. Open eyes quickly dispelled these misconceptions.

Our visit was timed to coincide with the Dia de los Muertos festival. On Sunday, November 1, deceased children are honored. We strolled past several blocks of street vendors en route to the cemetery. They offer everything needed to create shrines and decorate tombs for the dead. The cemetery was packed wall-to-wall with celebrants. Men were scraping and repainting the white gravestones. Children played nearby, even sitting on the tombs. Artistic shrines were created from the petals of yellow magnolias, colored sand, and photos and personal items of the dead.

Howard, 80, is funny and uncommonly irreverent, and he gets away with it. He will say or do something outrageous, and the recipient will say, "Oh, Howard! You're such a pill." Anyone else would be clubbed to death like a baby seal. Bill, 72, is the son of a barber growing up in Mexico, Missouri, later creating confusion when in the process of becoming a Mexican citizen. He is a decorated combat Vietnam War veteran, a one-time escort to Imelda Marcos, and now a celebrated jewelry designer. He has a calming influence on Howard.

Howard, Bill, Bob, and I would spend several days together for story-telling sessions, but the time spent traveling and socializing with Howard was equally revealing. He doesn't own a cell phone or a computer, but he stays in touch with the world with frequent visits to pay phones. He stops to pick up trash. He never passes a beggar without giving generously. He recognizes and knows someone everywhere he goes. He is kinder to and infinitely more solicitous of the powerless than he is of the powerful.

The stories that follow are Howard and Bill's accounts of some of their adventures. *Author's note: unless otherwise attributed, statements in quotes are Howard's own words.*

SALLY RAND
1904 - 1979

As young men, Howard and Bill were active in various Kansas City charities, one of which was the Historic Kansas City Foundation. In 1974, Joan Dillon, a prominent Kansas City woman, was committed to saving the Folly Theatre, an aging but elegant building most notable for its mention in the Rodgers and Hammerstein's, *Oklahoma*:

"Ev'rything's up to date in Kansas City.

They've gone about as fur as they c'n go.

They got a big theayter they call a burleeque.

Fer fifty cents you c'n see a dandy show."

She sought Howard's assistance organizing a benefit for the final fundraising push to purchase and renovate the crumbling structure, which was slated to become a parking lot. Howard perused old rosters of those who had once performed at the Folly, a veritable "Who's Who" of show business. Two names caught his eye, both with Kansas City roots: Lucille LaSueur and Helen Beck, better known as Joan Crawford and Sally Rand. Both were born in 1904, and both modeled coats for Spaulding's Department Story as girls, and Sally had once graced the stage at the Folly. Howard knew the wife of a *KC Star* columnist, who had danced with Sally. He asked if she'd call to see if Sally would perform at the benefit. "We'll pay your airfare and put you up at the Muelhbach Hotel, but we don't have funds for a performance fee."

Sally jumped at the chance. She arrived and performed before an appreciative sellout crowd. She did her famous fan dance to Debussy's Clair de Lune. Sally was totally nude, offering mere glimpses when the fans crossed. "It was brilliant. She was 70, but if you didn't know her age, you would think you were watching a 25-year-old perform."

After the show Bill and Howard went to Sally's dressing room to offer their thanks and to congratulate her. She was sitting on a theatre trunk dressed in a little pink chiffon dress, into which she had changed for her encore, and they were surprised to find her in tears. "Oh Miss Rand, why are you crying? The audience loved you. It was wonderful. You've saved the theatre."

"Howard, you cheap bastard. You only gave me two days to spend in my old home town."

"If you'd like to stay longer, you're welcome to be our houseguest."

The tears stopped in a heartbeat. Fully composed she said, "I'll go to the Muelhbach, pack, and meet you out front." She came out with her dresser, a cousin who lived in town. Howard and Bill picked them up, dropped the cousin at her home at 180th and plowed ground, took Sally to their Hyde Park home, and got her settled in one of the guest rooms.

Anna was an elderly, black lady who oversaw the operations of Bill and Howard's 8,000 square foot mansion in the Hyde Park neighborhood of Kansas City. They would explain, "Anna ran the household, she just let us live there." Howard was in the kitchen with Anna and was equally startled when Sally walked in totally nude. "Good morning. Got any coffee? Do you have any garlic salt?"

Anna handed her a cup of coffee and poured some garlic salt in Sally's hand and she disappeared.

On the third day Howard encountered an irritable Anna in the kitchen. "What's the problem?"

"Mmm! Mmm! Mmm" she exclaimed, "We're sure going to be seeing a lot more of Miss Rand than we want to. I have a feeling she is going to be here for some time." Sally followed the same routine every morning for the next five years, much to the delight of the gardener who timed his coffee breaks accordingly. But after the prickly start, Anna and Sally developed a deep friendship becoming inseparable.

BECOMING SALLY RAND

According to Bill, "Sally was 4'9" tall and weighed 98 pounds when she was 16 years old and was 4'9" and 98 lbs on the day she died." Sally's family moved from the Ozarks to Kansas City when she was in grade school. She studied classical ballet at Miss Brown's, housed in the third floor of an elegant mansion at the corner of Armour and Charlotte. Serendipitously, it was located only three doors from Bill and Howard's residence. This did not go unnoticed by Sally. "She literally shrieked with joy as she recognized her girlhood home away from home."

After graduating from high school, Sally worked as a machine operator for Tension Envelope in KC. She later ventured to New York City in search of fame and fortune, only to arrive in the early days of the depression and to discover there was little demand for a classically trained ballerina. But she did catch the eye of Agnes DeMille, a talented choreographer at the time, but more noteworthy for being the niece of the movie mogul, Cecil B.

Agnes took Sally to California to meet her uncle. He thought that she had great potential, but during their first meeting stated, "Helen Beck wouldn't look sexy on a marquee. We need to change your name." After rejecting several suggestions offered by Cecil B., she noted a Rand McNally atlas sitting on his desk. She thought of her favorite aunt, and proclaimed, "Why don't we call me Sally Rand?" And she became one of many chorus girls under contract to Cecil B. DeMille.

In 1933 she was sent to dance in the chorus at the Chicago World's Fair. The lead dancer failed to show up for their first performance. Sally noted, "She was having an affair with a Chicago mobster at the time." The stage manager told Sally, "You've got to do this." She thought of her childhood when she would visit her uncle in Hermitage, Missouri and of seeing the giant egrets fly. She went into the prop room and found two large feathered fans roughly her size and visualized the dance she would perform. She went to the music director and asked if he could play Clair de Lune. He replied imperiously, "What key?" Sally said, "In the key of dance, you fool!"

She also recognized that merely dancing with fans wouldn't stand out, so she decided to appear totally nude covered only by the fans. Her skillful teasing, plying the audience with glimpses of bare flesh, insured their rapt attention. Overnight she went from an unheralded chorus girl to a sensation.

In 1934 she returned to the Chicago World's Fair, this time introducing her bubble dance. She used a transparent balloon, made partially opaque by the stage lighting, exactly 4'9" high behind which she would appear stark naked. She and the bubble would glide onto the stage. She would titillate with her nude silhouette and conclude her routine floating off stage with the aid of a hidden wire, as though she were being carried by the wind.

She would be arrested numerous times for public nudity, but never charged, with the attendant publicity only adding to her allure. She would later bristle at being labeled a stripper, "I never stripped. I always started out nude." She was also quick to quip, "The Rand is faster than the eye."

Author's note: Readers can view these remarkable routines on YouTube.

LIFE AS A STAR

Howard recalls, "Sally's biggest problem was her unbelievable generosity. After she became an overnight star, she bought houses for her parents, her brother, and other relatives and moved them to California." She built a Frank Lloyd Wright house that was situated on a five-acre orchard that she called the "Blue House". She spent most of her time in her mansion on Glendora Boulevard in Glendora, CA. Sally would become real estate rich, but cash poor.

She married and later divorced a film cowboy, Thurk Greenough, the longest lasting of her four husbands. He was a product of the 101 Ranch in Oklahoma that trained many of the cowboy stars of the era. "He could ride every horse in the rodeo, but he couldn't ride me," Sally recalled with a hearty laugh.

While with 'the boys', as Sally would affectionately refer to Howard and Bill, she would consume a book a day. She was a graduate of Christian College in Columbia, Missouri, and at the age of 43 went back to school to get her masters degree in history. "She was a brilliant woman. She was interested in everything and could converse intelligently on almost any topic."

Gypsy Rose Lee and Fanny Brice were contemporaries and close friends of Sally's. They were all the same size, all wore expensive clothing, and they shared the same dresser (assistant), an attractive black lady, also their size. The custom of the day was that burlesque performers would stay until the last act and 'count the house' before they got paid. After a matinee in NYC, Sally journeyed to Southampton for an evening show. She had a 12-cylinder Lincoln and a driver. She hopped in the backseat with her two Pekinese and her dresser. When they arrived she was uncharacteristically without makeup or her typical elegant attire. Instead, her dresser was wearing the finery Sally shared with Gypsy Rose and Fanny. Sally emerged from the Lincoln disheveled and some older ladies observed, "Look! It's Josephine Baker and her maid."

She never had children, so while still in her 40's she moved to Florida, then the only state that would permit a single woman to adopt an infant. One of the showgirls she knew became pregnant and agreed to give up her newborn. Milton Berle was rumored to be the father, but Sally disputed that claim. The relationship with her son was never smooth. By the time he reached adulthood, they were estranged. Her son preferred that his mother be the grandmother who sits in a rocking chair, not the one who rocks nude on stage. Howard remembers him as, "The most ungrateful son of a bitch I ever met." But to be fair he also concedes, "Sally would not have been a candidate for mother of the year."

SALLY IN KANSAS CITY

It was almost like *Mary Had a Little Lamb*. Sally was included in every social event, of which there were many, attended by Bill and Howard. "She was never a high maintenance guest, but she was involved in everything we did." The three attended the grand opening of the Houlihan's restaurant on the Country Club Plaza. Howard introduced Sally to a young man at the greeting table. He looked at the tiny woman and said, "That name sounds familiar. Who is Sally Rand?" Sally put her hand on Howard's shoulder and, in an instant, leaped on the table. She pulled the hem of her evening gown up to mid-thigh and said with a laugh, "These are Sally Rand's legs. Don't you ever forget it!"

After their morning coffee routine, Bill noticed that the nude Sally would often don his trench coat along with a blue scarf and leave for a morning stroll. He followed her on a few occasions and observed that she would walk to the former home of Miss Brown's dance studio. "Even in the winter she would just stare at the building, sometimes for as long as half an hour. Then she'd return home." Years later Bill wore that coat, felt into the pocket, and recovered a note that Sally had written to 'the boys'.

She was greeted warmly into Kansas City society. Whenever she left the house she was always impeccably attired in Chanel suits or Garavani gowns, always the latest fashions. Two of Howard's socially prominent friends often included her in ladies events. On one occasion they arranged a luncheon at the Rockhill Tennis Club in Sally's honor. One of the attendees was new to the group and new to Sally. The newcomer sat next to Sally and said haughtily, "Miss Rand, tell us the story of your life."

After Sally shared a socially acceptable and brief version, the newcomer asked, "Miss Rand, did you ever regret not having a career as a classical ballerina?"

"F__k yes." She replied, and silverware dropped at each setting.

While in Kansas City Sally continued dancing and would receive $1,000 per show. She would disappear for 3-4 days and dance multiple matinee and evening performances and return. She once asked Bill to retrieve her fans, and he was surprised how heavy they were. While performing she carried them as though they were feather-light, but that was but a tribute to her remarkable upper body strength.

To keep in shape, she exercised daily and vigorously. Bill and Howard's house had numerous arched doorways leading from room to room. Bill remembers seeing the totally nude, 4'9" Sally doing stretching exercises with one leg straight up, her foot reaching the top of the arch, her head touching the extended knee, and her hands gracefully reaching beyond her toes. While she was agile, she was not healthy. She continued a three pack a day habit and suffered from emphysema.

During the first of her many hospitalizations at nearby Trinity Lutheran Hospital, Bill received a call from the night nurse at 2 am. "You have to come down here and do something. Miss Rand is stark naked, and she has wandered down to the kitchen in the basement of the hospital!" Bill reminded the nurse that she was probably just hungry. She ate small amounts throughout the day and night, and was merely acting like she was at their home. Howard called Sally's son to inform him of his Mom's hospitalization, and he replied coldly, "Take good care of my Mother."

Milton Berle and George Burns were frequent callers. Howard recalls hearing one side of Sally's telephone conversation with an aging cowboy star, "G_dd_m it, Tim. Don't call here again without your hearing aid. You're not understanding a word I've said." Sally was an earthy woman, but she limited her use of profanity to the comfort of home. When in society, she was the epitome of decorum.

Blanche Thebom, mezzo-soprano who headlined at the Metropolitan Opera Company of New York for 22 years, was a close friend of Howard's and a frequent houseguest. When he learned she would be appearing in Kansas City, he informed Sally that they would have to move her to another room, because the one she currently occupied was Blanche's favorite. Sally said, "Who in the hell is Blanche Thebom?" Blanche subsequently and graciously deferred to Sally's room preferences, and, after a rough start, joined the legion of Sally's KC friends and fans.

Howard continued his duties on the board of the Historic Kansas City Foundation. A female board member approached him and inquired if Sally would perform at another benefit to be held at the Midland Theatre. In a Mickey Rooney-Judy Garland-like moment she enthused, "Howard, let's get Sally! We need to replicate an old-time vaudeville review!"

Sally immediately agreed and informed Howard, "I want it to be spectacular!" And Howard remembers unwisely replying, "You don't have a budget. I want this to be the real deal."

The next few days, Sally could be heard on the phone speaking with some of her contemporaries, who had once been stars. "Allan, (Jones, singer and father of singer Jack Jones) are you available on such and such a date? The boys will send you tickets and put you up at a nice hotel. We don't have much money, but we can pay you a $500 performance fee." And he agreed, and along with an aging comedian from Las Vegas, singer Betty Rhodes, and the Lenore Sutton dancers.

Local jazz singer Oleta Adams agreed to open. Howard called a local bandmaster, Warren Durrett, to ask if his orchestra were available for the show. He listed the scheduled performers, and Warren asked, "Are they still alive?" He agreed, but said, "We have to get paid union scale."

Howard, Bill, and Sally handled the logistics for plane tickets to minimize trips to the airport. First they picked up Allan Jones and told him they'd be waiting for another performer. He whined, "I don't do waiting well," but waited. Last to arrive were the Lenore Sutton dancers. Howard observed three elderly women getting off the plane. One used a cane, and another was walking unsteadily with the aid of the third. Serious doubts emerged about Sally's judgment of talent.

They eventually assembled the antediluvian cast in a van and dropped them off at the Bellerive Hotel, on Armour Boulevard a few blocks from Howard and Bill's. Allan ‿

here 30 years ago, and it was a dump

a party that night for the visiting perf‿

the event.

They started running through t‿
suggested, "Sally, why did you stop doing
the story of how the factory that made he‿
designed specifically for her, had been ‿
make weather balloons. She was asked t‿ ... the
Bubble dance, and she agreed, but explained, "Honey, I haven't done
that act in years. I'll do it, but I won't use the flying wire."

The Midland Theatre was originally built in 1927 for the staggering
sum of $4 million and had been newly remodeled by local movie
mogul, Stan Durwood. It was known for its Renaissance Revival style
and being home to over 500,000 feet of gold leaf. The cast gathered at
the site two days before the show and observed there were no seats in
the theatre. Stan assured them that would not be a problem, he'd have
them in place on time, and he delivered as promised. He told the story
of the three brothers in the movie business arguing over the choice
of upholstery. The first said, "I want blue velvet on those seats," The
second said, "I want red velvet on those seats." The third said, "I want
asses in those seats."

Next, the performers viewed the various backdrops in front of
which they would perform. As the stage manager dropped them,
each unleashed large quantities of construction dust and debris. All
agreed a gauzy, pastel choice would make the performers look 25
years younger. Rehearsals began, and, much to Howard's chagrin,
went hours over budget owing to the many peccadillos of the finicky
former stars.

Howard received a call from an elderly man. He said he was a
friend of Thurk and Sally's from their days at the 101 Ranch. He
said he had come to see the show, was staying at the Muelhbach, and

Sally. Howard told her of the caller, and she said,

itch. I don't want to see that mother f____r." The man

it, but she never talked to him. The next morning Howard

own to meet him and found the elderly cowboy performing

at tricks in the hotel lobby. He invited him to the Midland and gave

him a complimentary ticket.

The afternoon of the show, Sally and Bill encountered a major problem when they tried to inflate the pre-WWII balloons from her stage trunk. One after another popped until there were no more. Bill suggested they contact the national weather service for a large balloon. He called the head of the local agency, Alan Pearson, and told him of their plight. After first thinking it was a joke, he almost hung up. Once he realized they were serious he agreed and delivered balloons a few hours before show time. Sally assured Howard and Bill, "I guarantee you this will be spectacular."

Some seats were made available to the general public, and a long line formed under the 'Sally Rand' marquee continuing around the block into an alley. Sally arrived backstage at 5, and Howard took her to a spot where she observed the line stretching as far as the eye could see under her name in lights. "She broke down in tears."

As planned, Oleta Adams opened to the sold out crowd of 3,573 on a Saturday night in Kansas City in 1978. Allan Jones followed with a few songs for which he was known and ended with *Donkey Serenade*, which he sang in the 1937 film *The Firefly*. The crowd roared their approval, and he followed with an encore, brilliantly singing the same song again. The place went ballistic. The Las Vegas comedian came on stage and began a routine first assailing Howard for lodging him in a crappy hotel and then following with material true to old vaudevillian traditions, but pretty darn vulgar. The crowd's reception was tepid.

Next Sally flowed gracefully onto the stage and performed her fan dance routine. The audience was enthralled as she expertly teased them as she had so many others. Betty Rhodes appeared and sang a medley of classic Broadway show tunes. She returned for an encore after the audience expressed their approval. Then came the Lenore Sutton dancers. Howard was in a state of high anxiety, not knowing quite what to expect. The three came on stage wearing black patent leather shoes, bowties, and black tuxedos. They looked 25 and opened with a synchronized tap dance, followed by a Rockettes-like routine with perfect can-can kicks. The audience wouldn't let them off the stage.

For the finale, Warren Durrett struck up the band and Sally floated on stage behind her 4'9" semi-transparent weather balloon. Bill recalled, "It was so graceful. Her silhouette was gorgeous." She danced, and she teased. At the end of her routine, she pushed the balloon away, held her hands elegantly aloft, stood totally nude before the audience, and walked off the stage. The audience sat in stunned silence for what seemed like minutes then broke into exuberant cheers. In a matter of seconds Sally reappeared, wearing her pink chiffon dress. She grabbed a mike moved to the edge of the stage, sat with her legs dangling, and spoke, "Now I want to talk to you about my beloved hometown, Kansas City." And she entertained them for another half hour.

Afterwards, Howard went to Sally's dressing room to gather her for a post-party. But there was no Sally. He was directed to a commotion in the lobby of the Midland. There he saw Sally and the old cowboy continuing to captivate the departing guests with a lariat routine. He would lasso Sally and rope her towards him seductively.

Howard mistakenly thought all was well between the two. He asked Sally if it would be acceptable to invite the old fellow to the party and spend the night at the house. Sally brusquely told him she never wanted to see the man again. When told of the rebuff, he told Howard, "I don't have any money." Howard took him to the bus station, gave him some cash, and bought him a ticket to Tulsa.

Sally's health deteriorated rapidly after the dazzling performance at the Midland. Howard and Bill received a call that she had been readmitted to Trinity Lutheran. They came directly from a funeral, walked into Sally's room, and were stunned to see a sheet pulled over her head and body. Thinking she had died, they approached, one on each side of the bed, and in unison pulled the sheet down over her face to gain a parting glance of their dear friend. They first noticed the resistance of someone pulling against them and then viewed unfamiliar red hair. Finally, they heard a shriek. "I'm not dead! I'm not dead!" Sally had been relocated, and the woman in the bed thought they were undertakers. Bill and Howard apologized profusely and were redirected to Sally's room.

Several months later, Sally recovered sufficiently to accept a three-day engagement at the Kimo Theatre in Albuquerque. Howard and Bill planned to come to see the evening performance on the last day and then take her to their Santa Fe home. Howard called several times a day by phone to check on her and noted she sounded weaker each time they spoke. He was concerned, but she had always rebounded.

He received a call from the manager of the Kimo to say that Sally performed beautifully during the first day of shows, but she fell on the second. She was mortified by the incident, but she was also terribly ill. She was sent by air ambulance to a hospital near her Glendora, CA home. Sally Rand died of congestive heart failure two days later on August 31, 1979 at the age of 75.

Her son, from whom she had been estranged for many years, quickly took over the funeral arrangements and control of her affairs. Money management had never been one of Sally's strengths. Howard had helped her in disposing of some of her real estate and then managing the resulting funds, but she died in debt. Sally's son organized a funeral service befitting his faith. Bill and Howard attended, and were displeased to see that Sally, a lifelong Episcopalian, was buried in an unmarked grave and was referred to as 'Sister Sally'.

George Burns interrupted the service once to say, "I don't know who this Sister Sally is that you're talking about. I came here to honor my friend Sally Rand."

Howard and Bill remember Sally fondly, "She always treated us like the sons she never had. She was interested in everything, and there was never a dull moment."

Years later, Howard received a call from Penny Singleton, the actress who played Blondie Bumstead in the Dagwood movies. She had undertaken the task of placing appropriate gravestones for former Hollywood legends. Penny located Sally's and had it marked in a fitting manner.

HOWARD

Howard was born in 1935 to a prominent Kansas City family. His great great grandfather, John Haynes, came to the settlement that would become Kansas City by way of Virginia and Iowa. In 1820 the Haynes family traveled by flatboat down the Ohio River and then poled up the Mississippi River to the site of what would later become Burlington, Iowa, where they established the first gristmill in Iowa on the Skunk River. Due to Indian troubles, the family relocated the mill further downriver to Quincy, Illinois. In 1843, 21-year-old John decided to roam further west, landing in the Town of Kansas at the confluence of the Missouri and Kansas Rivers and the starting point for the Santa Fe, California, and Oregon Trails.

John earned his living as a scout for the Santa Fe Trail and made seven round trips before heading to Sacramento in 1849 to join the Gold Rush. A few years later he returned to Westport, a few miles south of the still named Town of Kansas, bought a farm, established a few businesses, and raised a family including Howard's grandfather, Forrest Lee, born in 1873.

In the early 1900's Forrest Lee Haynes was one of the first surgeons to practice medicine in Kansas City. He would not operate at St. Luke's because they refused to treat blacks or Jews at the time, and instead worked at St. Mary's and German Hospital, later renamed Research during WWI. Dr. Haynes pursued many hobbies, one of which was acquiring art, including a collection of Thomas Hart Benton paintings. Howard would later inherit his grandfather's collection, add to it, and subsequently donate it to his alma mater, Baker University in Baldwin City, Kansas where he earned his degree in 1957.

If there is a common thread throughout Howard's life, it is the world of horses and horse people. Dr. Haynes was a horseman and an early member of the Missouri Hunt and Polo Club, established in 1902 and one of the oldest foxhunting clubs in the U.S. It was located in what is now Loose Park. Thirty-eight years earlier, the pastoral setting had been the site of the Battle of Westport, one of the bloodiest civil war engagements fought west of the Mississippi where 30,000 men fought and 3,000 men died.

An eastern foxhunting publication of the era spoke of the Missouri Club, "Foxes are plentiful, and it seems a pity to not make the best of a good opportunity. Best in the western states."

Howard began riding at age 5 and rode in his first foxhunt at 12. By the late 1940's the club had moved south and was renamed the Mission Valley Hunt Club. The club would produce the first U.S. junior Olympian horseman, Carol Duran. August Busch, Sr. would later give her Miss Budweiser, a horse that he declared, "would match her talent."

The etiquette of the hunt dictates that the rider is properly dressed, and the horse is well-groomed, aka manure free. The hounds are let out in the open fields and the riders follow. The typical ride lasts for 2-3 hours covering miles of terrain and multiple jumps. Howard remembers an encounter with a new member, newly wealthy, that showed up shabbily attired and riding a horse speckled with horseshit.

Howard greeted him snootily, "How chic to ride in a stocking cap."

Howard's maternal grandparents also lived in the same Westport neighborhood and interacted daily. Howard's family moved to St. Louis when he was in high school, a time he recalls as, "The biggest disappointment of my life." He matriculated to Baker University, 40-miles southwest of Kansas City, to be close to his grandparents, and it was a time he remembers fondly as, "The best experience of my life."

"The professors were great. At age 80, I remember them like it was yesterday. They could have taught at any university in the country. Sissy Hively taught literature, and she made every class exciting. She would become the character about which we were reading. She would often say, 'The trouble with the world is that children should be buried when they're born and dug up when they're 25.' I remember being invited to the home of my English professor, Vera Lavelle and her companion Grace Irwin, Dean of Women for dinner and discussions. We stayed in touch until their deaths."

But Howard was not a strong student. He spent more time at the hunt club than with the books. As graduation approached, the president of Baker called his mother, "We have a problem with Howard. He's the only student in the graduating class that hasn't been placed in a job or graduate school." Howard's Mom replied, "Then why don't you hire him?"

It never occurred to Howard that he would ever have to work, but upon his graduation in 1957 he was hired as the director of admissions. He married his college sweetheart, and, shortly thereafter, their first child, Valery, was born.

In 1958, Howard was selected to participate in a summer program at DePauw University in Greencastle, Indiana sponsored by the Eli Lilly Co. for 40 admissions people from universities around the country. Howard became acquainted with one of his fellow attendees, the director of admissions at the University of Cincinnati, who later recommended Howard for a similar position at the University of Akron. Howard was interviewed, offered the job, and accepted. Shortly thereafter, he added housing and financial aid to his responsibilities. And Howard and his wife added two more children to their brood, Lee and Sarah.

Dr. Norman Auburn (University of Akron president from 1951-1971) was a world-class fundraiser, and wisely introduced Howard to the scions of the Firestone and Goodyear families to pursue their shared passion for fox hunting. "They would do drag hunts where a scent laid out in a gunny sack was dragged along for a timed two hours, event. It wasn't as challenging as a live hunt, but the Firestone's wanted their executives back at their desks at a prescribed time."

THE BUCKEYE

Early in the Kennedy administration, Dr. Auburn became the undersecretary of state under George Ball. He returned to Akron after a two-year stint and was in demand as a speaker. He asked Howard to travel with him and make introductions. "Dr. Auburn was 5'7", 130 lbs, and bald, but he was dapper beyond belief."

They would fly around the country in the comfort of the private air fleet provided by the rubber companies. Howard would give an introduction listing Dr. Auburn's many accomplishments and recite the positions he held. One evening at the University of Pittsburgh, Howard tired of the routine and changed the script. "Coming from the Buckeye State I often pondered the origins of that nickname. I looked it up in Webster's and learned it is, 'A smooth, hairless nut of little commercial value.' I give you Dr. Norman Auburn." It took several minutes for the audience to regain their composure.

Nary a word was spoken between the two until they were halfway home to Akron. Then Dr. Auburn said warmly, "I want you to use that exact intro from now on."

Laura Trexler was one of the people Howard befriended at the DePauw program. She had been a lieutenant in the WAVES in WWII, later founded a private high school in New Jersey, and then went to work in the education section of the Department of Health, Education, and Welfare department in Washington, DC.

She called Howard and said, "I'm talking to the next headmaster of the Grafton School in Virginia. They need someone who can raise money, fox hunt, is willing to become an Episcopalian, and can run a boarding school." When asked by a board member, "How successful can you be at fundraising?" He replied, "I can pick pockets from the top of a horse as well as I can from the ground." And he was hired.

At the age of 29, Howard and his family moved to the hunt country in rural Berryville, Virginia to become the headmaster of the boarding school serving children with learning disabilities aged 8-16. "The school was in horrific shape. Had I known how bad it was, I would never have taken the job. They were effectively bankrupt, and the former headmaster was inept at fundraising. It was early in the field of learning disabilities, so everyone was flying blind."

Horses were the primary draw. The campus is located on a magnificent estate in the midst of the beautiful Virginia hunt country. It had been donated for the purpose of founding the school. The site alone made it a socially acceptable destination for the difficult children of the wealthy. Most came from families of the rich and powerful in the DC area. "So many of the children arrived here on Ritalin. They were like zombies. We told parents that we were going to medically withdraw their kids from the drug that was used primarily for the parents' and teachers' convenience. Over 80% never went back."

Laura Trexler fed Howard an endless list of contacts for fundraising, almost all horse people. Howard inherited a good faculty, added a psychologist and a speech therapist, and told parents not to interfere. A girl from a prominent family had a severe speech problem that no one could solve. The girl returned to her home one weekend a month. On one such occasion the chauffeur brought the girl's long time nanny for the trip. The speech therapist was present during one of the farewells, heard the nanny speak in an unrecognizable foreign dialect and concluded, "Now I know the problem." The girl was separated from the nanny and within a year spoke perfectly.

Howard loved the life, loved riding with the Mellon's, Warner's, and other aristocratic families from the east coast, and loved that the school was succeeding. Over 50% overcame their learning disabilities, many had hidden talents that emerged, and all benefited from the break away from their previous schools. The one common denominator among the kids was their difficulty with the printed word.

Four years after his arrival, Howard received a book from one of the board members, the widow of Wild Bill Donovan, the founder of the OSS during WWII, the organization that later became the CIA. Inside the cover was the inscription, "The miracle you have performed at the Grafton School deserves a medal too." Ruth Donovan.

While still headmaster, Howard, along with friends Alex McKay Smith and Lida McGowan, co-founded North American Riding for the Handicapped in Battle Creek, Michigan. He raised the first $1 million to build the center. But he was also going through a bitter divorce. "My goal was to become the president of a small liberal arts college. My wife wanted no part of that."

Howard's father died a few years earlier at the age of 50. In 1969 his grandfather, Forrest Lee, passed away, and it was time to return to Kansas City.

Howard met Bill through a mutual friend. It took three months before Bill would see him again. Howard is an acquired taste. Bill had just returned from a four-year tour of duty with the Air Force including two years in Vietnam traveling throughout various combat zones as part of an inspector general team. When not in Vietnam, he was stationed in Manila where he met a Swiss-German hotelier who was close to Imelda Marcos, wife of the then dictator Ferdinand Marcos. He subsequently befriended Imelda and frequently served as her escort. Imelda was renowned as the largest accumulator of shoes in the world. She confided in Bill that she did love shoes, but never purchased a pair. Shoe designers gave her a constant supply of their new wares in the hope she would wear them publicly. Bill agreed to a lifetime ban from discussing his war intelligence work. Military personnel would visit him often during the years after the war to check in with him.

Bill grew up in Mexico, Missouri, about halfway between Columbia and St. Louis. His Dad was a barber and dabbled in trading farms and horses. Bill spent much of his childhood on a horse, and remembers his Mexico childhood fondly. He and his Dad traveled to horse shows most weekends. After the war, he followed in his Dad's footsteps and leased the barbershop from Joyce Hall in Hallmark's newly opened real estate jewel Crown Center.

Coming out as openly gay was not commonplace anywhere in the country, and certainly not in the Midwest in 1970. The Kansas City gay community included many prominent civic and business leaders, most of whom were not yet 'out' and many who would never do so. The social norms were that gay men could have lunch together but not dinner. The most accepting restaurants were Putsch's 210, The Golden Ox, The Majestic Steakhouse, and The Savoy.

Discerning citizens quickly learned of Howard's philanthropic inclinations and fundraising prowess, and within a few years he was on the boards of the Lyric Opera, Kansas City Symphony, Prime Health, Planned Parenthood, and the Historic Kansas City Foundation. He had also assumed responsibility for Haynes Family Investments.

Howard invited two of the most socially prominent women in town to lunch at the Rockhill Tennis Club. He told them, "I've met the person with whom I will spend the remainder of my life. We're moving in together. His name is Bill. Will that be a problem?" And of course the answer was no, nor was it with any one else that mattered to Howard and Bill.

QUESTOVER

In 1973 a local municipal judge, with the un-judge-like moniker of Skinny Meyers, called Howard. "You're going to run a program to help retarded (sic) first-time juvenile offenders." Howard told him no, delicately but firmly. Two days later a social service worker knocked on the door with two special needs teenage first offenders and dumped them on Howard's doorstep.

Over the next year, Howard and Bill acquired and rehabilitated seven aging homes in the Hyde Park neighborhood. Several of them were once grand mansions, had subsequently been converted into multi-family dwellings, and were in varying states of disrepair.

Howard was not a NIMBY kind of guy and located three of the homes adjacent to his. They tore out 27 kitchens and reconfigured the seven dwellings to house a total of 44 residents and 6 live-in staff members. They also enlisted the aid of special needs educators, vocational rehab specialists, and other professionals, all with the mission of helping these young people to live independently. Howard recruited a valued volunteer, Mr. Fleischaker, a retired milliner, to provide art therapy for the kids.

Howard and Bill founded, funded, and operated Questover, as in 'their quest is over', from 1973 - 1990 when they turned it over to the Jackson County Court. During that period they housed over 400 kids, with over 80% graduating from the program to live independently.

They would host the higher performing kids at their home in Santa Fe, introducing them to a broader world. Bill and Howard were responsible for the introduction of special education programs and the concept of mainstreaming of mentally challenged students at Westport High School, part of the Kansas City Public School system.

Employment was arranged for several of the kids at the upscale Alameda and Raphael Hotels on the Country Club Plaza. Howard was touring the popular destination one afternoon with friends from Santa Fe. On several occasions, they'd greet young people who would approach and hug Howard, and say, "Hi Dad." After a few such encounters the Santa Fe guests asked, "Do you know anyone who is normal?"

THE BUS TRIP

Howard's brother lived in Jefferson, Texas. Through him Howard knew of a state park that they decided would be the ideal destination for a 7-day get-away for the 44 teenagers and 6 staff members of Questover.

Bill knew how to drive a school bus and cook for large numbers of people, so off they went. The first accident occurred six feet into the trip when the rear end of the bus clipped a car as they pulled onto Charlotte leaving their home. They arrived at Queen Wilhemina State Park in Mena, Arkansas late the first night. Park rangers warned them to be on the lookout for black bears.

Undeterred, each kid had a blanket and pillow and was sleeping in, under, and around the bus when a fierce thunderstorm unleashed its wrath on the unprotected campers. It was 4 am, everyone was soaked to the bone, clothes were strewn every which way, and it was pitch dark. The staff gathered everyone and everything as best they could and drove down the mountain and found a 24-hour truck stop in Mena.

One of their charges was a boy named Harold. He was nicknamed the Shadow because he followed close behind Bill everywhere he went. "If I stopped, he'd run into me." He was mentally challenged, not by an accident of birth, but because his father once beat him senseless in the head with a sock loaded with a bar of soap.

Followed faithfully by Harold, Bill reconnoitered the truck stop, which was staffed by one cook and one waitress owing to the early hour. They negotiated a deal where Bill would help with the cooking, staff members would serve, and all were fed. Howard and Bill explained that several of the teenagers were naked and wrapped in blankets because their clothes couldn't be found in the rainstorm.

The group then descended upon a laundromat and spent $50 in quarters getting blankets and clothes dried, and later found a store to replace lost clothing. Before leaving Mena they went into a grocery to purchase snacks. A friendly clerk spoke to Harold with an extreme southern drawl, "Where y'all from?" And Harold replied, "That yellow bus over there."

As they rolled on, Howard pointed out the changes in terrain, and the teens yelled excitedly and in unison, "Train! Train! What train?" And they rolled on.

When they finally arrived at the Caddo Lake State Park they encountered curious fellow campers. While provisioning at a nearby store, the owner surveyed the motley assemblage and told Howard and Bill that he wanted to introduce them to a friend. Upon meeting the man they were told, "I'm going to bring everything needed for a catfish feed for your entire crew." And he did. Bill got verklempt when he reminisced, "Our host and his family were fabulous. They served us a delicious dinner like we were royalty. Our kids were overwhelmed, being unaccustomed to such kindness. It was wonderful to be embraced so warmly."

The next day, one of the boys was missing. They notified the park rangers, and everyone spread out searching for 16-year-old Billy. A park ranger found the boy later in the day naked and scratched. To prevent further wanderings they tied a rope to the back belt loop of his pants and then to a tree. The parents of Tommy, another of their charges, lived nearby in Louisiana and asked if it would be okay if they visited their son. They were welcomed warmly and enjoyed their time with the unique group. Upon noticing Billy, they inquired, "Do you tie many of them up?"

THE NYMPHOMANIAC

Howard received a call from a wealthy man in St. Louis, "I need your help. My 18-year-old daughter is currently confined in a mental hospital. She is a nymphomaniac, and she is beautiful." Howard went to St. Louis to meet with them and discovered that the girl was gorgeous beyond belief. After their first encounter, the girl whispered seductively to Howard, "Can you come back later so we can f__k?"

Howard told the father, "We'll keep her on birth control, but no guarantees," and reluctantly brought her back to Kansas City. They placed her in one of the homes and got her a job at the Jewish vocational rehab.

Sally Rand was then living with Howard and Bill, and she took a great interest in all of the girls in Questover. She helped them with basic cleanliness, make-up, and social skills. She took the newcomer under her wing, and they became close.

One day Howard received a call from the police, "Doris* has been raped in the alley behind the Jewish Rehab building. I called your house and someone answered who said she was Sally Rand. What's with that?"

Doris later confessed that she hadn't been raped, and in fact had seduced an unwitting boy, but it was a continuation of her destructive behavior. The family was apoplectic, and she agreed to a sterilization procedure. She returned to her family in St. Louis, stayed close to Sally through the years, and is now successfully married.

SAN MIGUEL DE ALLENDE

Inexplicably, Howard and Bill abandoned their mansion and lifestyle in the gentile Hyde Park neighborhood and moved to a suburban lake community north of the Missouri River. They purchased and redecorated a lovely home, but it was a monstrous mistake. "The people of Riss Lake didn't understand us, and we didn't understand them."

Concurrently, a friend, the manager of KC Marriott's, told them of a place he visited in central Mexico, San Miguel de Allende. It's a charming town with a year-round moderate climate, exquisite architecture, relatively low crime, and a vibrant arts community. More importantly, the town is home to a large community of interesting expats, many of whom, like Howard, are more than a few bubbles off plumb.

The city is renowned for 2,000 doors, behind which there are 2,000 courtyards. The dominant architectural feature of San Miguel is the Parroquia, located in the center of a 64-square block section of town dating back to 1520. It towers over the Jardin (Garden), the largest of the town's plazas, ringed with laurel trees manicured in the shape of giant drums.

Seventeenth, and eighteenth century haciendas border the square. They were once the homes of the wealthy owners of the silver mines in nearby Guanajuato. Most, but not all, have not been repurposed as hotels, restaurants, museums, government buildings, and retail shops. They are typically two-story edifices built around a large courtyard.

Entry is gained through a wooden or metal gate sufficiently large for carriages, and each stone threshold reveals the wear of centuries of carriage traffic. One can almost imagine the grand lifestyles enjoyed by their 17th century inhabitants of New Spain.

San Miguel de Allende was recently designated a World Heritage Site by UNESCO. Many U.S. veterans came to San Miguel after WWII to study art on the GI Bill. Situated at 7,200 feet, it is known for its moderate temperatures, blooming flowers year round, and steep cobblestone streets. There are no stop signs, stoplights, fast food restaurants, nor motorcycle helmets in use. The town is home to 150,000 including a large expat community estimated at 5,000 full time and another 5,000 seasonal residents. The restaurants, shops, parks, and plazas bustle with activity.

Bill and Howard first visited in 1996 and purchased their first home a year later to become year round residents. They quickly applied their philanthropic energies to their new home and subsequently obtained dual citizenship.

Their second, and current, SMA home is one part art gallery, two parts Architectural Digest gracious living, and three parts world-class botanical gardens, all enclosed in immaculate 9' high white adobe walls with tile coping. The garden has over 100 different species of trees. A museum quality display of American Indian and pre-Columbian artifacts fills the entryway. The living room is long and narrow with art covering the interior wall.

The exterior wall of the living room/art gallery features a large fireplace bracketed by glass doors, which lead to a spacious veranda and on to the gardens. The fireplace is used infrequently in December and January, and the house has neither a heating nor a cooling system. Howard and Bill's Mexican lifestyle is greatly enhanced by the presence of a butler (mozo), cook, maid, and two gardeners.

Bill's jewelry studio occupies one corner of the hacienda with a separate entrance off the front courtyard. All of the home's windows and doors are bronze-framed with beveled glass giving the feel that one is living in a chandelier.

FOUNTAINS

San Miguel is built on the side of a mountain. For centuries this topography provided an abundance of building sites with magnificent views of the city, lake, and valley lying below. The lanes are exceedingly steep and narrow, most allowing one small car to pass, some wider allowing two cars to pass (as long as one stops), and some larger thoroughfares sufficient for buses and trucks and a normal flow of car traffic. The smaller lanes are paved with cobblestones, the larger arteries with mortared stones. It's hugely charming, but also worrisome, save those with experience as a cabby in Beijing. It is a miracle any cars retain their side mirrors.

Since colonial days, gravity supplied water from the plateau flowing through a chain of 46 fountains down to the central city. When Bill and Howard arrived, none of the fountains worked, so they set about solving the problem. In a pattern that was to follow, they didn't just write a check, they rolled up their sleeves, and fixed the fountains. They enlisted members from their own staff, hired electricians, masons, and plumbers, and added their own labor. Every weekend, they'd load up a truck with ladders, tools, mortar, and other necessities and take on a fountain project. After restoring 23, the city government, having been embarrassed by the ambitious Gringos, began the process to restore the remainder.

LUIS

Shortly after moving to San Miguel, Howard and Bill's mozo, Abell (pronounced Ah bell) told them of a young man who had been disowned by his mother because he was gay. Luis was one of eight children of a devout woman struggling to raise her large family. Public education in Mexico is free through the fifth grade and after that the family must pay tuition. Luis' mother stopped paying for his education. Abell knew of the lad and knew he held promise. Based on his recommendation, Howard and Bill provided the funds for Luis to continue his education through preppa (the equivalent of junior college in the U.S.).

Howard and Bill would take Luis, and his mother and siblings, to Mexico City for outings to tour museums and see performances of the *Lion King* and *Phantom of the Opera*, insuring that they enjoyed the best seats situated on the aisle.

Early on, they realized Luis is a prodigy. He learned English quickly and currently speaks, and even banters in English almost as though it were his first language. But his real gifts are in the arts. He does everything well, and he is now Bill's equal partner in the jewelry business which operates out of their compound.

Once Luis started earning money from his artistic talents, he began helping others. He is currently funding the education of twelve relatives, built his mother a home, and, with some help from Howard, built a church near his mother's home. He painted world-class frescoes on the ceiling, and was immediately dubbed Michelangelo, Jr. Each year Luis is called upon to decorate the Parroquia Cathedral for the Dias de las Muertas festival. Although still in his young 30's, he has become a prominent man in SMA.

Luis converted the casita in the corner of Howard and Bill's estate into his home. It is a splendid two-story, uber-modern dwelling with open spaces, chic chrome kitchen, and sleek metal staircase, but decorated with contrasting gilt-framed, dark, religious themed paintings. The designers of the Crystal Bridges Gallery in Bentonville, Arkansas would be impressed.

Luis's art decorates every room of Bill and Howard's house. Papier mache statues are one of his more frivolous, but inventive, venues. Luis created a skeleton statue to display during the Day of the Dead festival. He is also funny and quick. His barbs are usually in response to Howard's jabs, and they are accepted good-naturedly.

Luis stated with confidence, "I will be famous when I'm dead." *Author's note: I wouldn't bet against it, perhaps well in advance of his departure.*

HOSPITAL RECEPTIONIST

A Mexican physician friend called Howard one day to tell him about a bright woman who was answering the phones at the hospital whose talents were being grossly under-utilized. Howard and Bill met the woman and were impressed. They said they would help her, but only with her husband's permission. Machismo plays a major role in family dynamics in Mexico. Howard and Bill knew their time and money would be wasted if the husband would not be supportive. Fortunately, he was, and they began funding the woman's education. She finished preppa, earned a university degree, and then her masters. The family arrived on Howard and Bill's doorstep several years later to announce that she had just accepted a position as a university professor.

A year in a Mexican university costs about $1,200 per year U.S. 'The boys' are currently funding the education of twelve promising students, and several hundred have preceded them.

FAT GUESTS

Howard and Bill frequently donate one-week stays in their San Miguel home for various charity auctions. Successful bidders are undoubtedly pleasantly surprised when they discover the treasure upon which they have stumbled. A few such guests were exceedingly troublesome, but most were fun and appreciative of the experience.

One of the latter had a slow build. Heavy hors d'oeuvres were laid out in the dining room in anticipation of the newcomer's arrival. The staff was shocked by the obesity of the guests and silently mumbled in Spanish their concerns about damaged furniture. As Howard arrived to introduce himself and welcome his guests, he noted the man had already finished the food and was licking one of the serving plates.

The next evening, Howard rushed to the dining room in response to a noisy commotion. The corpulent visitors were stark naked on opposites sides of the table shouting at full volume. He calmed them down, and they returned to the guest quarters.

It was going to be a long week, until it wasn't. Over time, Howard, Bill, and the staff warmed up to the new guests. They learned that the man had been the chauffeur to a rich lady in California. When she died, she left him $10 million.

On the last day of their visit two 4' x 4' x 4' packages arrived addressed to the guests. It contained school supplies and high quality children's clothing. They asked Howard if he could find a home for these items and handed him a check for $10,000 U.S.

THE ROBBERY

House etiquette calls for the housekeeper, Beatrice, to answer calls at the front door. Howard and Bill's property covers approximately one acre surrounded by a 9' adobe wall topped with handsome clay tile. The metal front door has a 6" x 6" peephole. Beatrice, the maid, answered the bell, peered through the opening, and viewed two impeccably dressed men, one about 30 the other 45. They asked to see Señor Howard.

Not knowing either man, Beatrice called upon Abell, who arrived and assessed the situation. Unannounced visitors are commonplace, all appeared well, and he invited them into the courtyard. He informed them Howard was busy and suggested they take a seat in one of the front garden patios. They looked Mexican, but spoke perfect English. Later, the older man asked if he could use the bathroom. This request was granted, and he was shown to the employee's bathroom, which opens to the front courtyard.

Minutes later, he emerged brandishing a pistol. They forced their way into the kitchen, and the younger man placed a knife to Abell's side. They encountered the cook, maid, and a man sitting in the breakfast room that was the driver of five female jewelry customers currently out of sight and touring the garden with Howard. The strangers ushered the three into the employees' bathroom and told them to stay put. Oddly, the robbery was conducted in English.

Bill maintains a jewelry studio and workshop in the front corner of the property. Guests can enter directly from the front courtyard or through the breakfast room from the house. The robbers led Abell from the kitchen, through the breakfast room, and confronted Bill in his studio. The older man pointed the pistol at his head and demanded his watch. As a combat veteran with prior experience being on the receiving end of gunfire, Bill was angry at the intrusion and shouted, "No you can't have my watch!" took it off and put it in his pocket. Then he started waving his arms wildly.

The younger man, with his knife still held to Abell's side, demanded, "Where is the safe? Where is the money?" Abell is 51, but looks 30, and he has been accurately described as 'movie star' handsome. He replied, "If you knew how much these people paid me, you wouldn't ask such a stupid question. There is no safe! There is no money!"

A few minutes earlier five women from Beaumont, Texas, now in the garden with Howard, had been in Bill's gallery and made their purchases. From the studio and through the breakfast room, customers can view a corner of the magnificent grounds that dominate the property. Howard happened to be at home at the time and graciously took them on a tour. The women's driver, a large man, was the fellow caught unawares earlier and was now locked in the bathroom.

Howard was chatting amiably with the ladies as they turned the corner around the large veranda intending to reenter the house by way of the breakfast room. He noticed the man with the pistol aimed at Bill and the knife in Abell's ribs before they saw him. He instructed the Texas ladies to enter the master bathroom using a separate entrance and lock themselves in. They didn't need babysitting, and they moved quickly to the safer setting. Then Howard pressed the panic button on his key chain. This set off a series of loud alarms. Bill was still gesticulating wildly with the gunman trying to create confusion, almost daring the robber, "Are you really going to shoot me for a watch?" The 30-year-old bolted and his partner quickly followed.

Once the alarms went off, neighbors appeared from behind their gated walls with their guard dogs. The would-be robbers were picked up by an accomplice in an awaiting car and sped off. Had they been familiar with the English term 'cluster f'__k', it might have aptly described their morning.

Howard knocked on the door of the bathroom full of the Texans and gave the 'all clear' signal. The ladies began searching through stacks of towels looking for the rings and jewels they had secreted. The staff and the driver were retrieved from their cramped quarters. The stunned shoppers gathered their petrified driver and left. The police arrived, but long after the miscreants had fled. They asked a few questions and departed.

Several days later, two detectives came to interview Howard and Bill. "Are you worried they might come back? Are you concerned for your safety?" Howard, with a well-developed mischievous streak replied, "No not at all. But if the 30-year-old were to come back I would plead, 'Would you have sex with me before you kill me?'" The detectives just shook their heads.

A few days later Howard and Bill met the Texas ladies for drinks at one of the more elegant rooftop bars in San Miguel to decompress. Bill brought leather holsters and plastic pistols for each of the ladies to serve as a Girl Scout badge-like reminder of their intrepidity. They thanked him and noted, "We all carry in Texas. Had we had our weapons, we would have opened fire on the bastards."

Several days after the incident, Howard read news of an armed robbery on an inter-city bus leaving nearby Queretaro. Two well dressed bandits, one about 30 and one about 45, attempted to rob the passengers on a bus en route to San Miguel. A security guard happened to be one of the passengers. He shot and killed the two men.

Thinking these might be the same two, Howard alerted the local police in an attempt to get pictures of the deceased. The police from Queretaro informed the police in San Miguel that they don't share information on such matters. In Bill and Howard's eyes, the case is closed.

MISCELLANEOUS PHILANTHROPY

Howard and Bill were responsible for opening the first hospice unit in Mexico. They overcame opposition from the local Bishop who thought it was a form of assisted suicide. They overcame his objections by rallying hundreds of Mexican families who knew otherwise.

While walking on a side street in San Miguel during the Dias de las

Muertas festival, a tiny, elderly woman greeted Howard warmly and gave him a hug. After they finished their brief conversation, Howard explained she is one of the people who periodically appear at their front door seeking alms.

Howard and Bill often speak of the Rose family. They later explained. There is a large family who sells roses throughout the city. They live in a dwelling without running water or electricity. It has come to pass that they arrive at Howard and Bill's every morning and sweep the front courtyard and leave roses. In return they are fed breakfast and provided use of the employees' bathroom and electrical outlets to charge their cell phones.

Not all of their attempts at philanthropy went smoothly. Years earlier while in Kansas City over the Christmas holidays Howard came out of a meeting with his attorney and accountant at the Union Bank building. He noticed a woman wearing a sleeveless summer dress and no coat, even though it was wicked cold. She was holding a styro-foam cup outstretched in her right hand with her left hand supporting her right elbow. Howard was feeling the Christmas spirit and dropped a $20 bill in her cup. The woman was shocked and rudely said, "Hey, asshole you just ruined my coffee."

POSTSCRIPT

The politically and socially active New England Puritan pamphleteer, Cotton Mather (1663 - 1728), never knew Howard, but he described him well:

"He that will write of Eliot must write of charity, or say nothing. His charity was a star of the first magnitude in the bright constellation of his virtues, and the rays of it were wonderfully various and extensive.

"His liberality to pious uses, whether publick (sic) or private, went much beyond the proportions of his little estate in the world. Many hundreds of pounds did he freely bestow upon the poor, and he would, with a very forcible importunity, press his neighbors to join with him in such beneficences....

"He did not put off his charity to be put in his last will,...; but he was his own administrator; he made his own hands his executor; and his own eyes his overseers. It has been remarked that such men are often long-lived men; so do they after many days find the bread with which they have been willing to keep other men alive."

CHAPTER 4

Dr. Adam Stone

In most small communities the local hospital bears the burden of recruiting physicians. The business model where physician practices were able to sustain themselves as independent units was rapidly disappearing by the mid 1980's. In days long gone, an older doc, or group of family practice docs, would hire a new graduate to join their practice, train him/her for many years, turn some patients over to his/ her care, and eventually look to the younger physician to buy him out. As more and more institutions such as hospitals and insurance companies started employing primary care physicians, starting salaries rose, and older docs discovered that the new graduates expected more money than the seasoned docs were earning, thus breaking a cycle that had endured for several generations.

The inability of physicians to hire their own replacements exacerbated an already severe shortage of docs in much of rural America. Most sane hospital administrators would rather crawl naked through a mile of broken glass than willingly employ physicians, but that's what happened with few exceptions.

The typical arrangement between a newly employed physician and their hospital employer involved a fixed salary, often with a productivity bonus. The physician's employees became employees of the hospital and started receiving hospital benefits and wages, almost always substantially higher than before. The new employer would be responsible for the paperwork portion of the medical practice, billing and collecting, compliance and reporting requirements, negotiating contracts, maintaining insurance, etc. In theory, the physician was then relieved of the burdens of being a small businessman and could concentrate on patients and medicine. In reality, the result was abbreviated to the term 'Tahiti Effect.' Once relieved of the economic pressures of meeting a payroll and other fixed expenses, the physician often mentally retired. Instead of squeezing 30-40 patients into their daily schedule they would now see 15-20, citing concerns for patient quality, presumably of little concern in their former circumstance. The newly employed docs would vigorously advocate for greater pay and less work for staff, and their parking lot would be empty every day by 3 pm. Concordantly, losses to the hospital would average $100,000+ per year per employed doc. But a simple syllogism governed the transaction: no docs = no hospital = no medical care or safety net = no economic viability = no community.

Community members were complaining that they couldn't get an appointment to see a physician for months. Residents would then drive nearly 70 miles to a larger city where one might receive care on a timely basis. The results were bad for the community and bad for the hospital, but plausibly good for the local physicians who had no competition and could be picky about their patients. The shortage of doctors could also be seen in hospital market share. As a general rule of thumb, a rural hospital can capably provide 60% of the services needed in their market, lacking tertiary services such as cardiology, cancer, transplants, burns, etc. If the hospital was garnering 30% market share, then it followed that the hospital was getting 50% of its potential and a majority of the local residents were doctoring elsewhere.

Such was the situation at Community Hospital*. The CEO was under a lot of pressure to recruit more physicians to town, but also realized he was dealing with a politically volatile situation. Outsiders provided political cover for the hospital CEO and board in dealing with these adversarial contests. If everything blew up, the outsider could take as much of the blame as could reasonably be deflected.

Consultants would analyze basic demographics of the population in the hospital's service area, match that to industry guidelines regarding physician manpower planning, compare the result to the existing composition of the medical staff, and make recommendations regarding recruiting priorities. They'd interview existing physicians and community leaders to learn their perspective about community needs and analyze market share data to determine where those leaving the community were traveling for their medical services.

The analysis merely quantified what everyone already knew intuitively. The community needed and could support nine full time primary care physicians (family practice or internal medicine) and they had five. It wasn't a close call. Presentations were made to the city commissioners, service clubs, and a host of other community meetings and were received warmly. But as was almost always the case, the real drama was boiling below the surface.

I was favorably impressed by Dr. Stone* after our first encounter. He looked like Huck Finn in a lab coat, was in his mid to late 30's, and greeted me in a personable and engaging manner. He was from a small town in an adjacent state, had graduated from a prestigious medical school, finished a residency in family practice, and had been practicing in the community for ten years. He was the youngest member of a four-person group with offices located in an attractive new building adjacent to the hospital. Their practice was burgeoning. During our interview he confirmed that their practice was virtually closed to new patients, it would take over a month for an existing patient to get a non-emergency appointment, and yes he was aware that a lot of people in town had given up and would go out of town for care. He was the only member of the group that would speak to me, giving some clue of the difficulties that would lie ahead. Later the hospital CEO told me, "You just saw the Dr. Jekyll side of his personality. Wait for Mr. Hyde."

Shortly after that relatively benign interview, the young doc burst into the hospital CEO's office, sat down across from him and threatened, "If you persist in bringing my competition into this town, I will do everything in my power to destroy you and this hospital. I won't rest until your f___ing head is on a platter, and you're heading out of town hanging from a pole." His face was red with anger, and he was nearly frothing at the mouth as he slammed the door, glared at anyone nearby, and stalked out.

This was but an extreme example of a common occurrence. Similar versions of this threat occurred in virtually every community where a hospital was involved in recruiting primary care physicians to their communities by either employing them or providing incentives such as a salary guarantee and moving expenses. All hospital CEO's dreaded this confrontation, and their response varied greatly depending on their survival instincts, age, level of self-confidence, and their perceived support from their board of directors. The insecure would vacillate, postpone, and pass the problem along to their inevitable successor. The young would be eager to make their mark and hadn't yet experienced the flagitiousness of a scorned physician. The veterans would plan, cajole, nurture, dodge and weave, and try to manage the crisis before it boiled over.

The physicians' side of the argument was not without merit. They perceive their local hospital using their resources to unfairly bring competitors to town. Medicine is a business, and the local attorney, dentist, or car dealer didn't suffer this indignity, why should physicians?

The hospital proceeded to hire three new family practice physicians and provided financial support to assist them in getting their practices started. The young doc and his group, delivered on the promise to hurt the CEO and the hospital by staging a virtual boycott. They referred most of their patients to a regional medical center 75 miles distant. Patients were told that physician concerns over quality of care necessitated these extreme sanctions. The boycott lasted for nearly a year and resulted in a technical default on the hospital's outstanding bonds. Several services were closed, and layoffs affecting more than 40 families were implemented. The young doc conducted a full court press with his patients, the board, and anyone who would listen about getting the CEO fired. The town was split; some believing Dr. Stone's argument that he was the only line of defense between an unsuspecting public and an incompetent, evil hospital administrator.

In the case of open warfare between passionate rural docs and a hospital administrator, the docs almost always win. Consider the potential for public relations damage within a small community that can be caused by four mightily pissed off docs, each seeing 25 patients a day, reaching nearly 500 people per week, and espousing their version of events to their captive audience. Amazingly, the board backed the CEO, and he withstood the assault on his character and livelihood with uncommonly good grace.

The doc's ended their boycott after one year, not because they had given up on their goal of revenge, but because it was costing them money. Many of the patients, once sent out of town, didn't come back. The docs were conceding the revenue they would have ordinarily received providing follow-up care in the hospital. Interestingly, morale among the staff improved immeasurably during Dr. Stone's absence, as he was notoriously unkind to nurses.

TEN YEARS LATER

One Saturday afternoon I received a call from the CEO at Community Hospital. He had survived the many crises that are commonplace in his line of work. We'd stayed friends and maintained a client relationship in spite of the events of ten years earlier. He said,

"Do you remember Dr. Stone?"

"Of course, I'll never forget that name as long as I live."

"Well, you won't believe what he's been up to now."

Try me."

And he told me his version of the latest events: "As everyone in town knew, the Stones were having marital problems. By outward appearances, he was one of the wealthiest guys in the county. He owns a large, well-tended farm with a beautiful house, stables, and barns. It's a veritable show place. A couple of weeks ago he went into his fancy barn, took a baseball bat and knocked out the rear window on the driver's side of his pickup truck. Then he rigged a shotgun in a vise in the barn, so that he could shoot light buckshot into the back of his right shoulder. In case there is any doubt that there is a God, he screwed up that part of the scheme and actually blew his right arm all to hell. Then he got back in his pickup, drove about half way down his half-mile driveway, and called the county sheriff to say, 'My wife just tried to kill me!'

"Apparently, he was concerned about losing a portion of his wealth, so he tried to set up his wife for attempted murder in advance of divorce proceedings. An ambulance was called to take him to the hospital, and the sheriff arrived at the house and arrested the wife. One does not have to have to be Columbo to figure out what happened. After a few days, the local law enforcement folks figured it out, he confessed to his misdeeds, and the wife was cleared of any wrongdoing. She was, however, one exceedingly pissed off woman. It's unclear whether she chose not to press charges or exactly what happened, but the county attorney took no further legal action. Within a few weeks, any hint of scandal had blown over. Dr. Stone got a free pass except for the crippled right arm and a weakened negotiating position in his divorce proceedings."

I later talked to the chief financial officer of the hospital to ask her take on this story, knowing both she and her mother were patients of the schemer. Her response was, "I always knew he was an asshole, but he's a really good doc." She then mimicked her Mom's reaction (imagine a Monty Python character's voice imitating an older woman) saying, "I've always just loved him, he's such a fine young man and all, and such a wonderful doctor. We all go through a bit of a bad time, now don't we? I just couldn't risk trying to find someone else who could take as good of care of me, knowing my medicines and history and all. I'm so relieved this has all blown over, and he's going to be all right. I'm so sorry about his arm, the poor man."

Several thousand patients must have had similar sentiments, because he was back in business with a full practice shortly after recovering from his self inflicted wound.

ANOTHER FIVE YEARS LATER

Once again I received a call from the CEO, who had shown amazing resilience surviving several decades at the Hospital. "Want to hear the latest?"

"Of course."

He explained, "You're really not going to believe this. Dr. Stone walked into my office a few weeks ago and said, 'I know I have wronged you many times over the years. I've consistently taken actions to harm you and the hospital, and I'm here to apologize for this behavior. I don't expect you to judge me by my words, as they have not always been truthful, but instead by my deeds through which I hope to earn your forgiveness.'

"Then an even more amazing thing happened. Over the past few weeks he has behaved like a normal human being. When he came to see me, he didn't just barge into my office. He stopped, visited pleasantly with my secretary a few minutes, asked if I was free, and if I could possibly see him. He's started to treat nurses and other hospital staff decently. He asks their opinion on caring for patients, he doesn't shout and throw things. They don't know what to make of him. The ones who've been around here a long time are still wary of him and are afraid he'll return to his former persona if they show any sign of weakness. We'll just have to see if this is for real or not."

AND ANOTHER FIVE YEARS LATER

I ran into the Community Hospital CEO at a meeting, and we exchanged pleasantries, and I asked about Dr. Stone. He obliged, "You remember when I told you about his asking for forgiveness and saying judge me by my deeds not words. Well he was true to his word and has become one of the most supportive docs on the staff. He really did change for the better. But here's the really astounding part of the story. It turns out that our now not-so-young friend was just the stalking horse for the others in his group. Once it was apparent that he was really cooperating with the hospital, the other three asked him to leave. He is now practicing solo and has moved to another town."

CHAPTER 5

John Fontenot

PROLOGUE

John has been a polished and professional waiter at Galatoire's in the French Quarter of New Orleans for the past 48 years. There he has served and masterfully entertained legions of patrons. His stories, delivered rapid-fire in his heavy Cajun accent, are always funny and fun.

"I served Mick Jagger once. He's a little bitty guy, but his lips are huge. If he licked them, and you threw him at that wall, he'd stick."

"I grew up in the bayous around Ville Platte, LA. We'd pick cotton as kids. Got paid 2 cents a pound. We'd pee on the cotton to add weight. I once put a bolt in my sack, but I got caught."

"Me and my brothers would hunt gators and frogs in the bayous. You'd see the red eyes of the snakes slithering to get the same frog you were after. You learned real fast to not mess with a Momma gator with little ones nearby. One followed me five miles to my house."

"Probably the dumbest thing I ever did was to crawl through the window of one car into another, while the two were racing down a country road at 50 mph. To this day, I can't believe I did that."

And these snippets were offered during the first few minutes of a recent lunch. Galatoire's is an elegant Bourbon Street restaurant famous for not taking reservations. Wealthy diners have been known to send paid surrogates to assure their place in line. The Fridays before Christmas and Mardi Gras are particularly coveted lunch dates and are auctioned off with proceeds going to local charities. One can expect to pay $500 per person for the privilege of buying a $150 lunch and for the prospect of being entertained by John.

John enjoys a large following and has achieved a modicum of fame. He has been featured in several articles in New Orleans newspapers and periodicals. He also recorded a 45-minute interview for the National Archives of Storytelling. John has rebuffed the requests from several writers who have approached about telling / selling stories about the famous people he has served. But he graciously agreed to spend a few days with me when I told him, "I'm not interested in the famous people you've served. I'm interested in you."

On the first of the two days we spent together, John asked me, "Do you like boudin?" Boudin (boo-dan) is a gumbo-like mixture of sausage, rice, and spice stuffed into casings. Having sampled the regional cuisine a few months earlier, I told him, "No?"

"What! You don't like boudin? Where'd you eat it at?"

"Commander's Palace."

"No wonder. Let me get you some real Cajun boudin."

And he left, went to the Rousch's grocery store on Royal and St. Peter and returned with a package of spicy boudin. He cooked the gooey substance, and it was plate-licking tasty. I'm now a convert. "Now that we've had some boudin, I can tell you some stories about growing up as a Coonass."

CAJUN COUNTRY

The British defeated the French in the middle-18th century war known as the French and Indian War in North American History and The Seven Years War in Europe. French speaking occupants of Acadia, now Nova Scotia and eastern Quebec, were on the losing end of the conflict, and many filtered to the friendlier confines of the vast Louisiana territory still ruled by France. They were eventually dubbed Cajuns, a bastardization of the word 'Acadian', and many settled in the southwestern corner of what is now the state of Louisiana.

The first Fontenot's came to Cajun country directly from France, first landing in Mobile, Alabama, later moving to New Orleans, and then migrating west to Ville Platte, 172 miles northwest of New Orleans and the county seat of Evangeline Parish. John explained, "People think all these Cajuns came from Canada. It's not true. There might have been a few boatloads, but most came from France, Ireland, all over the world. They just say that to make the Canadians happy."

John remembers family lore about Evangeline Parish's very own serial killer, Euzebe Vidrine. One day Euzebe was milking the family cow. His sister stood nearby holding its calf making the milking easier. He told her, "I think I feel like killing you." The little girl was appropriately alarmed and ran to tell her Mother, and they went to the sheriff. He questioned Euzebe who confessed to killing twelve people. He was arrested, convicted, and was the last person hung in Ville Platte. And the memory of Euzebe has been used to scare little children in the parish from that day forward.

DILAN AND CARRIE FONTENOT

John was the youngest of eight children born to Dilan and Carrie Fontenot: Wesley, Myrtis, Glenn, Pearl, Ola, Versy, Clarence, and John. Carrie was a 'redneck hillbilly' from the hills of North Carolina.

They met in the 1920's when Dilan was returning from an overseas assignment. She was a Baptist and he was a Catholic, and they came from different worlds. "Back then, the Daddy made all the decisions, so we were all raised Catholic." Dilan was one of twelve kids growing up, all in and around Ville Platte yielding an abundance of Fontenot aunts, uncles and cousins in the small town.

Dilan worked for the government in mysterious ways about which John didn't elaborate, but he would disappear for long periods of time then reappear. Dilan was an intimidating man and his children learned early not to sass or speak back to him. "You were almost afraid to meet his eye. All he had to do was give you 'the look', and you knew you were in trouble. He was different from others. His gaze would go right through you. He would just clear his throat, and you knew you were being dismissed. He was quiet, but always carried a gun. People were afraid of him. They were afraid of my family."

Carrie's Dad was a giant of a man standing 6'8", and he would travels the hills and hollers of NC locating illegal stills and sawmills. Later the revenuers would appear. At 5'4", John picked up his maternal grandfather's toughness, but not his height.

John speaks proudly of being a Coonass, as distinct from a Redneck. I asked for a definition, and he explained, "A Coonass speaks French, Rednecks speak English." John spoke French the first five years of his life, learning English only after starting school. Several of his older siblings spoke English well, presumably a function of more time with their Mom. By the time John arrived, Carrie had undoubtedly tired of tending babies.

None of the kids wore shoes until they entered school. They had a washtub outside the front door where feet would be washed before entering. The family raised cows, pigs, and chickens, which, along with a big garden, kept food on the table. Butchering the animals in the yard became a regular part of the family routines. A few weeks before an animal was to be killed, the children would set it apart and feed it nothing but corn, to cleanse the body.

Pork would be salted after butchering. Then they would wrap the meat in cheesecloth, tie it tightly with twine to squeeze out the moisture and store it under their beds. Beef had to be eaten shortly after it was butchered, so family and friends gathered to share in those feast days. "Everyone had a smoke house in those days, about 10' high, no fire, just smoke." The family didn't acquire electricity until John was in high school. They used an icebox for refrigeration, a well-insulated chest cooled by blocks of ice delivered by incredibly strong men. When electricity came to their house, it was direct current with two wires running parallel to the house, but they still used coal lamps for lighting to save money. The family didn't have indoor plumbing until John left home. It was a one-holer serving the family of ten, but the boys used the back of the barn and a shovel.

On the few occasions when John was emboldened to ask for candy, his Dad would point to the pocketknife in John's pocket and direct him to a fig tree in their backyard. The figs were good, but getting them involved going into a tree full of hornets. In spite of learning to first use a torch to smoke the nest, John would still get stung, and Dilan would treat the wounds with tobacco spit.

As a child John was a 'bleeder' and suffered from uncontrollable nosebleeds. Dilan took him to a 'traiteur (treater)' in nearby Carencre. Ville Platte was home to another treater, but Dilan didn't trust him. The Carencre traiteur would lay hands on John, chant, and pray, and he was cured. The traiteur didn't take money, so Dilan paid him with tobacco. One of John's grandsons now suffers from the same affliction, but he receives treatment from an otolaryngologist and a hematologist.

There was little money for clothes. John's Mom washed what garments they had on a scrub board and hung them out on a clothesline. She would often use the barbed wire fence that kept cows out of their yard for extra line. When rain clouds appeared she'd whistle loudly, and all kids would arrive instantly to help bring in the wash. "Death was the only excuse for not being on time." If John accidently tore a garment while retrieving it from the barbed wire, his sisters would, "slap the shit out of me." Then they'd go in to tell their Mom who would "slap even more shit out of me." John learned to be careful when bringing in the wash.

"Momma baked bread every day. If you were in the house you had to be sleeping, otherwise any movement would make the bread fall, making Momma mighty unhappy. No one wanted to be around when Momma was angry. The best thing we ate was sugar cane syrup on pecans. You can't climb a pecan tree because the branches are too brittle, so you have to use long poles. Momma would stir the pecans in the boiling syrup until it became a hard candy. It was the best thing in the world, but you had to have good teeth."

One of John's brothers was a good guitar player and singer. The family also owned a wind-up record player and would buy discarded records from a local bar with a jukebox. They'd host dances at their home. In preparation they'd push all the furniture to the side of the main room, and the kids would set about polishing the floor with old army blankets. At age 6, John served as a human mop. He would lie on an army blanket, swim around under the furniture, and then one of his sisters would pull him out.

The family purchased their first television in 1964, John's last year of high school, but the reception was poor. Whenever their parents left the house, John and his brothers would remove the metal springs from their beds, link them together, and use the contraption to wire the TV to the rooftop, making an ersatz antennae. Amazingly, it worked, but had to be disassembled before bedtime.

The cotton harvest started in August and continued through October. Dilan would drive all of his kids to a cotton field owned by one of his brothers, drop them off at daybreak, and pick them up at sunset. Glenn, the most cerebral of John's brothers and who later became a physicist, wanted nothing to do with the heavy labor, and would disappear spending his days walking along railroad tracks. John, not wanting to be left home alone, asked to be taken along at age eight. By the time he was ten he was picking 70 lbs. of cotton a day, and by twelve could pick 150 lbs. It was hot, nasty work, and the fields were full of snakes and bugs. Every morning the Fontenot children would bring a mason jar full of ice water and hide it in the weeds hoping to keep it out of the sun. By mid-morning, when they'd have their first break, they'd return to find it near boiling.

They were paid 2 cents per pound, and they tried every trick possible to increase the weight including peeing and spitting on the cotton. John went to the trouble of acquiring and carrying several large iron bolts. He hid them in his sack, but his uncle quickly detected the ruse. Cotton is picked twice during the harvest, and the first pick cotton is heavier. "For the second cut, you work much harder for even less money." The kids would also be hired out hoeing the cotton fields for which they earned $3 for a day lasting from sunup to sundown. John's father always collected their pay relieving the children of the burden of managing their meager wages. The children never saw a dime of their 'cotton-picking' earnings.

"Picking that cotton ball out of the boll would tear up your hands." Later, John's became so tough you could put a cigarette out in his palm. They'd pick alongside several older Negro women who would sing gospels and chants while working, "Their singing put me in a trance that took your mind off the heat, the bugs, and the monotony of the work."

The job was tough on hands, but even tougher on the neck and back. The pickers carried a long canvas bag strapped over their neck. "You'd be stooped over picking the cotton out of the boll dragging that heavy bag." John passed the time trying to think of how to build a machine to do this labor.

BUSINESS BOY

John wised up at age thirteen and started a paper route to get out of the cotton fields. "Picking cotton was worse than Vietnam. And Vietnam was bad." His Dad took him to the local bank where he obtained a loan to buy a bicycle, and was soon earning $20 per month delivering the Times Picayune. But the payments went first to the bank and then to his Mom. He delivered papers at 4 am every day, and once a month he would make a return trip on the route in the afternoon to collect $1.97 from each subscriber. Riding around town during the wee hours, John would observe cars parked in places where they shouldn't be. At an early age, he was learning who was sleeping with whom and many of the little town's secrets. John also started mowing lawns. He borrowed another $20 from the bank to buy a Briggs & Stratton power lawn mower. He was earning $3 mowing a single lawn for the 'rich' people, the equivalent of a full day's work in the cotton fields.

"Mom made shirts for me out of flour sacks. I wasn't going to wear that stuff to school anymore." With his newfound wealth, John treated himself to store bought clothing, and he acquired and wore muscle shirts, ala James Dean. "I didn't smoke, but I'd roll a pack of cigarettes in the sleeve of my 'muscle shirts'. We didn't have any money for weights, so we borrowed some concrete sacks from a construction site and made our own." He told his Dad he needed tennis shoes so he could play basketball. He was taken to the Army surplus store and his Dad bought him olive drab green shoes for two bits ($.25).

John delivered papers to Mademoiselle Jean Vidrine, an elderly lady who lived in a grand old plantation home. John took special care to deliver her paper on her doorstep, making it easier for her. In return she tipped John generously at Christmas. She also allowed John to retrieve pecans from a large tree in her backyard. There, John captured a flying squirrel that became his pet and constant companion for a year. John kept the squirrel in a buttoned shirt pocket while in school. Years later, the house was torn down and the land was donated to the nearby church. The demolition crew found a package under the porch containing $50,000 in small bills. "I can't believe I walked on that porch and over that treasure every day for years."

"We were expected to be tough and stand up for ourselves. If I ever backed away from a fight, word would get back to my brothers and sisters, and they'd kick my ass." It was easier to just take your beating when it came. Even though John was little when he graduated from high school, 5'4" and 120 lbs, he was strong and relentless. "People only f___d with me once."

HUNTING AND FISHING

May is mating season and the best time for froggin'. John and his brothers would wear headlamps, walk along the levies bordering the rice fields, and grab frogs by hand. "Some people would use a long pole with prongs, but we'd just use our bare hands. You learned to watch for the red eyes of the snakes slithering in to compete for our catch. We would catch frogs the size of my two hands spread out. We'd get $1 for each pair of legs. The leg is the only part you can eat, so we'd cut them off and skin them. If you threw a bunch of legs into a boiling pot, you had to be sure to put the lid on, otherwise they'd jump right out."

"We'd hunted rabbits at night. We'd just club them with a stick. They were so plentiful. Sometimes, we'd use a BB gun or a shotgun with #8 buckshot.

"Blackbirds were delicious. We'd see a flock on the ground and shoot a round of buckshot above their heads. They'd fly up and form a tight ball. We'd fire the second round into the ball, and they'd fall like rain. The thing about bird hunting is to make sure they're dead. I'd always touch the bird with the tip of the shotgun barrel. If alive, they'd go straight for your eyes with their claws."

John and his brothers hunted alligators in nearby Rapides Parish on Bayou Teche. First they'd kill a poule peu (a little duck also good for gumbo) and cut it up so it would bleed. Then they'd put it on a 4" hook, drop it in the water and wait. It wouldn't take long for a gator to bite, and then the fight would begin. One of the boys would lasso the snout, and another would shoot it in the head with a .22 rifle so as not to damage the hide. "You gotta watch out for that tail. Those gators are mighty dangerous." They would sell the skins for $1/foot to an outlaw-guy that would come around in his truck. The Fontenot boys would keep the tails for the meat.

John's brothers told him to never mess with a mother gator that had babies nearby. They are dangerous under any circumstances, but even more so when protecting their young. 10-year-old John failed to heed this warning, and he picked up a baby gator while out and about. He walked five-miles home, and put the little gator in the foot tub outside their front door. He covered it with a board on which he placed a large rock. Later that night, the family heard a commotion and discovered a large gator banging its tail against the house. It had trailed John and retrieved its offspring.

Squirrel season opens the first Saturday in October. Schools are closed the preceding Friday acknowledging that no one would attend anyway. Boys would head to their favorite hunting spots and set up camps. Fires would be made and all would enjoy a feast of poisson etouffe (made of catfish, flour, tomatoes, and spices) and play cards, booray being their favorite game.

On Saturday morning the hunt would begin. The leaves would still be on the trees, but dozens of the squirrels would be bagged with shotguns and #7 shot. The catch was cleaned and thrown in a communal pot for the second feast of the weekend. The first basket of squirrels became Sauce Piquant. Priests would hold mass early on Sunday so people could get out for the hunt. "Squirrels are mighty tasty even though they only eat nuts."

The Fontenot boys would hunt for turtles in the mud of the Atchafalaya River basin. They'd poke steel poles in the mud until they hit a turtle. Then they would poke around its edge and pry it out. Sometimes they'd get lucky and land a loggerhead. "The only problem would be the snakes that would fall on you out of the trees." John was familiar with snakes, but was once bitten by a cottonmouth. His hand swelled the size of a basketball. Dilan treated it with tobacco spit, and he lived to tell the tale.

John and his brothers would set up trotlines across the bayou. They'd use crawfish for bait, and set hooks every few feet about 12" deep. The boys would run the trap every hour and would bring in large hauls of goo fish, blue catfish, yellow catfish, spotted catfish, eel, and gaar. "The gaar was the best eating."

The boys rigged a sled out of 2"x 4" boards to carry a large iron pot. They'd drag the contraption behind one of their horses to use on their crawfish hunts. There was a spring fed swimming hole adjacent to the bayou and the nearby rice fields. The rice farmers would pump the spring water into their rice fields that were bordered by small levies. John and his brothers would breech a levy, screen the flow, and it would quickly fill with hundreds of crawfish. "We had to be careful to not let the breech get out of hand." Then they'd boil the crawfish and make a dipping sauce out of vinegar, salt, and pepper. To complement the meal they'd bury sweet potatoes in the mud, build a fire on top, cook for several hours and then eat. The Fontenot family did not go hungry.

When John's Dad retired from his 'government' job, he started a local cab company. He was always dabbling in various businesses, some legal, some less so. At 5 am every weekend, 14-year-old John would be picked up by one of his Dad's cabs, along with a local doctor and a maid, for the 20-mile trip to a whorehouse in Oakdale, LA. The doc would examine the girls, the maid would clean up, and John would earn the tidy sum of $5 for a few hours work restocking the beer boxes.

By listening to nearby adult conversations John would learn more. "All the girls came from California. No local girls were involved because Cajun fathers could be expected to kill any son of a bitch pimping their daughters." Even though the song *Hotel California* was still decades in the future, girls were welcome anytime, but they could never leave. Cab drivers were forbidden to take any girls out. Young John would hear talk that the local sheriff and police and politicians were all on the take. Busloads of soldiers came from nearby Fort Polk, for which the commanding general was rumored to receive compensation. Every now and again there would be a faux raid, but the proprietors were warned well in advance, and the girls would be relocated for the occasion. This provided a few comforting, but phony, headlines to appease the citizenry.

Sheriff Cat Doucet, was a colorful and controversial character and a minion of Huey Long. The Kingfish once famously predicted, with little fear of contradiction, "Someday the people of Louisiana are going to get good government, and they're not going to like it." Cat supported the registration of African American voters in Saint Landry's Parish as early as 1952 and was rewarded by their votes for the remainder of his political career. He owned a 'high yella' whorehouse in Opelousas, the Parish seat, staffed by mulatto and Creole girls. According to local legend, Sheriff Cat was the inspiration for the term 'Cathouse.' And he was John's Dad's friend and business partner.

The sheriff, another man, and Dilan owned all of the pinball and slot machines operating in Saint Landry Parish. John remembers being held by his Dad when he was a small boy, pulling the lever on the one-armed-bandit serving as a good luck charm. He also helped his Mom and siblings count and pack the nickels and quarters from the machines.

Blacks and whites lived in separate worlds in 1950's Louisiana. Blacks respected John's Dad because he treated them with respect. He would tell his children, "You leave them people alone." He was tough but had a big heart. During elections, many blacks would ask John's Dad who they should vote for, to determine who was the least racist among those running. "Dad would answer in French, because most of the blacks spoke French back then, 'pap bon' meaning someone was no good."

REVENGE

"I was a sneaky little shit. I'll admit it." While most people dealt with John fairly during his paper route days, a few did not. One stood out. The brother of the town's most prominent doctor would regularly dodge John when it was time to pay. He didn't like John, and he didn't like the Fontenot family. He would occasionally sic his Irish Setter, Rusty, on John when he would ride by.

John told one of his uncles about the problem and was instructed, "Go to the feed store, buy a mason jar full of lye, put the lye in your water gun, and use it on the dog if he bothers you."

A day later, Rusty chased John and received a squirt of lye. The dog howled, ran home, and never troubled him again. Unfortunately, the spectacle was viewed by Rusty's owner, and he wasn't happy. He got in his car, and gave chase. John kept circling back on him, cut through some back yards, and finally made it to the safety of his home, where the pursuer would not venture. The guy called John's paper route boss and tried to get him fired, but without success. "People would push me, I'd push back."

Another paper route customer also made a habit of regularly stiffing John. He wouldn't answer the door even if he were home. He just wouldn't pay. The miscreant purchased a brand new 1957 Chevy. He was obsessive about the car and would wash it every day. John would bicycle past his house most afternoons and was intimately familiar with his habits. One day the man unwisely left his car unlocked. John happened to have a sack full of crawfish heads. He crawled in the backseat of the car, and using a screwdriver, forced the stinking detritus between the back seat and the armrest. He cleaned up the upholstered area leaving no visible trace of his mischief.

Days later he rode by and noticed the car in the driveway with the doors and windows open. He later overheard the man screaming at his wife accusing her of doing something to the car. He eventually sold it because he couldn't get rid of the lingering stench.

The owner of a country western bar joined the ranks of those earning John's teenage wrath. After collecting his $1.97 monthly subscription fee, John would usually buy a bottle of pop and a bag of chips. On one such occasion the snack was stale, and he complained. The merchant refused to either refund his nickel or replace the chips. The man was also obsessive about keeping his front porch swept clean. Later that day, John crushed the stale chips into dust, and sprinkled them on his porch.

He was later confronted by the bar owner, "TJ, you sneaky little shit! I know you did that. If I ever catch you in the act, I'll whip your skinny ass." The accusation, though well founded, motivated John to build a small bomb and blow up his mailbox. "I was little, but people didn't mess with me."

After high school, John went to work for a company that repaired used rail tank cars and boxcars. They'd sandblast and paint the interior of the cars, and it was a hard, unpleasant job. "Some of the older guys took to messing with me. They'd want me to pad their time sheets and do their work. I'd always end up with the worst jobs. One day I caught five Blue Runner snakes and put them in a sack. I threw the sack into the bathhouse where everyone was showering after their shift. When those snakes slithered out, the black guys turned white, and the white guys were assholes and elbows getting out of there. They never figured out who did it."

"My Mom later taught me to turn the other cheek."

COTTON FESTIVAL

The Tournoi de la Ville Platte Cotton Festival would be held at the end of the cotton harvest and would feature various horse races. In one, men would ride their horses around the high school track holding long wooden lances, like knights of old, and try to spear large metal rings hung from a stationary pole with a clothespin. The rider who gathered the most rings in the least time won. It is also very dangerous with many horses and riders falling on the cinder track.

Bush track races were also part of the festival. These are unsanctioned, informal horse races on makeshift tracks with Quarter horses, ridden by amateur jockeys, with the judges standing on the bed of pickup trucks. Louisiana is notable for having produced many top jockeys who got their start in these events. John was ten when he started riding, usually quarter mile sprints. At the time, he weighed 80 lbs and had strong legs to grip the horse, making him a good jockey. He earned $3 to race, $5 if he won. His uncle once tied him to the horse, thinking it would be safer. When John's mother learned of this she forbade the uncle from ever again setting foot in their house. In later life, John would learn that the doctor who accompanied him to the Oakdale whorehouse was also known for doping the horses before the races. "I was too big by the time I turned twelve, ending my career as a jockey."

At the age of 17 John graduated from Ville Platte High School, having been kicked out of the Catholic High School a year earlier. "I was a good student, but I was a bad student if you know what I mean. I picked things up quick, but I was sneaky. My Dad taught me how to play chess and how to walk around the board and look at things from different angles. That's how I looked at the world."

John moved to New Orleans and lived in the projects with his sister and her husband. "Back in those days the projects were full of white people, mostly WWII veterans." He got a job as a busboy at Antoine's in the French Quarter. Before he turned 18 he knew he would be eligible for the draft. His Dad advised him to enlist, and he did, for a four-year stint in the Air Force.

John was still 5'4" tall and weighed 120 lbs when he arrived for basic training at Lackland Air Force base in San Antonio. He lined up with other trainees, was asked to salute and sound out his name. Unfortunately, his heavy Cajun accent made Fontenot sound like 'f__ you'. The drill sergeants would ask him to come forward and repeat that. Then they'd ask others to come and listen to the diminutive Cajun's apparent epithet. "Once I got through basic training and into the rangers they stopped f___g with me."

Basic training was relatively easy for John. The drill sergeants marveled at the toughness of his hands and feet. "I could have done basic barefoot, and you could still put out a burning cigarette in my hand. We'd run everywhere, and would have to do chin-ups before chow. The fat boys had a lot of trouble with that. They couldn't do even one. It was comical watching them hang from the bar kicking their legs in the air like that would lift them. I first heard the word 'profanity' in basic, and I didn't know what it meant, but I quickly learned."

Because of his French fluency John was assigned duties as a translator. After basic, John went to the Jungle Warfare training in

Panama. "They taught us to live off the land. We ate iguanas and snakes. For me it was just like growing up in Ville Platte. It was harder on the city boys." Special-forces candidates with highest IQ's were often tapped for medic training. John was sent to Ft. Sam Houston for a six-week medic course. John could still recite hundreds of medical terms from this training and would later deliver babies in the bush in SE Asia.

After completing their training, John's unit flew to Clark airbase in the Philippines. "It was 800 miles from Vietnam and was like living in the Humphrey Bogart movie *Casa Blanca*." Massive shipments of war material went in and out of the base theoretically headed for U.S. troops in Vietnam, with, "Much going to the black market and eventually used against U.S. troops." John's unit oversaw the loading of pallets of U.S. currency loaded onto a cargo plane. They were told the dollars came from the casinos and whorehouses operated by the military in Vietnam.

Then his unit was told to remove their dog tags and all identification, and they were flown into the bush. "We knew we were screwed if we were ever captured. No one would own up to our being where we were. We did some bad stuff. I don't want to say no more about that." After a pause, he reflected, "You saw things, but you never said anything or corrected anybody. Everyone was armed. It was unbelievably dangerous. I was scared to death all the time, especially when you were on point. You were told to volunteer, 'you, you, and you just volunteered.' I got a multi-million dollar education, but I wouldn't ever go back there again."

John's worldly father gave him some of the most useful advice about jungle survival, "Don't ever pick up something you didn't drop. Take salt and pepper."

Many years after the war, a friend of John's was working for Wal-Mart and recommended him for a well paying job setting up distribution systems in Southeast Asia. John declined.

John's father died of emphysema while he was in the bush. The military flew him home for the funeral. The Red Cross gave him $500 in travel money. The money came in American Express Travelers checks, which John had never seen. They explained how to use the checks, and he found his way back to Ville Platte using a combination of military and civilian flights, a bus trip, and hitchhiking. After the funeral he met with a gruff colonel and was told he had the choice of returning to his unit or getting an early out. He opted for the latter. He was given a physical, where they found and ignored blood in his urine, was debriefed by military intelligence, given an honorable discharge, and Staff Sergeant Fontenot returned to the civilian world.

BACK FROM THE WAR

"One day, they asked me to run bets for them. I was in college then, could use a little extra money, and I accepted, but I had no idea what 'running bets' meant." *Author's note: I asked John who 'they' were, and he said, "Let's just use the words they and them."* The owners of certain racehorses would use straw men to place bets on their behalf before the windows would close to disguise their interests and manipulate the odds. The horse, a hidden ringer, might open at 50-1 odds. John would be given $10,000 in cash to place 5-10 minutes before the race. He'd move from the $50 window to $10 window, betting various 'win, show, or place' bets on the 50-1 horse. The oddsmaking wasn't computerized in 1968, so the odds might only drop to 30-1. John would then go into the men's room, put all the racing tickets in a paper bag, hop in a cab, and return them to his employer. "Those guys made a lot of money."

At the end of the season (Mid-November - Early January), John's contact took him aside. "How much you pay for that house of yours?" John was in college on the GI bill and had just purchased a home for

$17,500. John told him, and the guy handed him $20,000 in cash and said, "Go pay that off."

"I knew he had me on a string. I could have become one of those wise guys I later heard about on television shows, but fortunately they let me go."

PATRICIA

John married Patricia shortly after returning from Vietnam in early 1967. "I used to run on the levy near the French Quarter to keep in shape. I'd see her sitting there on one of the benches, so one day I brought her a rose, and the rest is history. We didn't drink or smoke, so we didn't go to bars, we just liked being out." She was one-quarter inch taller. Andre Paul (aka Andy) was born in 1969. Four years later daughter Helen was born.

"I got hooked on cigars in the bush. I needed something to cover the smell of the C-rations. When I got back home, my wife told me there would be no smoking in the house. Hey! It's my house isn't it? So when she goes out one day, I open all the windows and doors, and light up. I was reading the racing form, watching a football game, and smoking a cigar when she returned. She started pulling the drapes down and put them in the trash. Hey that costs a lot of money! We bought new drapes, and I gave up cigars. I only won one argument with her, but the price was too high. She was a bitch, but God love her, she was my bitch."

"She had accumulated a lot of stuff. She was addicted to QVC. She owned five sewing machines. One day we were sitting on the front porch when an 18-wheeler pulled up and stopped in front of our house, blocking the entire street. Pat disappeared to the back of the house. The driver gets the removable forklift and then places two huge packages on my lawn. I tell him he's got the wrong house, but he shows me the manifest. I yell for Pat. She doesn't come out, until the truck is gone. She doesn't want it to go back. Once open I see it's a bright red Troy Bilt tiller and shredder she paid $1800 for. She said, 'I know you like cucumbers, now you can have a garden.' We had a garden one year, and I ended up giving the tiller to my brother."

"In 2002 Pat's car was t-boned by a semi, and she was taking Vioxx, a muscle relaxant no longer on the market, to manage the pain. I returned home from work one night around 11. I called a greeting to her, and went in to have a diet coke and unwind. When I walked into the bedroom, she was lying in bed with her glasses fallen down from her eyes and a book on her chest. She would read four books a week, but it was unusual for her to fall asleep with her glasses on. I brushed my teeth, undressed, and climbed into bed. I touched her arm, it dropped lifelessly, and she was cold as ice. I tried CPR, but she was gone. I called 911, and after the medics arrived, I went into the yard, and cursed her for leaving me here alone." An autopsy was performed, and it would reveal that she died three hours earlier. Her heart stopped, presumably attributable to the Vioxx. She was 56."

"In an odd way, Katrina was a blessing. Our house was under fifteen feet of water, and I lost a lot of photos and things that were important to me. But I also got rid of the massive amount of crap that Pat accumulated."

GALATOIRE'S

There were ten Fontenot's working at Galatoire's in the late 1960's. One of them a first cousin, and he helped John get his first job as a waiter. "Back then, the waiters had a lot of influence over who was hired. The boss man would ask, 'Is he a good guy?' and that was that."

The other guys didn't warm to John because he was educated. Most hadn't graduated from high school. Some couldn't even write, and they used their own code with the kitchen. "They said I was overqualified."

Early on John saved a man's life executing the Heimlich maneuver as he was choking on his lamb. "I know I bruised him pretty good, but he's alive." In the summers John worked for Grand Hotels in Mackinaw, Michigan and upper New York State in the summer. "Back then you'd starve in New Orleans in the summer. There was no business." By the 1980's things improved, and John built up a 'call for you' clientele of locals and could survive year round.

Over the years John earned a modicum of fame as headwaiter at Galatoires, where he has worked for the last 48 years. One travel writer gushed about the restaurant and closed his article with the line, "And if you go, make sure to ask for John."

The wife of a prominent local man knew of John and some of his stories. She conducted a 45-minute interview with him and submitted the finished product to the Story Telling Archives in Washington, DC. It was one of forty submissions accepted from thousands. John used the line about the encounter with Mick Jagger's sticky lips in the interview. A New York Times' reporter discovered the quote and printed it, with attribution to John. This led to a filmmaker contacting John and making a documentary. John was wired and filmed during several shifts. Clips from this effort have been shown frequently on the food channel. In spite of the lip-quip, John remembers Mick Jagger fondly, "I got to know him over the years. He's sharp as a tack, a really good guy."

"I waited on Mike Wallace, famous for hosting the TV show *60 Minutes*. I walked up behind him and sounded out 'tick, tick, tick, tick (mimicking the audio lead-in to the show) and told him, 'You have 60 seconds to order.' He didn't find that funny at all."

Jackie Gleason was one of his favorites. After John would regale him with jokes and stories, he would laugh appreciatively and say, "You need to lighten up."

"Jackie was a big man and ate copious amounts of food. He always had a dessert of chocolate ice cream with chocolate syrup, along with the promise, 'I'm going on a diet soon.' "

John served at private parties when Frank Sinatra or Tom Jones would come to town. "Sinatra hated waiters, but for some reason he liked me." One time John waited on Clay Shaw, reputedly involved in the assassination of John F. Kennedy. "He looked like something out of a James Bond movie. I also waited on Jim Garrison, the New Orleans author who wrote of the conspiracy about the cover up of the Kennedy killing."

TJ'S PEARLS

In two years, John will celebrate his 50th year working as a waiter at Galatoire's. Those fortunate to have been served and entertained by John can observe firsthand the skills he has acquired.

"I'm a waiter. I love my job. I'm living well. I love my grandkids more than anything."

"For most people the sound of their own name is one of the sweetest things they can hear. I remember peoples' names and use them. I also remember what they drink and what they typically order. I'll try to have their drink ready for them when they arrive if they're with friends. If they're with a different group, new to me, I'll wait for their order. I don't want to make them look like a lush, if they're with a group of teetotalers. You've got to be attentive. Be nice to people. It's an art being a waiter."

"I kill them with kindness. You don't worry about the tip. The big ones help offset the times when you get nothing. Sometimes people split the check, get their arithmetic wrong, and your tip disappears."

One of the waiters received a $10,000 tip from the founder of PayPal. For a while the biggest tip John received was $700. "Back in the 1980's three guys from Texas came in and bought every bottle of

Dom Perignon we had in stock. The final bill was $1,000 and they left a tip for $700. Another guy asked me about the biggest tip. I told him it was $700, and he upped it to $701. Later another guy asks the same question, and he tipped $800. Some customers send you Christmas bonuses. It's greatly appreciated, but don't think that happens often. The big tips are a rarity, every few years or so."

"You're on your feet 12 hours for a full shift. There is no place to sit for the wait staff. You've got to be alert to the needs of your customers, so you're watching them all the time. I use the mirrors. I buy Red Wing double-soled shoes. Got to take care of your feet."

"The hardest people to wait on are the solo guys. They'll see me bantering with larger groups, then feel they're being left out. I try to treat everyone the same. You've got to be nice to everyone. People that only go out for special occasions, anniversaries, birthdays, etc. are difficult to serve. They don't know how to act, to eat, to order, to tip."

"Back when smoking was allowed, it was the pipe smokers who were the worst. Their taste buds are gone. They have no appreciation for food."

"I wash my hands a gillion times a day. Got to stay clean. Nails have to be short and clean. You're handling food. It's serious stuff."

"A lot of the young guys keep asking me when I'm going to retire. They think they'll get my 'call for you' business, but you've got to build that up on your own." And John answers their question with a grin and a wink, "Maybe another couple of years."

John may have never heard Walt Disney's advice to those seeking the key to success, but he's living the message, *"Do what you do so well that others will want to see it again and bring their friends."*

CHAPTER 6

Mardi Gras

PROLOGUE

It has been my good fortune to attend Mardi Gras over the past dozen years as a guest of a good friend who maintains an apartment on the second floor of a building on Royal Street in the French Quarter of New Orleans. The balcony provides views of a streetscape reaching down towards Canal in one direction and to the St. Louis Cathedral in the other. My host has become nearly a native of the Crescent City affording his guests access to people, places, and experiences not readily available to the typical Mardi Gras celebrant. Most relevant, my host is a handsome and mysterious man. It has been my good fortune to be his 'wing man' during the festivities thus introducing me to a host of interesting characters.

2012

Generations of New Orleans school children have been assigned art class projects to build a Mardi Gras float out of a shoe box, a Louisiana version of Pinewood Derby. Now a few artist and art teachers, one of whom is the son of friends, have decided to take some of the better renderings of these replicas and form their own parade. They move the tiny, but intricate, floats around a small room. An exuberant crowd lifts the shirts of assembled Barbie dolls and in turn receives Lilliputian trinkets. They have named the miniature event 'tit Rex. But it's not what you think.

In Cajun parlance, John's son becomes t'John. This is short for petite John, shortened to 'tit John, pronounced tee'John, or t'Bob, t'Beau, etc. Rex, the king of carnival, is the most socially prominent of the several dozen parades, and they convene on Mardi Gras morning, the premier time. Thus 'tit Rex impudently challenged the mighty and noble Rex. One of the trinkets dispensed at the 'tit Rex parade was a 12-page comic book, each page being the size of a postage stamp. In the final frame, the cartoon King declares, "Mockery is afoot."

The 'tit Rex people requested that a local features editor run a story on them, but he said, "I can't put 'tit' in print," demonstrating a remarkable level of sensitivity in a city known for public nudity and obscenely high murder rates.

The biggest drawback to chilly weather is the reduction in outdoor alcohol consumption that sadly leads to semi-sane behavior, although there were still plenty of women eager for a temporary respite from social convention. Fortunately, Mardi Gras day was sunny and warm, and we enjoyed the first of hundreds of flashers at 9:45 am. The body-painting kiosk was operating at full capacity throughout the day, producing abundant titillation for all, save a few moms trying to shield their offspring from premature anatomy lessons.

Some thoughtful folks opine that our society has coarsened over the years. I'm not sure this is correct. We've now had sufficient experience to anticipate a 50% success rate in our beads for boob bartering. Interestingly, a majority of those choosing not to disrobe in public apologize before moving on. "I'm so sorry, I just can't do that."

Sunday we attended an elegant brunch in the French Quarter hosted by friends. Walking along the street one might pass by a nondescript building without giving it a moment's thought. However, once inside the gates of the 1830's vintage home, we beheld a beautiful courtyard, swimming pool, and elegant gardens. The top floor offered stunning views overlooking neighboring gardens and green spaces, all hidden from public view.

After dinner on Sunday night we went to a wine bar recently opened by a friend. We were greeted warmly, opened a bottle of wine, and settled in for a relaxing evening. From this vantage point we viewed our transgender acquaintance sashaying down Rue Bienville accompanied by a large, young man dressed like a centaur. She held a leash attached to his neck. His costume was elaborate, with his legs, chest, and head serving as the front portion of the horse enhanced with a papier-mache torso, and hindquarters trailing on roller skate hooves.

On Mardi Gras afternoon we observed her again holding a leash around her male companion's neck. Her yellow and red wig added about three feet to her six-foot frame, mindful of Old Faithful. She was wearing a bright red dress similar in style to the one worn by Marilyn Monroe when she sang Happy Birthday to JFK, and the 3" straps barely concealed her melonious breasts. Predictably, she wore a neck collar. The overall effect was eye-catching. We espied her before being espied ourselves and retreated into the confines of our apartment. Unfortunately, she must have seen us and stood outside of our balcony yelling, "I know you're in there." I never heard Bronco Nagurski speak, but her mournful calls sounded something like my imaginings of the former gridiron great. Resorting to skills learned in junior high, we hid and ignored her pleadings until assured of her departure.

One of our balcony visitors was wearing a costume I'd never seen. It resembled prison attire, but the stripes were wide and the colors honored Mardi Gras with purple, gold, and green. A multitude of 2" strips of cloth hung randomly from the ensemble. "I like your costume, but I don't understand what it is."

He replied, "This is what they wear in Cajun country, in southwest Louisiana, on Mardi Gras day." He continued, "The men all ride horses in parades, often standing in their saddles. People go around to all the houses collecting sausages, shrimp, crayfish, veggies, and other delicacies for a communal pot of gumbo to feed the revelers. The highlight of the festivities is when a chicken is thrown off the roof of a house, and everyone chases the chicken and tosses it into the pot."

I inquired, "How does one get invited to such a festival?"

He replied, "You don't. One must be born to it."

My favorite costume this year was of an attractive, young androgynous person. He/she wore a male costume on the left side of his body with wing tip shoes, a brown plaid suit, and a short haircut. On her right side, she wore a high-heeled shoe, a red bikini bottom and top, and sported a shock of lengthy blond hair. It certainly didn't look like a wig, so he/she must have a mighty understanding employer. I recounted this story to a high school friend who reminded me that our classmate, Debbie Bryant, used this same technique as her 'talent' when winning the Miss America award. Debbie, as you may recall, was the only girl from the Shawnee Mission East class of 1963 to win such an award. She sat in a chair in a mock interview and when turned to the right presented herself as a woman, and to the left, a man. She switched her seat position in a conversation with herself. Go figure. Memorably, Debbie was nice to those of us who inhabited the lower nether-regions of the high school social strata. But I digress.

We observed six young adults, apparently sightless, walking with the assistance of canes. It's not uncommon to see people costumed as the blind, as in Three Blind Mice, but these folks were the real deal and deserving of uncommon respect for navigating the mayhem of Royal Street on Mardi Gras, presumably absorbing the sounds and smells. Being pretty darn nice guys, we didn't throw beads at them. Instead we quietly acknowledged the nobility of their presence in such an inhospitable setting.

Whilst enjoying an after dinner drink at one of our favorite watering holes, I couldn't help but overhear the following bartender's soliloquy told over a 30 minute span betwixt the mixing of multiple drinks:

Patron, "How are things going with you and your boyfriend?

Pretty blond female bartender, "We've talked about getting married, and I want so much to have kids and raise a family. I love him so, but I don't know if I can depend on him. What if I were to break my leg and not be able to work for six months? He says 'maybe when we get our credit card debts down to a manageable level, we can start thinking about marriage.' I've got mine paid off, but his debts keep growing. There are women in my family who started menopause by 35. I'm 32 years old, and time is running out for me. I've been with him since we were both 19. I've grown up, but he hasn't. What am I going to do?"

Police towers were a new addition to the Bourbon Street streetscape. They were situated every three blocks and featured a three-story boom with a watchtower, floodlights, and presumably cameras recording all in range. It was pretty darn Orwellian.

The evangelists were out in force again this year. It appears that someone must bring in busloads of guys seeking to help sinners find the Way. Pleasingly, they left their microphones at home. They do their thing, and the festival-goers do theirs. The primary distinction was that they now have giant crosses made out of 4" diameter PVC pipe. Whoever wrote "The Old Wooden Cross" would have been grievously offended.

Pete Fountain's Half Fast Marching Band entertained all in the French Quarter. Several hundred men escort the trolley carrying the band and the elderly clarinetist, and they toss an abundance of beads to the onlookers. This year the men wore striking canary yellow suits, hats, and shoes. Their appearance and the accompanying Dixieland music are one of the highlights of the day.

Our brunch hosts shared a few stories about the recovery from Katrina. New Orleans population dropped from 490,000 to 350,000 immediately after the storm and remains at the lower number today. Those with limited resources to rebuild or without strong roots to the community took off for more friendly environs. Homeless people from all over the country invaded NOLA in the storm's aftermath, gathered at City Park, and asked, "Where's the free food and clothes and stuff?" And they have stayed, one group of homeless replacing another.

Lunch on Ash Wednesday was a three-hour affair. Genteel is the only way to describe Galatoire's. The wait staff dress in tuxedos, and aside from me, the gentlemen diners appeared to have been en route to an Esquire fashion shoot. We enjoyed several bottles of wine, souffled potatoes (good, but not as perfect as Arnaud's), gumbo, and lamb chops. We passed on dessert, so as to not be excessive.

In between major dining experiences, we munched on muffaletta sandwiches from Central Grocers and Rouse's King Cake, all washed down with Abita beer. I'm now recovering by eating lettuce sandwiches and should be back in form for Mardi Gras 2013.

2013

I arrived for dinner at Arnaud's directly from the airport with a roller bag in hand. We encountered a young lady, a friend of my host, who queried, "What's in the suitcase gramps? Oxygen?" Having been suitably humbled, we were off and running.

My flight had arrived at Louis Armstrong Airport 20 minutes early, which was pleasing. I caught a cab with no wait, so all was going well until my knuckleheaded cab driver dropped me off eight blocks distant from Arnaud's. I knew he missed the correct turn when we passed the Super Dome on my left rather than on my right. Worse, I was on the wrong side of Canal Street, which at that moment was hosting the Endymion parade that follows a horseshoe shaped route through the central business district. I was in the middle of the horseshoe. The parade route was lined by steel barricades, behind which throngs of humanity were stacked 10+ deep. I called my host, now situated comfortably at the bar at Arnaud's, to describe my dilemma. As the crow flies I was about 200 yards from my destination, but I was no crow. He comforted me by noting, "You're screwed. Endymion goes on forever. Definitely avoid going upstream, as that will take you to some scary bad parts of town."

I navigated downstream with the flow of humanity, pulling my roller bag and was quickly reminded why we never go to parades. A few times I tried to get up to the barriers, but people wouldn't give an inch. I spotted a lady on a ladder and asked if she knew of any crossing points. She told me of such a spot 1/2 mile farther away from my destination, and I was off. The sidewalk afforded but one lane of traffic, so it was slow going. The lady was correct, and I found the intersection where the police let people scurry across at 30-minute intervals. I waited patiently until the allotted time, crossed through the tuba section of the LSU band, and eventually made my way across Canal into the French Quarter.

The detour around the parade delayed me an hour and added a couple of miles of hiking through a stew of beads, confetti, spilt beer, and human emesis, but I finally arrived at Arnaud's, an elegant oasis of civility where I was cordially greeted by friends and the highly professional staff.

Charles, the maitre de extraordinaire, arrived to take our drink orders and then returned with lagniappe he had personally prepared to take the edge off our appetites while we enjoyed our beverages. The dish he presented was a generous portion of chilled shrimp, cut into small pieces, blended with chopped, crisp yellow bell peppers, parsley, cilantro, olive oil, salt and pepper. Unpleasant thoughts of the previous hour's misadventure receded quickly.

After dinner we headed to Patrick's Bar Vin. Patrick greeted us warmly, brought a fine bottle of wine, and introduced us to some interesting people, including a travel writer who was checking out his place. She was overwhelmingly unimpressed when I told her of my own meager efforts with the pen. She haughtily explained, as though speaking to an auditorium full of rapt listeners, "Everyone says they want to be a travel writer, but it's like saying, 'I want to be a movie star.' You'll get over it."

We returned to our quarters in the Quarter around 1 pm and were pleasantly surprised to observe swarms of young people out at that hour. I encountered two college-aged couples from the NYC area were sitting on our doorstep. We chatted for a bit, and one of the guys said, "You'll never guess what I do for a living?" He then told me he was a professional pickler, which prompted me to share with him my ancient past life as a pickle magnate wannabe. It's truly a small world when pickle(d) people come together.

On Sunday, two young couples joined us on the balcony. The ladies quickly established themselves as cunningly skilled bead for boob traders. Our efforts paled in comparison, so we just stood back and let our attractive guests work their magic.

After attending nine Mardi Gras's one would think you've pretty well seen it all. Not so. Mid-afternoon we saw two young ladies promenading beneath our balcony attired only in G-strings and a few strokes of body paint, one of them had to have been eight months pregnant. This was undoubtedly instructive for the children present.

We paid close attention to a large black man costumed to resemble a menacing, homeless man with disheveled clothing. His hair appeared to have been styled with electric-chair-juice, and he held a sign saying, "Shitty Advice $1." This is truly a testament to absolute truth in advertising.

On Sunday, after a stroll around the Quarter, I returned by walking past our balcony and observed Patrick visiting with a large, dark haired woman I didn't recognize. When I entered the apartment I realized it was our transgender acquaintance. She greeted me warmly as I joined them and said, "Remember me?"

"Of course." And she gave me a big hug, indicating she hadn't read my book. Since she is substantially bigger, younger, and stronger than I, she might have first thrashed me and then thrown my bloodied carcass off the balcony in repayment for my unkind portrayal. I almost felt badly after her gracious greeting, but quickly recovered. As they were leaving, Patrick, the mischievous scamp, suggested he might share his copy of NNAOPP with his companion, insuring a future, unpleasant encounter.

The evangelists were out in full force preaching to the accumulation of sinners. Fortunately, they weren't using microphones and weren't too much of a distraction. I did notice one noteworthy addition to their banners listing the various classes of miscreants who are doomed to eternal damnation. This year, church gossips were added to masturbators, fornicators, adulterers, abortionists, Muslims, Catholics, Baptists, and a lengthy list bound to include most everyone.

From our balcony I espied a woman dressed (using the term loosely) as a nun. She wore a standard wimple and veil covering her head, but was topless with small painted black crosses serving as tiny pasties. I ordinarily don't take photos, but would have made an exception in this case, as I was thinking this would make a perfect posting for my blog www.nudenuns.blogspot.com. The site would no longer disappoint the porn seekers from the United Arab Emirates who occasionally visit. Sadly, she was walking briskly, and I didn't get a chance to capture the moment.

Before packing it in on Lundi Gras evening we walked by Pat O'Brien's and stopped to admire the work product coming out of the body-painting kiosk across the street. I chatted with a pretty young lady who was rightfully proud of her unclad, but painted, torso. She told us that she was a member of the KOE (Krewe of Elvis) and was eagerly looking forward to their upcoming parade. She said, "Look for me, I'll be dressed like Elvis." From our vantage point we could see the naked back of a whale-sized woman in the process of being artistically altered. Her unattractive back featured folds of fat. In an uncharacteristic display of cattiness, I asked the young lady, "Do you think they charge extra for circus-tent-sized paint jobs?"

She said, without a hint of approbation, "That's my Mom!" And it was.

Is this a great country or what?

2015

After a year's absence, I was fortunate to return to NOLA for Mardi Gras 2015. I arrived early as my host insisted I should attend his Friday luncheon. Another guest and I arrived at the same time and shared a cab to the French Quarter apartment that would be home for the next six days. Walking up to the second floor apartment, we encountered our adjacent-balcony neighbors taking their bulldog out for a stroll. She made my day by asking, "Hey, aren't you the guy that wrote the book about our Mardi Gras?" I thanked her. Good start, I thought to myself.

Shortly after our arrival we headed for dinner at a restaurant fittingly named NOLAs. Once there our host played a voicemail he received earlier from our transgender acquaintance. Her pleadings came in a voice blending the worst of Queen Elizabeth and Broderick Crawford.

"Darling! I hope this finds you well. I've prepared my costumes for Mardi Gras, and I think you'll find them stunning as usual, but sadly I don't have a place to stay. Any chance you'd have room for me at your place? I'm so sad to think I'll have to stay in LA while everyone is having so much fun."

She is a world class mooch, and her call was not returned. It did prompt us to once again ponder her gender. A female friend, new to the topic, weighed in and asked, "Does she have an Adam's apple?" "Yes, but it's usually covered by bejeweled, velvet dog collars." "Then she's a man." Then she listened to the voice on the message and said, "That's definitely a woman's voice." No one has ever been bodacious enough to pull a Crocodile Dundee crotch grab on the personage in question, so the matter remains in doubt.

After a delightful dinner of honey-roasted duck, several in our group ventured to the Muses Parade on Canal Street. We rarely attend parades, but the Muses event is special. It consists of 1,000 well-dressed women riding on floats, and each decorates 30 shoes that they dispense to friends in the crowd. Occasionally a miscreant will step between the Muse member and her intended recipient to run off with the treasure. Membership is highly coveted and limited to the extent no names are being added to the waiting list. The shoes that I saw are veritable works of art. On the previous night a group called Nyx does a similar parade only they dispense outrageously decorated purses. New Orleans is an extraordinarily welcoming place for women enjoying the company of other women with a penchant for fun.

The Friday before Mardi Gras is a big honking deal. We arrived at the Rib Room around 11:30 am for cocktails. We were surrounded by men wearing expensive suits, monogrammed cuffs and links, and crisply folded, colorful handkerchiefs accenting the ensemble. The women are equally and elegantly attired often wearing Kentucky Derby hats, and their numbers matched that of the gentlemen. Those present exhibited healthy doses of southern graciousness and hints of aristocratic privilege. Table arrangements are made years in advance.

The dining areas opened precisely at noon and we were seated at a table in a loge-like balcony affording us a view of the diners seated below and the crowds passing in the street. Our table for eight was adorned with ten bottles of exquisite wines, i.e. Cade, Duckhorn, Cinq Cepages, Chassagne Montrecet, and Jordan.

Our group consisted of three engineers, specializing in subterranean structures, and one construction executive. Early on the conversation was semi-business related and we got a mini-education on foundations in NOLA. The structural engineers explained how the brick corbelling beneath the centuries old buildings in the French Quarter would disintegrate once exposed to the elements making it difficult to build adjacent structures. "The only reason many of these buildings are still standing is habit."

After the ten bottles of wine were consumed, the conversation turned to earthier topics. One of our companions is a senior executive of a construction company. She is also an attractive lady. I complimented her on her success in what I perceived to be an industry not renowned for friendliness to her gender. She noted women are making strides in construction. Then she shared this observation about working in a male dominated environment:

"No offense, but men are basically simple creatures. They only care about women's body parts, games involving a ball, food, and drink. That's it. Women are infinitely more complex. We view layers in all things."

The seven men listening nodded in agreement as if to say in unison, "None taken. That pretty well nails it." Then I inquired at what age she made this discovery.

"I didn't figure this out until around 30. Then everything became less troublesome. When I was 16 I thought boys should think like I did."

We were feeling good after our lengthy luncheon, and we walked the several blocks from the Rib Room to Patrick's Bar Vin, accompanied by Patrick, one of our luncheon companions and owner of the eponymous establishment.

The Fridays before Mardi Gras and Christmas are his two busiest days. He caters to a local crowd and those are the days the locals celebrate. Even schools are closed from the Wednesday before Mardi Gras to the Wednesday after. The bar is relatively small, laid out like a sitting room with three groupings of furniture each serving as a conversation pit. The furnishings are nice, with leather couches and armchairs, oriental rugs, handsome wood paneling, and an attentive staff.

I spotted an empty space on one of the couches in the midst of a group of people and asked if I could join them. They graciously made introductions. All were members of the Krewe of Cork and regularly patronize Patrick's, as he is both the founder of the Krewe and its permanent King.

I stayed seated after the bacchants left. These fine folks were then followed by a succession of new and interesting visitors. I can only presume I was approached because I appear to be harmless, and I am content to listen to whatever stories people want to tell with minimal interruption.

THE LESBIAN

At first she was sitting on the couch across the coffee table from me talking to others. She was about 40, tall, bookish, and pretty with long dark hair and glasses. After her companions left she came over and sat next to me. My friend, Sniper, was sitting nearby. After introductions she told us that she had just moved to NOLA from LA. She was married to a man for ten years, but she moved to NOLA to be with a woman with whom she fell in love, but the woman dumped her after two months. She proceeded to tell us how difficult it is to be a single lesbian in NOLA vs. LA. Apparently, lesbians are more readily identifiable in LA than in the Deep South. She said if she gets desperate she could always go back to men. I told her I didn't think she looked like a lesbian given the lack of a girls' fast pitch softball haircut. She laughed and explained the distinction between dykes and lesbians. I'm not sure when I'll get a chance to deploy this new knowledge, but one never knows.

THE RICH MAN'S WIFE?

I sat alone for a while observing the crowd, content to stay put. The bar manager, a beautiful Vietnamese woman, periodically checked on me and told me a little about her background. She was born in the U.S. shortly after her parents arrived as 'boat people' fleeing the communist takeover of Saigon. She received a degree in finance, then worked for Morgan Stanley but tired of it and entered the hospitality world. Before her story could unfold, she was beckoned by other customers.

I noticed a youngish couple sitting across from me. The man was about 45 and the woman 35. They were handsomely dressed and appeared to be deeply engrossed in their conversation and were holding hands in a loving way. He looked like a conventional NOLA aristocrat, and she looked like an exotic creature recently escaped from the New Orleans zoo. Then he left. After a bit of time she moved to the chair next to my corner of the couch and introduced herself. She cut a striking figure wearing blood red lipstick, an extremely short skirt, white stockings, and expensive jewelry. She sat at the only possible angle one could sit while still maintaining a modicum of modesty.

She said, "So what's your story?" I told her I had totally mastered the art of being an invisible nobody, and I spent my free time sitting in wine bars listening to other people's stories. She then told me that she was of Puerto Rican descent, grew up in Brooklyn, got a degree from Columbia University, almost went to Columbia law school, but instead became a grade school teacher, married a rich NOLA attorney, and now runs a restaurant in the French Quarter.

Then she looked around the room conspiratorially as though someone might surreptitiously listen in on our conversation. She leaned forward and whispered, "But you know what I really want to do?" "No." I replied. "I want to be a writer. I have stories I must tell."

I informed her of my hugely unsuccessful efforts as a scrivener, and she asked if I would read some of her work. I told her I'd be pleased to do that and shared the title of my book that has my contact information. Patrick would periodically glance our direction with a mischievous grin. I later asked him if he set that up. He smiled and denied any culpability.

Our evening routines are pretty simple. We stroll four blocks to Patrick's for cocktails at 6, dinner at 7 at varying restaurants. On Saturday it was Arnaud's, possibly my favorite. We were greeted by the owner, an attractive young woman, and received inter-planetary air kisses. Once again I feasted on the petit filet Lafitte, a dish featuring fried oysters and a slightly peppered and tender filet. As the maitre d' accurately boasted, "We serve nothing that cannot be cut with a butter knife." By 10:30 we'd done all the damage we could do at the dining table, and it was time to leave.

We had been invited to a party on a balcony overlooking Bourbon

Street by one of Patrick's best customers, a wealthy industrialist. We accepted, but Patrick declined and returned to his bar.

Getting to the party, lamentably, required walking two blocks on Bourbon Street on a Saturday night. The partygoers one finds on Bourbon Street would not be confused with visiting yachtsmen. The crowd was massive, unruly, and often downright frightening. The entire scene provided a full frontal assault on all of the senses.

None in our group of five could be mistaken for youthful. One has an injured back and knee, and he walks slowly and awkwardly. It was a huge mistake for us to have entered that dangerous milieu, but we did safely make it to the balcony. Verily one could observe no shortage of licentiousness from the safety of our new perch, but I was too stressed from the two-block walk to enjoy the moment.

Our host and I left early with our injured comrade. We navigated one half a block on Bourbon before we could cross to the friendlier confines of Royal, but it was slow going. Our friend was in obvious pain as we inched our way back to the apartment. When we were within one block of our destination, we stopped so he could rest against a lamppost.

She may have been a sincerely concerned Good Samaritan, as she appeared ghost-like out of nowhere and inquired, "Do you guys need some help?" We explained the situation and thanked her for her concern. She asked where we were from, and when we said "Kansas," she became animated and said, "No way! No one is from Kansas! What is that all about?" We accepted her joshing with good humor and explained it was an acquired taste.

She was not a pretty woman, more like the female equivalent of Larry the Cable Guy. She wore a camouflage ball cap and an unflattering form fitting tee shirt. She had long stringy hair, was 40ish, and told us the following, implausible story:

She's a college professor in Fairbanks, Alaska, couldn't see Russia from her house, couldn't understand why anyone would want to live anywhere other than Alaska. She was surprisingly articulate, given her unkempt appearance. Then in the midst of regaling us with her academic achievements and the joys of Alaska she changed directions, "Omigod, I had sex with one of my 21-year-old students last night. I'm afraid he might say something to someone that could jeopardize my job."

I opined, "So the kid now owns you?"

She became irritated and replied, "No! If he ever said anything they'd find his dead body in the river."

"Well, it's sure been nice chatting with you."

By now my two chums had started walking the final block, and I was left alone with the professor. She calmed down and inquired, "Are you boys staying anywhere around here? I could help him with his back if you'd like."

I thanked her for her concern and trotted along.

I don't live a particularly cloistered life, but I rarely encounter anything as consistently bizarre as I do during the evenings in the FQ during Mardi Gras. In the day I am invisible, but in the evening, and in the company of my host, and while dressed nicely, we can almost count on meeting strange people. I truly hope this continues.

This year my favorite street performer was Transformer Man. He fashioned a little yellow car body that he wears like a tortoise shell backpack. He has wheels attached to each of his ankles, and he holds a battery-powered front wheel/axle unit that propels the little device. He gets down on his hands and knees, rides around giving the appearance of a normal little car, then he stands up, flips the yellow car body back from his head and shoulders, holds up the front axle/power unit in his right arm, and poses like a super hero. I heard one little boy shriek with joy when he saw the little car transform into a man. It was pretty darn cool, but an extremely difficult way to earn a living, as his act requires getting up and down from the pavement several hundred times each shift.

He performed just down from our balcony so I watched him try to draw a crowd. During one of his breaks I took him a bottle of water, and we chatted. He was a little guy with quarter-sized holes in his ears filled with hollow green rings, Ubangi like. I told him I liked his act, gave him a few bucks and commented he must be in great shape. He said his costume, including the battery packs, weigh 90 lbs, barely less than his 135 lbs. frame.

We noted a paucity of painted, topless women this year. The weather was really nice on Saturday and Sunday and the crowds were large, so we couldn't account for the decline. The entrance to our apartment is on Rue St. Peter, just off of Royal. Our immediate neighbors down St. Peter towards Bourbon are Pat O'Brien's and Preservation Hall. Both of these venues draw huge crowds from the eddies of humanity swirling around the intersection with Bourbon Street. A local artist paints women's torsos in the narrow alley across the street from Pat O'Brien's. It's a perfect location as the bar emits an endless stream of impaired young women holding plastic hurricane glasses filled with some sugary concoction. But he wasn't doing any business this year. Being an inquisitive fellow, I decided to learn more.

He was a rugged looking man, about 50, wearing a black leather outfit with a doo rag. When I asked him why things are so slow this year, he said, "If anyone ever tells you to paint within the lines, do it. I've spent my entire life painting outside the lines, and this is where you end up."

Within earshot of our balcony one could hear the strains of a gifted clarinetist, opera singer, violinist, and my favorite, a ragtime group featuring two open-backed banjos. They drew large, appreciative crowds and their tip jars seemed to be filled to the brim.

A memorable flash occurred when a young woman was cogitating the trade of beads for boobs. She looked at her husband/boyfriend for either a way out or encouragement, and he said, "Go ahead. I'm going to be an old guy some day."

CHAPTER 7

Art Ditto
Copper in the Congo

Art Ditto and George Forrest, Lubumbashi, 2007

PROLOGUE

We met at a hospital board meeting in Wickenburg, Arizona during a discussion of some import. An animated debate occurred, and I observed an older gentleman sitting silently on the sidelines. Then someone inquired, "Art, what do you think?" All secondary conversations stopped, the room quieted, and heads turned deferentially. Art is trim and athletic with thinning, whitish hair, and was dressed in modest khakis and a golf shirt. Art spoke in a quiet and thoughtful manner, and all present nodded in affirmation to his comments.

Later, the hospital CEO told me that Art is a billionaire, and he earned his fortune developing gold and copper mines around the world. His last and biggest deal was restoring a copper mine in the Congo. He is also highly inquisitive, and I was pleased to receive an invitation to join him for dinner, as he sought to pick my brain about healthcare topics. We spent a cordial evening, giving me an opportunity to learn a smidgen about his Congo project.

A year passed, and I returned to Wickenburg to again work with the hospital board. It occurred to me that Art's story would be a perfect fit for the book that was starting to boil in my head. This time I invited Art to dinner, and he graciously agreed. While waiting at the Los Caballeros Golf Club, I noted his name prominently displayed on a wall plaque as the club champion two out of the last five years, as if the guy didn't already have enough going for him. During our four-hour dinner, he told me more about his life and work, and I asked if he would consider letting me write about this Congo adventure for inclusion in a future book. He called a few weeks later and agreed.

Several months passed, and I traveled to his summer home on Puget Sound and listened with great interest as he told me how his career evolved from a boyhood growing up in frontier mining camps in northern British Columbia to the restoration of a multi-billion dollar mine in the Katanga Province of the Democratic Republic of the Congo.

Art and his wife Gail were gracious hosts and we spent the better part of three days together. Unlike many powerful people I've encountered, Art does not suck the air out of the room. He is economical with words, and his demeanor is quiet and calm. He even cooked blueberry pancakes, made from scratch, for our breakfast. What follows is Art Ditto's remarkable story.

Author's Notes

When we first sat down I inquired in a mildly gee whiz fashion, "Are you really a billionaire?" He replied with a wry smile, "No, but I can pay my bills." Concordantly, I will not refer to him as such.

I have frequently used the convention of quoting / paraphrasing Art. Wherever quotes are used without specific attribution, Art is speaking. I've taken the liberty of blending bits and pieces of various conversations to fit the flow of the narrative.

Wherever the $ sign is used the reference is for U.S. dollars.
I have relied on Adam Hochschild's King Leopold's Ghost, for background information about the colonization of the Congo, first by King Leopold and later by the Belgian government. Direct and paraphrased quotes from this source are noted "KLG".

THE CONGO

"The Congo is possibly the most blessed place on the planet in terms of natural resources. Tragically, that wealth has brought little but misery to its inhabitants." (KLG)

Prior to meeting Art, my impressions of the Congo had been formed from reading King Leopold's Ghost, Heart of Darkness, How I Found Livingstone, and several other books describing the search for the source of the Nile. I was also influenced as a child watching Tarzan movies from the 1950's where crocodiles slide ominously into dark waters. It always seemed unimaginably foreign and sinister.

Until the later part of the 19th century, few Europeans had ventured into the Congo River basin. The impenetrable jungles, swamps, and accompanying malaria and other tropical diseases, such as sleeping sickness, made it inhospitable for European exploration and exploitation.

The British typically colonized areas that would be attractive to their citizens seeking places to live with their families as administrators, farmers, and fortune seekers. South Africa, Rhodesia (now Zimbabwe), Northern Rhodesia (now Zambia), and Kenya fit the bill, but the Congo did not.

In 1876, King Leopold II of Belgium organized the International African Association with the cooperation of the leading African explorers and the support of several European governments for the promotion of African exploration and colonization. After Henry

Morton Stanley explored the region in a journey that ended in 1878, Leopold enlisted his aid to promote his interests in the Congo. (KLG)

King Leopold II made this last parcel of un-colonized Africa his personal fiefdom and became the de facto owner of the colony he dubbed Congo Free State. Belgians would soon learn that their new colony was seventy-six times the size of Belgium; larger than England, France, Germany, Spain, and Italy combined; or roughly the size of all the states that lie east of the Mississippi River.

Ironically, one of the more forgettable American presidents, Chester Arthur, comically described by journalists of the era as 'a gentleman with a well developed waist....evidently a good feeder' (KLG), was the first of the world's powers to recognize King Leopold II's claim to the Congo in 1884. The King subsequently plundered and pillaged the land for wealth seeking first ivory and then rubber and palm oil.

During this period, missionaries and adventurers traveled to the southernmost part of the Congo, the Katanga province, and discovered an area featuring rolling plains, abundant water, fertile fields, a temperate climate, and readily accessible minerals. They learned that indigenous peoples had been smelting copper for generations for local coinage* using easily obtained copper ore and charcoal fires. Word eventually reached the King and his agents of the untold mineral wealth lying beneath his dominions.

* Katanga copper coin. Later used as the logo of Katanga Mining, Ltd.

By the turn of the century, the violence used by Congo Free State officials against indigenous Congolese and a ruthless system of economic extraction led to intense diplomatic pressure on Belgium to take official control of the country, and in 1908 the Congo Free State became the Belgian Congo. But the King exacted his own version of sweet revenge by selling 'his' possession to the Belgian government for 200 million francs.

COPPER AND COBALT

Many contemporary Americans are increasingly disconnected from the underpinnings that make their lives pretty darn comfortable. Nearly every electrical device relies on copper wiring: automobiles, cell phones, motors, and many other items essential to our daily lives.

Copper is a ductile metal used as a conductor of heat and electricity. It possesses anti-bacterial qualities that make it highly suitable for use in coinage and for transporting potable water. Until 1982, the American penny coin was 95 percent copper. Then copper became more valuable than the coin, so the U.S. mint changed to inexpensive zinc coated with copper. Copper is also easily recycled, and 20% of the world's total demand is met in this manner.

The symbol for copper, Cu, comes from the Latin word, cuprum, which is the ancient name for the island of Cyprus, home to some of the first known copper mines. The Bronze Age, lasting from 4000 - 3000 BC, was the second of three metallurgical systems (Stone Age, Bronze Age, and Iron Age) marking the development of prehistoric human societies. It could just as easily been called the Copper Age, as bronze is an alloy made by melting and mixing 88% copper and 12% tin.

An important physical property of copper is its color, reddish-brown. Chemical properties turn the color to a tint green when mixed with oxygen and water, the most famous example being the copper-clad Statue of Liberty in NYC.

Cobalt is usually recovered as a byproduct of mining and refining copper. It is used to make powerful permanent magnets, high speed and high temperature cutting tools and dyes, stainless steel, and alloys for jet engines and gas turbines.

At one time it was possible to find copper lying on the ground, but now that is rarely the case. For the past 8,000 years copper has been extracted from the earth by mining. It's a safe bet that there are more third-world people lacking the conveniences afforded by basic metals than those living a first-world life style desirous of abandoning them. Yet John Denver co-wrote the mega-hit song *Rocky Mountain High* in 1972 lending his considerable lyrical gifts to promote the notion that modern societies can function without disturbing the earth.

Now his life is full of wonder
But his heart still knows some fear
Of a simple thing he cannot comprehend
Why they try to tear the mountains down
To bring in a couple more
More people, more scars upon the land

This story will not change the minds of those who view miners as exploiters of Mother Nature, but it might lend balance. As Art lamented, "Our society couldn't function without copper, and most of the objections to mining are based on 19th century practices that no longer exist. Twentieth and 21st century mining is radically different in terms of reclamation, resource sustainability, safety, and efficiency."

ART

"I told my sons early on, you must get a first-rate education and prepare yourself well, if you are to make something of your life."

1941 - 1963

Art's personal history is a testament to this advice. Whether by destiny or serendipity, each stage of his life, from his birth in 1941 and boyhood in mining camps around Bralorne, British Columbia, led to the capstone project of his career, restoring the copper/cobalt mines near Kolwezi, Democratic Republic of Congo (DRC).

Art's grandfather Harry McPherson emigrated from Scotland to British Columbia in the early 1900's. He earned a degree in civil engineering from St. Andrews University, and his name was listed as a one-time member of the famed Carnoustie golf course. He was part of the Scottish diaspora that motivated the landless to leave, owing to lack of opportunities at home.

He was one of the engineers charged with carving the newly created city of Vancouver, BC out of the forest. Along the way, he designed three of the city's golf courses. Then, in keeping with the centuries-old dictum, 'When England goes to war so goes the Commonwealth,' he joined the army and served in WWI working in Whitehall and living in Surrey where his daughter Ruth was born in 1918. After the war he returned to his promising prospects in British Columbia.

Ruth enjoyed a relatively privileged upbringing in their formal Victorian home. Victorian parents expected their daughters to be proper ladies, and sons were expected to get an education. Time spent with her father required an appointment. Ruth's mother died when she was 11, coinciding with the onset of the worldwide depression. Shortly thereafter, an unloving stepmother arrived and dominated the family scene. Ruth was encouraged to fend for herself, 'stiff upper lip' and all. And she did.

One of the few bright spots in the British Columbia economy during the depression was the development of the Bralorne Mines. Mine owners hired Art's grandfather to lay out the town surrounding the complex of mines located in Bralorne, about 200 miles north of Vancouver, and his daughter Ruth accompanied him. These mines would remain open from 1931 - 1972 and would produce over three million ounces of gold.

Gold was a refuge after the collapse of the world markets in the 1930's. Physical gold reserves backed U.S. paper dollars, but the reserves had shrunk as individuals accumulated gold to protect their own finances. To counteract this behavior, and to increase the Treasury gold stocks backing the issuance of more paper dollars, President Franklin Roosevelt signed a series of executive orders in 1933 banning private ownership of gold coins or bullion. The new laws mandated that all gold be 'sold' to the government at the price of $20.67 per ounce. The penalty for possessing the precious metal was severe, a $10,000 fine and up to 10 years in prison.

In 1934 Congress passed the Gold Reserve Act that revalued the price at $35 per troy ounce. In theory, this was done to stabilize faith in the banking system and to devalue the U.S. paper dollar. The ban on private ownership didn't end until 1975 when citizens were once again allowed to freely own and trade gold.

But gold mining continued to prosper during the era as the U.S. government maintained the gold standard, backing currency with gold at a rate of $35 per troy ounce for purposes of foreign exchange, until the policy was officially abandoned in 1971.

When England entered WWII, Grandfather McPherson was again called to duty. By then he was a colonel and spent the war in Ontario where he was responsible for the POWs interned in Canada. He died of cancer while on active duty at the age of 59.

Ruth met and married a local miner and stayed in Bralorne after the rest of the family moved back to Vancouver. In 1941 she gave birth to her first and only child, Art. She divorced her husband a few years later, and Art has no memories of his biological father. Ruth remarried another miner, Andrew 'Bud' Ditto, who subsequently adopted Art, and whom Art considers his true father.

Ruth always had a job, usually working as an accountant for one of the mines. In spite of her privileged upbringing, she was deeply seared by the hardships of the depression and was hyperactive every day of her life. Although she lacked a formal education beyond high school, she was bright and well spoken. "She carried herself as an upper class woman, though living in a working class world."

Absent the availability of daycare, toddler Art accompanied his Mom wherever her work duties took her. At the age of five he was given the task of delivering lunch to his stepdad. This involved taking a series of cable suspended trams from ridge to ridge, then through a mining tunnel to his underground destination. Once there he would help his Dad set explosives. "I have vivid memories of the pounding headaches that would occur if the nitroglycerin touched your skin and the overwhelming noise of the un-muffled drilling machines and explosions."

There were few children in the camps, so Art spent a mostly solitary childhood roaming the surrounding mountains and streams. "I grew up as a little kid in an adult world. The miners were decent, hardworking people eking out a living, and they were always kind to me."

The family never lacked for food or shelter, but Art retains vivid memories of being awakened at night by an explosion in their cabin (from a faulty heater) that burned their home to the ground and sent them shivering to neighbors. They lost all of their worldly possessions in the fire.

From the Bralorne gold mines, the Ditto family moved further north to a mercury mine in British Columbia and then to the Zeballos gold mine in western Vancouver Island, one of the most remote locales in North America, where Art first attended school and spent most of his time Huck Finn-like, fishing in the nearby streams and wandering in the forests.

As a mine supervisor, Art's Dad moved often because he was hired to manage small mines and to evaluate prospective mines for commercial potential. Some hit, some didn't, and they'd move on. Art attended three different high schools in three years. He took his junior year courses by correspondence, because he was working full time as a construction worker on a hydroelectric project in the Bridge River area of British Columbia.

Art's biological father later became a bush pilot running a fleet of floatplanes in northern BC. Once he called Art's mother offering to teach his estranged son to fly. Art declined the offer, and that was the last contact they had.

The family moved to Port Moody, BC for Art's senior year in high school, and he was eager to enter the adult world. "I was a driven guy. I wanted to get out and earn a living. I was always afraid I would miss the train."

He started his freshman year at the University of British Columbia in Vancouver thinking, whatever he did, it wouldn't be mining. But he soon changed his mind and realized that the university's mining engineering program had only one student. He checked his options and determined the best place to obtain a mining engineering degree would be the Montana School of Mines in Butte. "I knew I could work in the nearby mines while in school."

Butte has been called 'the richest hill on earth' containing commercial quantities of manganese, gold, silver, copper, zinc, and lead. Underground mines penetrate the hill from every direction and provided Art with gainful employment every weekend of his college career. "I started the Friday and Saturday evening shifts at 6 pm and worked until 3 am the following day. Laborers were paid a base pay of $3/hr. Contract miners were paid on a production basis and could earn up to $6/hr. I chose to be a contract miner and was making about $100 per week which was pretty good money in 1963, but I needed it, because I was married and had a newborn son, Todd."

When I asked, "Art, did you ever do anything frivolous while growing up?" His serious and thoughtful response was, "Define frivolous."

1964 -1970

Mining engineers study elements of geology, chemistry, and civil and mechanical engineering, all disciplines relevant to their tasks. Geologists identify fields with ore (rock containing sufficient minerals that can be economically extracted) based on their study of earth processes such as earthquakes, landslides, volcanic eruptions, and floods. They compile a geological map showing rock types and sediments prevalent in a specified area. Mining engineers look at the field three dimensionally and attempt to refine the economic analysis based on various methods of extracting the ore from the site.

On graduation, Art was hired by Anaconda and sent to the Chuquicamata copper mine in northern Chile where he worked as a shift foreman. At the time, it was the largest open pit copper mine in the world. The mine was so massive that they operated their own vehicle assembly plants. Chile charged a 300% import tax on vehicles. As auto parts and components were not subject to the tariffs, Anaconda assembled their own trucks, cars, and off road vehicles.

The workforce was primarily Chilean, and all communications were done in Spanish, which Art learned in a rudimentary fashion. Labor/management relations were reminiscent of the 1930's strife in the U.S., making every day a challenge. Their second son Mathew was born in Chile and quickly developed health issues. Doctors told the young parents that their baby wasn't thriving at the 10,000' elevation, and it was time to move.

The family sought to return to Montana, but Art was not a U.S. citizen, and his student visa had expired. He learned of a small prospect mine he could lease in British Columbia. Shortly after arriving, but before he started developing the mine, he was contacted and hired by Bechtel, a large engineering and construction company headquartered in San Francisco. After decades of declining mining activity in the iron range in northern Minnesota, the state legislature dropped the royalty fees on taconite to levels conducive for commercial mining. Bechtel hired 24-year-old Art as a project engineer and part of its team to construct the taconite processing facilities in Hibbing, Minnesota. He stayed 14 months. "I always liked trying new things."

Next Bechtel wanted him to help build a nuclear power plant in Georgia, but he declined, and instead returned to British Columbia to work for a mining equipment company. Within a year, Bechtel contacted him about leading the underground excavation team for the construction of the Bay Area Transit System (BART) in San Francisco, and he accepted. "It was a terrific job, technically challenging and a great place to live."

The project stalled over a financing delay that required approval from voters for additional bonds. Art was sidelined and wasting time sitting in Bechtel's San Francisco offices when he learned of another mining opportunity. "I leased a silver mine from a property owner in interior British Columbia in exchange for a royalty percentage. I quickly found high-grade ore. Silver prices were relatively high at the time, and I was able to raise the capital to start mining. For the first time in my life, I was making some serious money, around $30,000 per month, which wasn't bad for 1968. The mine produced well for about a year, and then it became necessary to extend a tunnel 2,000 feet. I approached the property owner about either sharing in the capital investment or reducing his share before proceeding with the costly move. He declined, and I moved on."

1971-1984

Anaconda hired Art to work on a new mine in Britannia Beach, British Columbia between Vancouver and Squamish. Then they sent him to develop an underground copper mine in an historic mining district west of Salt Lake City. The initial team consisted of 32-year-old Art and two others. They created the concept, budgets, and feasibility study. The Anaconda board then approved a $230 million commitment for the mine ($1 billion in today's dollars). The project was brought in on time and on budget, and the Carr Fork Mine became the most valuable of Anaconda's (later Kennecott's) holdings in the Bingham District.

"We sunk four shafts 4,000 feet deep capable of generating 10,000 tons of ore daily, and then built the mining complex to process the ore." When asked how he kept getting rehired from places he'd left, he said, "What I could do was get things done. I was great at building new things. Not so good at ongoing operations. My projects were like battle campaigns. A lot of people weren't comfortable with this. I was pretty hard-nosed. I wasn't interested in excuses. We set out the goals and held people accountable. We were at our best when we functioned like an athletic team."

When asked why he returned to the corporate world of mining after his success as an entrepreneur, he explained, "I was never motivated totally by the money. I loved technical and management challenges. I was attracted by the notion of a creating a mine out of nothing. And I needed to broaden my experience and knowledge."

KINROSS GOLD CORPORATION

1984 - 2003

ARCO purchased Anaconda and wanted Art to relocate to Australia to develop its coal operations, but he declined. "I wasn't much of a corporate guy." So in 1984 Art founded a company called Plexus Resources Corporation. "The original intent was to acquire nonstrategic mineral properties from large companies and to develop them. Mines take a long time to develop, so we needed to generate early cash flow to keep the doors opened. To do that, we participated in the development of some oil and gas properties knowing they require a shorter lead-time to become operational. Next we formed a 50/50 joint venture with Kiewit, a mining, construction, and engineering company in Omaha. They would put up the money, and we would find the mines. Our first mining venture was the Rawhide Gold Mine in Fallon, Nevada, a joint venture with Kennecott Copper.

The Kennecott data estimated that the Rawhide mine contained 1.25 million ounces of recoverable gold. "Kiewit and Plexus undertook a feasibility study and determined it would require $30 million to construct the mine and processing plants and provide sufficient working capital. Our share would be $15 million. After a global search and many turndowns, I found Elder's Resources, a group owned by John Elliott, a high-flying Australian, to invest the required amount collateralized by a 'call on future production'. We got the mine built, and in 18 months we were able to buy out their position.

In 1993 Kinross Gold Corporation, so named for a small village in Scotland, was formed from the consolidation of Plexus and two other mining companies and was listed on the Toronto Stock Exchange. Art was named President and COO. The company was soon operating several successful gold mines. In the late 1980's, the Canadian government created new tax incentives to encourage investments in natural resource companies, which aided the entity in raising $80 million in new capital.

Art served as President and Vice Chairman of Kinross for a period of 20 years and was actively involved acquiring, restoring, and operating mines all over the world, some of which were spin-outs from Kennecott. Art's work took him to Zimbabwe, Zambia, Russia, Haiti, Chile, Alaska, Ontario, British Columbia, Idaho, Nevada, South Africa, central Asia, and Brazil. *(Author's note: Art later asked me where I was going for my next story. When I told him I was headed to Central Mexico he said, "Oh shit! I wouldn't go there. That's too dangerous.")*

The Magadan, Russia project was noteworthy. "A total of $250 million was invested developing a mining complex 60 miles south of the Arctic Circle in the center of Stalin's former Gulag Archipelago, (a prison system of forced labor operated from 1918 - 1956). We invested $125 million and the remainder came from several governmental entities. The project presented many new demands and challenges. Working in an Arctic climate, building a network of ice roads, and establishing a procurement network leading from Seattle to Magadan was extremely complex. Working with the Russian bureaucracy and the various governmental agencies who were our co-investors was equally difficult. The Magadan gold mine truly tested our capabilities."

Art was accustomed to working in difficult environments. "Our strength was in taking mines that weren't doing well. We'd bring them up to modern standards, and make them work."

By necessity, Art also developed skills in dealing with the 'wolves of wall street.' "Miners view the world from a long term perspective. Traders don't, so it became essential to learn how to live with them. The history of the commodity businesses is that you raise capital and reap large rewards during the relatively short peaks in the cycle when prices are high. Then you learn how to survive during the long valleys by relentlessly working to reduce costs. You have to fend off the predators in both phases." Art discovered early what he did well and liked doing, and then spent his life doing it.

But all was not well. Art was divorced from his first wife, the mother of his two oldest sons, after 12 years of marriage. He remarried and fathered two children with Marjorie. In 1982 she contracted a rare form of brain cancer and was given months to live. Instead she lived with full time care in their home until 2002, the last 15 years not knowing her children or her husband. "You live with the hand you're dealt."

CONGO HISTORY

"There was no written language in the Congo when the Europeans first arrived in 1482, leaving the history of this tragic land to have been written by the interlopers. A Portuguese mariner stumbled upon the vast river, went ashore, and constructed a limestone pillar with an iron cross inscribed with the words:

"In the year 6681 of the World and in that of 1482 since the birth of our Lord Jesus Christ, the most serene, the most potent prince, King Joao II of Portugal did order this land to be discovered by Diogo Cao, and esquire in his household."(KLG)

And from that time forward the river and the lands beyond would be known as the Congo, a bastardized form of the discoverer's name.

Indigenous slavery existed long before the arrival of the Europeans, practiced between tribal rivals and by Arabs from the north. But the Europeans expanded the nefarious practice to the level of global trade.

The 1998 book King Leopold's Ghost by author Adam Hoschschild tells the riveting tale of the methodical plunder that occurred during the colonial reign of King Leopold II of Belgium. As an aside, Art shared the view that almost all of his Belgian friends and acquaintances with firsthand experience in the Congo believe the book lacks balance and fails to mention the positives that occurred during the colonial period, i.e. a literacy rate reaching 37%, the virtual elimination of sleeping sickness, creation of a transportation system, construction of hydroelectric power, et al.

In 1877 Henry Morton Stanley, the explorer most famous for locating Dr. Livingstone, and less well known for having fought on both sides of the American civil war, led an Anglo-American expedition from Lake Tanganyika down the Congo River, to the Atlantic coast. "His writings about the vastness of the region and his knowledge aided King Leopold II of Belgium, who was scouting for empire-building opportunities, in making the Congo basin his personal fiefdom." (KLG)

And a fertile opportunity it was. "The Congo River drains an area larger than India, has an estimated one-sixth of the world's hydroelectric potential, and the river and its tributaries constitute 7,000 miles of navigable waterways rivaled by few places on earth. And the King's agents would soon discover that the land was inhabited by over 200 different ethnic groups speaking over 400 languages, making conquest relatively easy." (KLG)

Geologists and miners quickly followed the early explorers of the Katanga Province and discovered what later became known as the Rhodesia Copper Belt, home to rich copper deposits over a swath of land running several hundred miles from the southern borders of the Congo into neighboring Zambia (formerly Northern Rhodesia). Art later explained, "The copper ore in that region is known to be six times more concentrated than today's best copper mines in North America."

Colonial administrators granted a mining concession to a Belgian mining company, Union Minière du Haut-Katanga (Mining Union of Upper Katanga) for all the mineral rights in the Katanga Province, a region rich in copper, diamonds, gold, tin, uranium, and zinc. They opened their first mine in 1912, and the Congo quickly became the richest colony in all of Africa. Wealth created in the Congo was largely responsible for funding the Belgian government in exile, both during WWI and WWII. After Malaysia fell to the Japanese in 1941, Congolese plantations became the principal source of rubber for the Allies. Additional mines were added over time in the area stretching the 187 miles from Kolwezi to Lubumbashi, along with mines in Northern Rhodesia, sharing needed infrastructure including rail lines, roads, and water and power systems.

The new Congo administrators continued King Leopold's practice of restricting access to Belgian concessionaires and Belgian citizens, the only exceptions being Cypriot miners and Italian craftsmen. They were diligent in keeping the English, Germans, and French out of their colony.

From WWI to 1960, the Katanga Province was a veritable paradise for the European colonizers. Agriculture flourished. Large farms produced grains, produce, and livestock in abundance. Food exports became a significant part of the economy, although overshadowed by mining. Even though the province lies 10 degrees south of the equator, the climate is mild, with summer (December - March) temperatures rarely exceeding 80 degrees, as the elevation is similar to Denver, Colorado. Occasional frosts occur during the brief winter, which is also the rainy season. Rainfall in Katanga averages about 49 inches per year, a little more than New York and a little less than Miami, Florida. Nearby lakes and streams provide abundant fish to feed the relatively small population. The terrain consists primarily of rolling hills and fields, "Mindful of Ohio" according to Art. Overall, the region has been uncommonly blessed by nature's bounty.

Katanga forms the southern Congolese border with Angola and Zambia. It also borders Tanzania by way of Lake Tanganyika. The province is roughly the size of France and is home to approximately 7 million people.

Union Minière was instrumental in constructing the Benguela Railway connecting the Katanga mines due west to the coast of Angola. Other rail lines connected Katanga to Northern Rhodesia and on to ports in South Africa to the south and Tanganyika (Now Tanzania) to the east. By 1919 they were producing and shipping 22,000 tons of copper processed by seven furnaces. By 1950, the Congo was the fourth largest producer of copper in the world. Hydroelectric power provided abundant cheap electricity required to operate the mining complex.

Lubumbashi is the capital of Katanga province and, benefiting from mineral wealth, was once known as a 'jewel of a city', much nicer than most European cities in the early 20th century. Many Belgians were eager to relocate to Katanga, and the tourist industry flourished with visitors attracted to nearby Lakes Tanganyika, Victoria, and Albert.

Jackie Kennedy's fortunes late in her life were linked to the Congo, by way of her companion Maurice Templesman with whom she lived from 1980 until her death in 1994. After her husband Aristotle Onassis died, she inherited a mere $26 million, a 'pittance' and clearly insufficient to sustain her lifestyle. Her subsequent companion thereafter was Templesman, an orthodox Jew and a Belgian American, whose family made their fortune dealing in Congo diamonds, first during the colonial period and later under the Mobutu regime. In 1957, when he was 27, Templesman traveled to the Congo with his then lawyer, Adlai Stevenson, former Illinois senator and two-time presidential candidate, and developed contacts, one of whom was Joseph Mobutu, gaining privileged access to Congo diamond sources. He later benefited from Mobutu's rise to power in the post-colonial Congo. The resources of the region attracted a legion of interested parties.

In 1960, the Belgians were caught by surprise when the demand for self-rule erupted in the Congo. Demonstrations in the capitol of Leopoldville were initially suppressed with bloody force by the Belgian Colonial police force, but the bird had fallen off the perch. "Colonial administration had done next to nothing to prepare the Congolese for their independence. At the time there were fewer than 30 Congolese university graduates, no army officers, engineers, or physicians. Eighty thousand Belgians fled the country during the first year of independence." (KLG)

Patrice Lumumba was the victor in the first election ever held in the territory. He was a charismatic speaker and openly hostile to western interests and actively sought sponsorship from the Russians. By this time U.S. mining companies were active in the Congo and were aligned with the Belgians in their antipathy towards Lumumba. Much of the uranium used by the U.S. in their WWII nuclear program was Congolese, bringing the region into play as the cold war with Russia heated up. In January 1961 Lumumba was assassinated, an act commonly attributed to the CIA, Belgian military officers still active in the Congo, and anti-Lumumba Congolese forces. One of the later was Joseph Mobutu, then a non-commissioned officer in the former Force Publique.

With the aid of the U.S. government, Mobutu staged a coup in 1965 and became the country's dictator and continued in that capacity until he was overthrown in 1997. He renamed the country Zaire and himself President Mobutu Sese Seko Nkuku Ngbendu Wa Za Banga which, in one of the nation's four hundred languages, means, 'The all-powerful warrior who, because of his endurance and inflexible will to win, goes from conquest to conquest, leaving fire in his wake,' or Mobutu Sese Seko for short. (IMBd.com biographies)

In 1961 Union Minière supported the secession of the province of Katanga from the Congo, but an independent Katanga was short-lived. Then secretary-general of the UN, Dag Hammerskjold took an aggressive stance against the Katanga secessionists seeking to support a unified Congo. He was killed in a plane crash in late 1961, with many believing the Belgians were responsible.

In 1966, Mobutu, following King Leopold II's example, acquired all of the possessions and activities of Union Minière transforming it into a Congolese company called Gécamines (Societe Generale des Carrieres et des Mines). With few exceptions, all enterprises in the Congo became the property of Mobutu and his cronies.

Mobutu's thirty two years of corruption, thievery, and thuggery would make him one of the world's richest men, with his personal wealth estimated at $4 billion. During his reign he was hosted and feted by left-wing politicians in America including Mayor Coleman Young of Detroit, and a then obscure NY politician by the name of Bill DeBlasio. The remainder of the Congo didn't fare as well. The Union Minière copper mines produced 400,000 tons of copper in 1960. By 1990 the Gécamines production declined to 25,000 tons. Virtually everything that could be looted had been.

ART AND THE CONGO

Knowledgeable people recognized the Congo as possibly the most metallagenic spot on the globe. Art established contact with two Czechoslovakians, one a rock mechanic geo-scientist and the other a mining engineer, both located in Tucson, AZ. For years the two provided technical support for Gécamines. They told him of the fabulous potential, specifically at the mining complex in Kolwezi, Katanga. Art hired one of them to keep him abreast of developments. In colonial times, Kolwezi was a relatively sophisticated city of 250,000 inhabitants, located northwest of Lubumbashi. By the late 1990's the population had declined, and the city was barely livable.

Gécamines (aka Mobutu's tribal cronies) kept expats, mostly Belgians, involved in technical and administrative functions until their expulsion in the early 1980's. The mines had long been dying the death of a 'thousand paper cuts' attendant to lack of capital, incompetent technical and managerial leadership. But mines don't die overnight. It took a calamitous event to serve as the straw that finally broke the camel's back. In 1982 the underground Kamoto mine, one of four comprising the Kolwezi mining complex, collapsed. "They were mining on two horizons as a room and pillar operation, one above the other, separated by fifteen meters of rock. In mining anything done in one part can impact others. They got out of sequence, and multiple layers pancaked down on one another in a manner similar to the World Trade Center. This catastrophic collapse, which fortunately occurred between shifts, brought the mine to a standstill."

The Marxist-led rebellion in nearby Angola in the late 1970's also wreaked havoc on Katanga's mines. In 1929, the Portuguese completed the Benguela Railway, connecting the Katanga mines westward to Port Benguela, Angola a distance of 1,085 miles. The eastern third of the railway was destroyed in the fighting and mining products were subsequently shipped by truck 2,150 miles south to Port Elizabeth, South Africa.

In 1997, ex-Gécamines officials contacted Art seeking help. Art knew of the history of these mines and their vast potential, so he was compelled to take a look. He was also aware of the potential in Katanga through the Tucson mining consultants. By this time Kinross, and Art in particular, enjoyed a proven track record of turning around failing mines. Kinross was principally a gold mining company, but Art thought it would make sense to learn more about the Congo mines.

Subsequently, Art flew to Brussels to meet with representatives of Gécamines, all Congolese. They asked him to fly to Katanga specifically to examine the Kolwezi mining complex, consisting of three open pit mines and the Kamoto underground mine that had collapsed. Production in the entire region had fallen to one-eighth of former levels, and the representatives were desperate. Art enlisted the aid of two Belgians, Ben Brabants, an elderly gentleman who once served as general manager of the mining complex in colonial times, and Rene Nolevaux, who had spent twelve years working for Union Minière as an engineer and manager in Kolwezi. Both were eager to return to their former home. The three flew to Johannesburg, South Africa and chartered a jet to Kolwezi, Zaire. "We checked out the geologic databases, and the potential was mindboggling. But the mines looked like a giant garbage pile. Everything needed was broken or missing. We met with the local management team who, barely concealing their lack of interest, said, 'Invest your money with us, and we'll fix everything.' We told them that was a nonstarter and left."

On another trip to Brussels in 1998, Art encountered people involved in the Kolwezi mines. Congolese held every meaningful position in Gécamines, and were selected from families of tribal royalty with close ties to Mobutu. They mostly devised various techniques for looting. Art recalled one example, "The Congolese CFO established a personal account into which the proceeds from virtually all copper sales were deposited. At times this settlement account held float in excess of $1 billion, where it was parked and earning interest for the clever kleptocrat, before being paid to Gécamines." Unrelated to mining, but still telling, is the story that the Zaire ambassador to Tokyo sold his country's embassy in a red-hot real estate market in the 1980's and pocketed the proceeds. (CIA report)

Later in 1998 Art returned to the Congo at the invitation of Gécamines to renew discussions about investments in the Kolwezi complex. He arrived in Kinshasha with the two Belgian miners and a lawyer. "Everything was chaotic. Mobutu had been overthrown, and Laurent Kabila maintained a tenuous hold on power. Young soldiers with automatic weapons were menacing and ubiquitous. I remember flying in and seeing the acres and acres of dilapidated warehouses that once held the treasures of the Congo. We were mistakenly greeted at the airport by South African consular officials, as there is also a South African company named Kinross. They were upset when they learned we weren't their countrymen but still delivered us safely to our hotel. The pilot of our jet said he wouldn't stay any longer than it took to drop us off, fearing confiscation. We had a local driver who spoke good English and became a vital part of our stay. He invited me to his home for dinner, and I mistakenly accepted. The hospitality was remarkable and gracious coming from extremely poor people. I had eaten a lot of exotic foods over decades of travel, but I was served something that I just couldn't get down. It tasted like chalk. I later learned that it was a root derivative with zero nutritional value. Its only benefit lies in assuaging hunger. After a week of fruitless discussions, we called our jet and left. They wanted the investment of foreign capital only, but were still unwilling to allow outsiders to run the mines."

Consider the following BBC contemporaneous articles painting a picture of the near-anarchic period at the time of Art's visits:

BBC

"A vast country with immense economic resources, the Democratic Republic of Congo (DRC) has been at the centre of what some observers call 'Africa's world war'.. This has left it in the grip of a humanitarian crisis. The five-year conflict (1997-2002) pitted government forces, supported by Angola, Namibia and Zimbabwe, against rebels backed by Uganda and Rwanda.

"Despite a peace deal and the formation of a transitional government in 2003, people in the east of the country remain in fear of continuing death, rape or displacement by marauding militias and the army. The war claimed up to six million lives, either as a direct result of fighting or because of disease and malnutrition. It has been called possibly the worst emergency in Africa in recent decades.

"The war had an economic as well as a political side. Fighting was fuelled by the country's vast mineral wealth, with all sides taking advantage of the anarchy to plunder natural resources, and some small militias fight on."

BBC MONITORING

"The history of Democratic Republic of Congo has been one of civil war and corruption. After independence in 1960, the country immediately faced an army mutiny and an attempt at secession by its mineral-rich province of Katanga. A year later, its prime minister, Patrice Lumumba, was seized and killed by troops loyal to army chief Joseph Mobutu. In 1965 Mobutu seized power, later renaming the country Zaire and himself Mobutu Sese Seko. He turned Zaire into a springboard for operations against Soviet-backed Angola and thereby ensured US backing. But he also made Zaire synonymous with corruption.

"After the Cold War, Zaire ceased to be of interest to the US. Thus, when in 1997 neighbouring Rwanda invaded it to flush out extremist Hutu militias, it gave a boost to the anti-Mobutu rebels, who quickly captured the capital, Kinshasa, installed Laurent Kabila as president and renamed the country Democratic Republic Congo.

"Nonetheless, DRC's troubles continued. A rift between Mr. Kabila and his former allies sparked a new rebellion, backed by Rwanda and Uganda. Angola, Namibia and Zimbabwe took Kabila's side, turning the country into a vast battleground.

"On assumption of power, Kabila inherited a country already involved in massive tribal infighting, partly arising because of the influx of refugees in 1994. His rule was quickly challenged by a Rwanda and Uganda backed rebellion in August 1998. Finally, troops from Zimbabwe, Chad, Angola, Namibia, and Sudan intervened to support Kabila's government. Even though a cease-fire was reached in July 1999 between DRC, Zimbabwe, Angola, Uganda, Namibia, Rwanda and the Congolese rebels, sporadic fighting continued unabated. Kabila was assassinated January 16, 2001 and rule of the country fell to his son, Joseph.

Joseph Kabila was successful in negotiating a withdrawal of the Rwandan forces from Congo in October 2002 and early in 2003, all combatant parties finally came to the table and agreed to cease the fighting. They agree to set up a government of national unity as a caretaker until democratic elections can be held in 2005."

GEORGE FORREST

In 1918, 16-year-old Malta Forrest left his native New Zealand signing on as a cabin boy on an Australian steamer headed for South Africa. He arrived penniless in Cape Town, but quickly found employment at a General Motors distribution company. His immigration papers mistakenly labeled him an Australian, which he had no reason, nor ability, to challenge. Two years after his arrival he persuaded his employer to sell him a truck on credit. He heard of the riches of the Katanga province of the Belgian Congo, and somehow got the idea he would start a one-truck trucking company. He successfully navigated the 2,200-mile trip taking him the length of South Africa, Rhodesia, and Northern Rhodesia, into the southernmost portion of the Congo. He arrived in Lubumbashi in 1921.

He went on to develop good working relationships with the Belgian colonial administrators and local tribal leaders and was known to all as 'the Aussie.' His trucking business flourished serving the Belgian operated copper mines. He later added construction, mining, and manufacturing enterprises. He married a Belgian lady, and they had three sons, Malta, Michael, and George. The senior Malta raised his sons as Congolese. He insisted that they learn the local dialects, the most dominant being Swahili, an artificial trading language originating with Arab slave traders along the Swahili coastal region and subsequently influenced by the infusion of German, English, French, and Portuguese. The boys also attended French-speaking schools. Malta was investing in the Congo for the long-term with his time and treasure and with his sons. He insisted that they grow up as locals with locals.

In 1940 Malta Sr. died, and Malta, Jr. became the head of Forrest enterprises at the young age of 19. Malta, Jr. also died young in 1960 leaving 20-year-old George to tend to the family's fortunes and to navigate the volatile and violent transition from colonial to post-colonial Congo. George sought to become a citizen of the newly named Zaire, but was told he could not because he was not black. To compensate for this slight, members of the local tribal hierarchy affectionately use the honorific 'Uncle George' and referred to him as a white Congolese. George later told Art, "My relationships are with the chiefs. The politicians come and go, but the tribal hierarchy remains." While George prospered during this era, it wasn't without difficulty, twenty percent of the people employed in his vast enterprises were dedicated to security, often referred to as George's army.

He soldiered on and continued to keep his businesses operating. He established a financial center in Brussels, both as a hedge to the troubled times and owing to the necessities of conducting international business. He survived the Angolan invasion of the Katanga Province in the 1970's when his Kolwezi home was shelled during the fighting. He preserved the remnants as a reminder of the frightening experience.

In the early 1980's, Mobutu nationalized all of George's businesses, and George packed up his family, including his now young son, Malta, and moved to a village 30 miles outside of Brussels. Within a year of his departure, Mobutu's minions called him to return. George said he would, but only if he regained total ownership and control. They agreed, and the Forrest family traveled back to their home. And he raised his sons in the Congo the same way he was raised.

Art reminisced about his subsequent dealings with George, "He was a man of his word. He had power but used it gracefully. He was one of the finest men I've ever encountered."

KATANGA MINING, LTD

In 2003, officials from the Democratic Republic of Congo ministry of mines again contacted Art. They assured him, "We're now ready to accept your terms and conditions."

Art had already concluded that the only way he'd return to the Congo was with a Congolese partner. "There was really only one partner that I'd consider, George Forrest. I hadn't met him, but I had heard a lot about him. All good. A few years earlier, the transitional president, Joseph Kabila, asked George to be his personal representative on the Gécamines' board. He knew they were cheating him, and he needed someone he trusted to look after his and the nascent nation's interests. Ben Brabants knew George and arranged for us to meet in Brussels. George doesn't speak English, but he brought his son Malta who does. We spent several days together. I told him what I needed from him, and what I would do. I would restore and manage the Kolwezi mines. George would manage the in-country relationships."

A few weeks after the Brussels meetings, Art flew to Lubumbashi and received the green light to proceed. "We stayed at the home of a Belgian friend and drafted a joint venture agreement. I was retired from Kinross at the time, but they let me use the corporation as a temporary holding entity. Kinross and George Forrest formed KF Ltd with a 60/40 split. KF Ltd then entered into a 75%/25% joint venture with Gécamines. George, another Kinross principal, and I would maintain majority control of both the management agreement and stock ownership. It was still a lark. The obstacles were formidable, and we had no idea whether this was going to work."

The agreement had to be approved by governmental decree, requiring a meeting with acting-President Joseph Kabila subsequently arranged by George. "Kabila was 29 years old when we met. I was impressed. He spoke English well, and I later learned that he had been educated at English speaking schools in Tanganyika. He wore a western-style business suit, forsaking the military regalia commonplace for men in his position. His accent was more like that of an American. Like most African leaders of the post-colonial era, he was soft spoken, but carried a big stick. He told us of his vision for the Congo, and we told him of our plans for the Kolwezi mining complex. He summarized his offer, 'Our nation is bankrupt. I can't provide any resources for the mine. But we need people to invest in our nation. I will support you in anyway I can other than money. I know it will be difficult to get the mine operating. If anyone in my government creates obstacles for you or tries, in anyway, to enrich themselves, come to me, and I will deal with it.'"

"I wasn't going to raise half a billion dollars on the promise of a dictator who could be gone overnight, but I now believed I was dealing with the legitimate head of a government."

The decree was signed in 2004. "We formed a shell corporation, Katanga Mining Ltd, and raised the first $7.5 million of seed money to fund the technical teams to develop a budget and feasibility study for the restoration of the mines. We determined that we would eventually need over $600 million to bring the mines to their full potential."

By 2004, the 'World War of Africa' also had ended. Two years later Katanga Mining Ltd's began operations. The feasibility study and technical reports released in April 2006 confirmed the long-term viability of the joint venture. The reserves and resources of the mining complex were estimated at 5.67 million tons of copper and 614,000 tons of cobalt. The average copper/ore concentration was 3.50% vs. a worldwide average of .6%.

In a letter Art wrote to shareholders in his first annual report he stated, "...2006 was a remarkable year for the Democratic Republic of Congo. After years of instability, the country held its first democratic elections in 40 years, and Joseph Kabila was elected President. In early 2003, when negotiations to create the Kamoto joint venture began, a workable and financeable outcome seemed far off. Now because of quite amazing transformations - including a constitution adopted by national referendum; a popularly elected government; good work by the World Bank, the UN, and others; and a revived demand for commodities - capital in many forms is moving to the Democratic Republic of Congo."

On June 27, 2006, Katanga Mining, Limited (KML) exercised its option to acquire the position of Kinross Forrest Ltd for their 75% interest in the Kamoto joint venture with Gécamines (owning 25%) and was approved for a full listing on the Toronto Stock Exchange. That same day, the joint venture officially took control of the Kolwezi site. Four Congolese, one of whom was George, were selected to serve on the eight-person board of directors by the founding shareholders.

From the KML 2006 annual report:

"Katanga Mining Limited is rehabilitating a mine complex located on the Congolese copperbelt near Kolwezi in the Democratic Republic of Congo. The site comprises the Kamoto underground mine and the open pit mines of Dikuluwe, Mashamba East, and Mashamba West (together known as DIMA) and Musoneie-T17. Ore will be processed and refined onsite at the Kamoto concentrator and the Luilu metallurgical plant. The concession covers 15,000 hectares (60 square miles)."

The stars were lining up. China was emerging as a global power and massive consumer of commodities. Brazil, Russia, and India were also experiencing growing economies. Demand for copper was surging, prices were rising, and funding for new capacity was becoming a real prospect. World copper prices hovered at $1 per pound from 1980 to 2004, and then started a near meteoric rise reaching $4/ lb. by 2008 and $4.50/lb in 2012. The Kolwezi mines would have an average site cost per pound of copper at $.22 placing the company among the world's lowest cost producers.

REBUILDING THE MINES

Art was now responsible for restoring the mines while George handled 'in-country' issues. Mining involves drilling, blasting, and transporting vast quantities of material from either an open pit or underground setting. In the case of open pit mining, the overburden is removed to expose the ore deposit. The pits may grow to more than a mile in diameter with a road spiraling down the slopes of the pit. Underground mines, like the Kamoto facility, used a room and pillar approach to access the ore.

The work also involved the restoration of the mining complex's metallurgical processing facilities, essential in converting copper ore into copper by removing unwanted materials through varying physical and chemical steps, each yielding higher concentrations of copper.

"We opened an office in London, filling five positions: I was president and CEO, and I hired a CFO, corporate secretary, director of corporate affairs, and director of investor relations. We hired a Belgian general manager to start assembling a team in Katanga. An American, Rick Dye was hired to head up the engineering and construction management, and he located in Johannesburg where we set up a procurement office and staging area for the equipment and material that would be purchased. We leased a Boeing 737 and had it reconfigured to haul both passengers and cargo for twice weekly roundtrips between Johannesburg and Kolwezi.

"I always felt safer in the Congo than in South Africa. Race relations were infinitely more harmonious, as the Congolese never suffered through anything like the apartheid system in South Africa.

Johannesburg is a far more dangerous place to live. It's no longer just a schism between white and black, but between haves and have-nots. All of the engineers working for us in Johannesburg had their homes broken into one or more times. Security and safety became primary, making it difficult to recruit skilled workers.

"We established a procurement program preparing detailed engineering drawings and bid specifications. By the end of 2006, fifty-two separate contracts were let, and work had begun rebuilding the mining complex. It started with the removal of thousands of cubic meters of debris and material clogging the mine sites, and was followed by contractors building roads, anti-malarial programs, pipelines, electrical power, water and sewer systems, housing, schools, training facilities, catering operations, cell towers, farms, a hospital, and, most critically, the mining and processing operations.

"A temporary camp was set up during the construction period, housing 600 people. We eventually built a dormitory and mess hall facility to house single, non-local permanent workers. We constructed one hundred single-family homes for the foreign workers with families. The contractor workforce consisted of Americans, Canadians, South Africans, Indians, Belgians, British, and Australians. There is a universe of people in the mining world who follow job opportunities to the most remote locations on the planet. Once full, the camp resembled the bar scene in the first *Star Wars* movie. We hired three separate chefs: Indian, South African, and North American, to cater to the preferences of the work force. Agriculture had collapsed during the post-colonial period, and we were incurring great expense importing food, so we started our own farms.

"We had 1,700 people working by the end of 2006 with a local monthly payroll of $1 million per month. But nothing was easy. Many of the Congolese we employed returned from the north, having fled Katanga during the worst abuses of the Mobutu era. The northerners were attracted to the opportunities at the Kolwezi mines and we hired them, as they had proven themselves better workers. This led to substantive tensions with locals with different tribal affiliations.

"There was also a lost generation of miners. The ex-Gécamines workforce received neither formal education nor on-the-job training during the 45+ years they ran the mines. The investment in training required to rebuild the appropriate level of skills was massive.

"Early on we had to pay local workers in U.S. currency. There were no operating banks or ATM's, nor would there have been much confidence in them had they existed. This required the costly and risky proposition of flying millions of U.S. dollars in from Johannesburg weekly. Later, we were able to persuade the workforce to accept direct deposits. We were able to get banks to open branches in Kolwezi and to set up ATM's. We also established a system of pay using debit cards, with a portion of each weekly paycheck going to the wife of the employee. African men are not known for their reliability in sharing their paycheck with wives.

"The older Congolese spoke French, a by-product of the colonial era, but the young did not, as virtually all of the schools closed when the Belgians were expelled. Our technical and administrative work was conducted in French, and we used Swahili to communicate with the manual laborers.

"We complied with all of the same safety and environmental regulations that would have applied had the mining complex been in the U.S. This was just good business practice and stewardship from our perspective.

"I made over 75 round trips from London to the mines over a two year period, spending about one week a month on premises. I remember being in Cape Town, South Africa working with contractors when I received an urgent message requiring my presence at a meeting with the Democratic Republic of Congo minister of mining in Kinshasha.

From there I traveled to Johannesburg, then back to the mine. I spent 39 hours in the air in a five-day period. My time was spent non-stop dealing with conflict resolution within the DRC, Katanga officials, non-governmental organizations (NGO's), contractors, and our employees.

"The two Belgian mining engineers, Brabants and Nolevaux, helped me enormously. Renè is an outgoing, smart guy who had a real affinity for the people. His children were born in Kolwezi, he knew the local people and customs better than anyone, and he was critical getting things launched.

"We were extremely fortunate. There were no serious accidents, outbreaks of disease, or social unrest during the 18-month rebuilding project."

POWER

The concentrating, smelting, refining, and hydro-metallurgical facilities required to convert ore into 'four nine' copper (99.99% pure) requires an enormous amount of reliable electricity. Fortunately, the Congo is blessed with abundant hydro capacity and potential. Unfortunately, it had decayed from neglect during the Mobutu era.

In the 1960's the CIA built a hydroelectric facility on the Inga Falls, a series of cataracts on the Congo River lying between Kinshasha and the Atlantic coast. Smaller hydroelectric plants were also operational in Katanga, but just barely by 2006. Most problematic, the transmission and distribution systems that brought the power from the rivers to the mines were unreliable. "One of the first things we had to do was to rebuild transformers and hundreds of miles of distribution systems. We also had to invest in diesel powered co-generation capabilities. Intermittent shutdowns due to power shortages are extremely damaging and costly to the process of refining copper."

Concentrating removes waste materials from the copper ore by running the ore through a succession of crushers and mills producing successively smaller pieces. The process continues by mixing the ore with water flowing through increasingly refined mills. The slurry is then mixed with chemical reagents coating the copper and the resulting concentrate is pumped into tanks.

"Three concentrates were produced at Kolwezi; a copper oxide, a copper sulfide, and a cobalt oxide. Because of the relative uniqueness of the ore's mineralogy, a 'hydrometallurgical smelting' approach to extracting the copper and cobalt was developed. In simple terms, the concentrates were transported as slurry through a five km pipeline from the concentrator to the Luilu metallurgical plant. Moisture was removed from the concentrates by vacuum filtration. The filtered concentrates undertook three different paths of treatment. The sulfide concentrate is "roasted" to produce a copper sulfate that yields sulphuric acid and copper ions. The copper oxide concentrate is added to the acid solution and the copper ion laden is separated from the remaining solids that are sent to waste disposal. The copper ion laden solution then goes to electrolytic refining for production of approximately 98% pure copper. The cobalt concentrate flows in a similar way by using some of the sulfuric acid stream to put the cobalt oxide into solution so the cobalt ionic solution can be refined by electrolysis.

"Stainless steel sheets acting as anodes are placed in long troughs. The tanks are filled with the acidic copper rich solution. When an electrical current is passed through each tank, the negative copper ions are deposited on the stainless steel. The remaining impurities fall out of the acid solution forming slime that collects at the bottom of the tank. After 9-15 days the current is turned off, and the copper sheeting (cathode) is removed from the stainless steel anode. Each cathode now weighs about 77 lbs. and is about 99.99% pure copper.

The slime is refined further producing chips of marketable cobalt, a product with significantly greater value than copper. After refining, the copper cathodes are ready for transportation to world markets."

TRANSPORTATION

"We worked with the various state-owned rail lines to restore service from Kolwezi to Port Elizabeth, South Africa requiring a route through Zambia, Botswana, and Zimbabwe. All land-based transportation was complicated owing to the necessity of making four border crossings each direction: South Africa, Zimbabwe, Botswana, Zambia, and Democratic Republic of Congo. Crew changes were required to operate in each nation. The region's rail system was also cumbersome, operating on two distinct rail gauges, colonial and standard, which limited our options. For the most part, we used rail to ship copper cathodes out and trucks to bring materials in from Johannesburg."

Virtually all of the mobile equipment required for the mines and processing facilities had been looted, requiring that replacements be transported from Johannesburg. The 1,500-mile route through five countries consisted of paved roads and bridges in varying states of disrepair. "We worked with the World Bank to assist in rebuilding the roads and bridges along this route. Freeport-McMoRan, Inc. (formerly Phelps-Dodge) was restoring a neighboring mine 60 miles from Kolwezi, and together we invested $60 million in road construction."

In addition to the difficulties associated with four border crossings each way, the truckers were required to drive on different sides of the road, South Africa, Zambia, and Zimbabwe, all former English colonies, drive on the British side, and Botswana and DRC on the 'American/European' side. Each convoy took about a week.

"We had to build an assembly facility at the mine site. It took 7-8 truckloads to carry the parts for one ore hauling dump truck.

The tires alone are 12' in diameter. The same was true for every piece of heavy equipment required to operate a functioning mine and metallurgical facility."

"The mines were roughly equidistant from the Atlantic and Indian oceans, but the choice of rail or truck and the destination depended as much on the political situation of the day v. conventional logistical considerations."

NGO's

One of the greatest obstacles in restoring the Kolwezi mines came from the various non-governmental organizations, mostly those based in Europe. Their stated mission is to protect indigenous peoples from exploitation. The worse conditions are in their domains, the greater their fundraising opportunities, creating a perverse set of incentives. "The NGO's did everything in their power to undermine our project. NGO's are inherently opposed to the injection of foreign capital. They worked to get the UN to oppose the project. Idealistic young people who staff the NGO's, believe that government or NGO-sponsored programs are the only solution to a problem. Fortunately, President Kabila lived up to his part of the bargain and calmed them down. Still, I spent a lot of time away from the mines to manage their delaying tactics.

"In early 2007, a formal event was held to dedicate the re-opening of the mines. The Democratic Republic of Congo minister of mining, Joseph Kabila's personal representative, and other dignitaries flew in to Kolwezi. The five-mile route was lined with thousands of cheering people. Had the individuals from the NGO's who fought the project been present, I'm certain their lives would have been in danger from the locals. I've witnessed an African crowd turn into a mob in a flash. It's almost primal."

OPENING THE MINES

Excerpted from Katanga Mining, Ltd's 2007 annual report:

"Underground mining began at the Kamoto mine in March 2007, open-pit operations started in May, concentrate was produced in July, and the first copper cathodes were produced in December.

"Rehabilitation of the original Kamoto facilities was completed on time and on budget.

"Reserve and resource estimates were upgraded to 239 million tons of 4.45 per cent copper and .44 per cent cobalt.

"More than 4,000 Congolese nationals were employed in the mines with a monthly local payroll of $2.8 million.

"KML's market capitalization more than doubled (to $3 billion).

The resurgence of the mining industry revived the local economy. Enterprising people arrived from all over the world. More goods and services became available, commercial air services returned, and hotels and restaurants opened.

"When I first started traveling to Kolwezi, I stayed at the house of the local general manager, and we always dined well. One of the positive legacies of the Belgian colonial era was the French influence on food and the abundance of excellent Congolese chefs. Once the mining activity began, the first to open ancillary businesses were the Chinese. Their restaurants soon dotted the landscape. It was like sprinkling water on a desert."

WOLVES

"Cheese in the middle of the sandwich attracts a lot of rats."

In the early stages of development, the three principals in the deal, George Forrest, the Canadian financial partner, and Art made a gentlemen's agreement to not trade any of their shares until the mine was fully developed, thus maintaining voting control. Art's twenty years of experience as the President of a publically traded mining company gave him an understanding of the ways of hedge funds and stock traders and manipulators. Given the vagaries of mining and the volatility of commodity prices, it is not uncommon for traders to put such companies in play. "I was trying to develop a mining complex and needed to keep the traders at bay until we had a fully functioning operation."

But Art wasn't the only one to realize that the stars lined up. Chinese and Israeli suitors were the first on the scene. The Foreign Corrupt Practices Act of 1977 makes it a felony under U.S. law for a citizen or corporation to pay a bribe in the conduct of business overseas. Non-Americans are unencumbered by such restrictions in their business dealings in Africa.

"The share price was set at $.35 when we created the $7.5 million private placement to fund the preliminary work. Later, when we did our first public offering, I returned to North America for the 'dog and pony' shows in New York, Boston, and Toronto. We battled with the investment bankers over the opening stock price. They argued that $6.75 was as bold as they could imagine. People on our side of the deal were unfortunately agreeing with them, but I stuck with $7.25, giving us an additional $6 million in funding, and the offering was subsequently oversubscribed. Within a year of our initial public offering (2006) the share price reached $24. Everything was getting way ahead of itself, as we still didn't have an operating mine. Then my Canadian partner reneged on our agreement and sheepishly told me he sold two million of his shares. The three of us still retained control, but it was an unwanted and ominous development.

"If we're going to lose control, I thought it best to deal with a mine operator like Rio Tinto, not a trading company. I contacted their CEO, as we had worked together in the past, and told him of our predicament. They agreed to pay $5 million to my erstwhile Canadian partner for a 30-day option for the remainder of his shares. Before the option expired, the Rio Tinto CEO called to say that it wasn't a good fit. They had their hands full with a Mongolian mine. The Canadian sold all of his shares to traders, explaining, 'you can't believe how much pressure I'm under', and that put us in play.

"Other sharks were also circling our deal. The Congolese government pledged a portion of their Kolwezi assets to the Chinese to collateralize a loan unrelated to our mines. They were also reported to have sold the remainder of their 25% stake to an Israeli, Dan Gertler, a large KML shareholder and operator of other mining concessions in the Kolwezi region.

"We were eventually forced to merge with Nikanor, a company controlled by Glencore and several Israeli's." (Interestingly, Glencore was founded as a commodities trading company by Marc Rich, a Swiss American billionaire known primarily for his indictment on tax evasion charges and for illegal oil trading with Iran, and his subsequent pardon by President Bill Clinton on the last day of his presidency).

The Canadian partner earned $100 million from his premature sale, but in so doing, forced Art and George to concede potential future gains in the order of $100 and $250 million respectively, and insured that they we were no longer in a position to thwart a takeover prior to the full development of the project.

"Glencore invested another $150 million in the deal, and the Israeli firm added $250 million. George and I lost control, and the project doubled in scope. On the bright side, the company had a market cap of $3 billion on December 2007 at the date of the merger, and we had just started producing metal. There was also some satisfaction in knowing we created an enterprise with the potential to become the largest producer of copper in Africa and the largest producer of cobalt in the world."

Art resigned as CEO of Katanga Mining Limited in late 2008 and liquidated his position in 2009. "I was never much of a corporate guy, so once we lost control of the ownership structure, I had little interest in working for Glencore. I was done."

George returned to Belgium and turned the operations of his various enterprises over to his son, Malta. "One of my greatest regrets is that George felt betrayed by me, since I was responsible for bringing the Canadian financier into the heart of our deal, and whose premature sale of his position led to our loss of control."

"In 2008, the startup year, the operation fundamentally met first stage production targets. Unfortunately, 2008 was the year the credit markets seized, world economies started to slow, and financial markets were stressed to the extreme. In hindsight, it was good that Glencore purchased our position. Their financial strength gave the project more staying power through the financial downturn as metal prices returned to more historic trend lines of $2.50 copper and $15 cobalt."

The Democratic Republic of Congo profited handsomely from Art's efforts receiving a 3% royalty on the multi-billions of dollars of ongoing revenue and from the 25% corporate income tax, both rates consistent with international standards.

Sadly, Art is not optimistic about the future for Africa. "I will never understand the way Africans think. Everything is in the present. The concept of building for a better tomorrow is totally foreign. Centuries-old tribal customs and conflicts remain in place. If a Congolese walks into someone's home and sees something they would like to have, the owner must give it to them, and reciprocation is then expected. Property rights are virtually non-existent."

The author of King Leopold's Ghost, Adam Hochschild, wrote an afterward to his book chronicling the evils of colonization yet he concedes, "....much of history consists of peoples conquering or colonizing each other. Yet from Ireland to South Korea, countries that were once ruthlessly colonized have nonetheless managed to build reasonably just, prosperous, and democratic societies. The reasons most of Africa has not done so go far beyond the colonial heritage. One factor is the abysmal treatment of women, and all of the violence, repression, and prejudices that go with that. Another is the deep-seated cultural tolerance and even hero-worship of strongmen like Mobutu, for whom politics is largely a matter of enriching themselves and their tribe. Finally, perhaps above all, is the way the long history of indigenous slavery is still deeply and disastrously woven into the African social fabric."

Art summed it up, "All in all, it's pretty remarkable to realize what we accomplished. You just can't imagine how bad things were."

CHAPTER 8

Edward and Joe and Jim Saguaro

Saguaro, home to about 1,500 people, is located in the northeast corner of Arizona and in the south central section of the Navajo Nation. There is no main street, no central business district, no town square, nor much of anything that would give you a sense of community. The most prominent buildings include a school, the hospital campus, one gas station and convenience store, and widely scattered mobile homes and other modest dwellings. The hospital is located on grounds originally occupied by a mainline Protestant church in the 1870's. If it were well maintained, the campus might resemble a small Midwestern college with handsome brick buildings bordering a grassy common area. The missionaries apparently tried to replicate their homes of origin and planted dozens of shade trees that stand out starkly on the barren plain.

By the time of my first visit, the buildings were in a state of neglect, and the formerly grassy lawn was hard packed dirt nurturing only weeds. Dead trees had been left to rot, and the roads and sidewalks were crumbling. The land was still owned by the Church, and the hospital received continuing philanthropic support from congregants, but overall this ownership arrangement would prove mostly harmful to efforts at restoring the community's hospital to life.

The Navajo Nation is a large section of the country centered on the four corners uniting Arizona, New Mexico, Utah, and Colorado and is home to about 175,000 Diné (tribal members). The 26,000 square mile area is almost exactly the size of West Virginia. Their nation is bounded by four sacred mountains with a large island of land in their midst that is home to the Hopi reservation. If you've seen a John Wayne western you've beheld views of Monument Valley, Shiprock, Canyon de Chelly, or the Rainbow Bridge serving as the backdrop as riders raced to the sound of gunfire. Each of these majestic vistas along with many others is located within the boundaries of the Navajo Nation. The natural beauty of the Diñe homeland is breathtaking and without parallel. Among their many virtues, the Navajo are the only major tribe to not operate casinos.

Years ago I received a call from Joe, a long time client with whom I had worked when he was the CEO of a hospital in rural Kansas. He was advising and mentoring the new CEO of the hospital in Saguaro. The hospital was in serious jeopardy of failing, and Joe needed a finance guy on his turnaround team and invited me to fill that role.

We flew to Albuquerque and drove three hours west to Saguaro by way of Gallup, NM. It's a pleasing drive, and I could count on seeing something new and captivating each time we made the trip. En route Joe gave me a rough outline of the situation. The board had just hired Edward*, he was getting his feet on the ground, but quickly realized the situation was even worse than he expected. The facilities were old and poorly maintained. They did not meet minimum safety standards nor did they meet current building codes. The finances were in a shambles, Edward didn't trust his chief financial officer, and they lacked cash reserves to provide any breathing room during the turnaround. The board was fragmented into various alliances mostly concerned about the needs of their specific clan members. Many of the employees viewed their job as the source of a paycheck to be earned solely by showing up. The COO hated the chief nursing officer and vice versa. The service and work ethic of the nine employed physicians was dismal, with a few exceptions. And to add a sense of urgency, the hospital was operating under a death sentence from the state hospital licensing authority. Two years earlier they issued a mandate that the hospital facilities must be replaced or face closure. An extension waiver had been granted, but Saguaro Memorial Hospital continued to exist only by a thin thread.

Edward previously worked as an administrator of a nursing home in South Dakota where Joe served as his mentor and adviser. The board of directors for the hospital was elected from various Diñe clans surrounding their small town. The board would have preferred to have a tribal member serve as CEO, but lacking same they selected a Native American from another tribe. Edward was Sioux. I would later learn that the Navajo do not hold the Sioux in high regard, but any Native American ranks higher than an Anglo. On a competence scale of 1-10, Edward would score in the mid-range, and he knew his limitations and was willing to seek assistance.

Before I became a threat to Edward, we got along well. Based on first impressions he was a nice, gentle man. He was average size with a rugged appearance and might have been handsome save for the ill effects of acne scarring. He told me about growing up on a Sioux reservation in southeastern South Dakota. I had once visited that sad place on another business matter in the late 1970s to observe firsthand that it was one of the least hospitable parts of the country made even less habitable by successive generations of debilitating dependency. During that brief visit to Edward's former home, I observed young men drinking Colt 45 on dilapidated porch steps of WWII barracks style housing incongruously situated on the windblown plains of South Dakota. It was one of the most tragic and depressing places I had encountered. Everything was in a state of disrepair, yet idleness appeared to be the dominant activity.

Edward told me about his background: "When I was 18 years old I was walking down a two lane highway on our reservation with my closest friend. We were both excessively drunk and were staggering along the centerline. An equally drunk man was driving his pickup on the same highway at the same time and he hit my friend in the head with his side mirror, killing him instantly. Up to that point in my life I had no concept of living beyond my teens. There was no one in my family that provided even a glimpse of what life might resemble as a successful adult. I started each day drinking myself into unconsciousness. But that ended on the day I saw my friend's head explode on that highway. I knew it could just have easily been me, and decided I was spared for a reason. From that day forward I chose to improve my life, left the reservation, went to junior college, got a job working in a nursing home, eventually worked my way up to the administrator position, got married, had two kids, and outwardly I was doing well. Inwardly, I remain in turmoil. Joe helped me get this job, and I owe it to him to do the best I can to help salvage this hospital."

Under the best of circumstances, it would be difficult to serve a rural Navajo population. Language and cultural barriers along with low incomes and geographic remoteness conspire to make it difficult to deliver modern medicine. Many of the older tribal members do not speak English, they don't have access to telephones or to automobiles, and they don't have the same concept of time as Anglos. Setting and keeping a 10 am appointment is difficult, almost random, at the Saguaro clinics. The incidence of alcoholism, suicide, hypertension, meth addiction, and diabetes is many times greater than the average of the U.S. population. The needs were great, yet the results were poor. But the failure was not due to a lack of money.

Even the concept of a hospital is foreign to the Navajo. The Hogan (pronounced hoe-gone) is the traditional home for a Navajo family. There are no windows, and doors must face to the east to greet the rising sun. Should a death occur in the dwelling, either the body is buried there with the entry sealed to warn others away, or the body is extracted and the structure is abandoned and burned. Unfortunately, it is not uncommon for people to die in hospitals, rendering such a building spiritually at odds with Navajo customs, providing yet another barrier to many older Diñe. Somehow an uneasy truce evolved between the hospital and the community over this matter, and older Navajos would, in some cases, use the hospital when they were seriously ill. Later, when we initiated discussions about building a replacement hospital the community wanted to mitigate this legitimate concern by integrating a traditional Hogan in the design, an idea that would prove anathema to the church leadership who maintained veto power owing to their ownership of the only suitable land.

Upon arriving in Saguaro for the first time, Joe and I met with Edward, and I asked to see copies of financial statements, utilization data, contracts with insurance companies, and other documents that would help us better understand the magnitude of the problems. Edward told me he had not yet had time to review this information, and I would need to talk to their CFO. He walked me down the hall, made introductions, and left us to the arcane world of hospital data. The CFO was a friendly Anglo about my age. After dispensing with a modicum of social lubricant, I asked him, "What keeps you awake at night?" He was a little startled, thought a few seconds, steepled his hands under his chin, and sheepishly volunteered, "Well, for starters our cash losses are $300,000 per month, and we only have $500,000 in the bank."

"Have you informed Edward or the board of this?"

"No, I thought about mentioning it during last week's board meeting, but the board hates bad news."

"What action plans are you contemplating so you can meet payroll and keep the doors open?"

"I was kind of hoping that things would pick up."

I gave him a list of information I wanted assembled, he politely complied, and I returned to Edward's office where he and Joe were discussing doctor issues. I shared the gist of my conversation with the CFO. I suggested that the board needed to be informed immediately of the impending run on cash, the CFO should be terminated, and we begin thinking in terms of immediate survival. Edward was alarmed and said, "As bad as he is, I can't possibly find a replacement willing to come to Saguaro on short notice." I told him I had an idea.

Jim was a former partner of mine who had retired a few years earlier. He moved to an elegant 8th floor condo overlooking the Gulf of Mexico in Clearwater Beach, FL, grew a graying ponytail, and occupied his time serving as a beach patrolman. His work consisted of riding a Honda four-wheeler on the public beach and advising wrongdoers of their noncompliance with local regulations. In spite of the occasional titillation attendant to telling young ladies that they had to wear tops, he was bored out of his mind and responded quickly when I told him I needed help. His first question was, "Do I have to cut my ponytail?" I told him no and suggested it might even be an advantage. He later shared that many of the people at the hospital thought he was Navajo because of his long gray hair, un-tucked Jimmy Buffet shirts, and dark Florida tan. Several months after his arrival, a board member approached him to in inquire of his tribal affiliation.

Joe, Edward, and I arranged to meet with the board the following day to alert them to the magnitude of the problems. We sketched out a preliminary plan involving major reductions in staffing, productivity incentives for the physicians, renegotiation of several contracts into which they had entered, closure of some services, and the introduction of more aggressive billing and collection practices. This was my first contact with the board, and they were not pleased to have been inconvenienced by an unscheduled meeting. The first 15-20 minutes of business was conducted in Navajo, so all of the non-Diñe present, including Joe, Edward and me, were completely in the dark. When the board chair opened the English portion of the meeting he asked Edward to explain why the board had been assembled. Edward was desirous of having as little to do with this unpleasantness as possible and asked me to summarize. Unfortunately, I presented our preliminary findings in the style to which I was accustomed in the Anglo world. It had been my experience that bad news does not get better with age, so I would get to the point quickly. I was blunt with people to whom bluntness is rude. To make matters worse I used the phrase, "We found snakes under every rock." Instantly, there was a hush among the nearly 15 people in the room. You would have thought I just took a crap on the table. At first I didn't know exactly what I had done, but whatever it was, wasn't good. The board listened to my glum tale in silence, there was no follow-up discussion, nor any recognition that they grasped the implications of not having sufficient funds to meet payroll.

After the meeting Edward told me that I had violated several Navajo taboos during the course of the meeting, most significantly by giving voice to the word "snake." He later gave me several Tony Hillerman books to read and another on Navajo taboos and light heartedly suggested I study up before our next meeting with the board. He said he was too new to the situation to fully read the board, but thought the best course of action was to fully develop a survival plan to present within the next few weeks. He also conceded that an outsider would have normally gotten a pass for the 'snake' comment, but my basic bluntness compounded their moderately hostile reception. Edward also offered, "I'm sure glad that was you, not me."

I eventually learned to adapt to the most obvious cultural differences between the Navajo and Anglo world. Better late than never. The Diñe listen intently and without interruptions when others are speaking. They do not use validating nods, gestures, or words when listening and will let the speaker continue uninterrupted for as long as he or she wants to go. Once a person speaks on a subject they will not speak again until everyone has had an opportunity to express their opinion, no matter how heated the topic. Anglos rarely let a speaker say a few sentences before uttering, "Yes, I see" or "I know what you mean" or "un huh" or interrupting to redirect the conversation. These words are usually accompanied by a validating nod of the head or a smile of recognition or some other gesture. To the Navajo this is considered rude. The advantage of the Diñe style of communications is that every speaker is given free rein to state their views. The disadvantage is that meetings last a long time.

The Diñe would often switch back and forth from Navajo to English. I learned that when speaking from the heart they would use Navajo, yet use English when speaking analytically, particularly if there were Anglos present. Even when they take exception to another's comments, the Diñe almost always begin with conciliatory phrases such as, "I understand Joe Eagle's feelings on this issue, and often times I have felt the same, but ..."

The CFO was fired on a Thursday and Jim showed up the following Monday to serve in an interim capacity. Jim possessed a bombastic personality and attacked problems with the ferocity of a rabid bulldog. He was in his element and within his first few months had renegotiated pharmacy contracts with the state Medicaid program, initiated the radical concept of sending bills to people who had the means to pay, renegotiated contracts with the larger hospitals in the region who had benefited from Saguaro's lack of negotiating skills, and arranged interim financing through the Navajo Area Indian Health Services (NAIHS).

The Navajos are a matriarchal society, and their identity to clan derives from the females. Land and other possessions are handed down from mother to daughter, not father to son. Females also do most of the work. While unemployment on the reservation was nearly 50%, women held most of the jobs. Many of the women are still masterful weavers and potters, and tourists would pay premium prices for their wares. Even the most elegantly crafted rug would contain at least one flaw so that evil spirits could escape.

Jim inherited an office with 25 female employees. His highest priority was in establishing systems and procedures to properly bill Medicaid (state/federal program to fund healthcare for the indigent) and Medicare (federal program to fund healthcare for the elderly). He recalled his team fondly, "They were eager to learn and would try diligently to follow procedures correctly. Most were single mothers but still managed to get to work every day. Many did not have a car and relied on friends for transportation, but they never complained. One couldn't have asked for a better staff." And they were successful in quickly improving cash flow through renewed focus on billing and collecting.

Saguaro Memorial was an independent hospital that received funding from the NAIHS along with more conventional forms of funding such as Medicare, Medicaid, and commercial insurance. Most hospitals located in the Navajo nation are owned and operated directly by NAIHS, which in turn is funded by the Bureau of Indian Affairs. Saguaro was the red headed stepchild and didn't receive funding as generous as their counterparts owned by NAIHS. Saguaro was paid on a 'capitated' basis by NAIHS, meaning they received a fixed amount per year per individual covered under this arrangement. Saguaro then either provided all needed health care services to those covered at their hospital and clinics or, for more complex services, they contracted with larger regional facilities. If they ran out of money before the term of the contract, they were still responsible for providing care. Like virtually every other hospital in America, the leadership team at Saguaro didn't possess the infrastructure required to undertake complex contractual arrangements of this nature. They had no way of assessing their true actuarial risk, nor in effectively contracting and monitoring the costs incurred at the larger hospitals

It is not widely publicized, but nearly 50% of all physicians graduate in the bottom half of their class. The operating losses incurred in the physician clinics were a major source of the cash drain. At the time, a newly graduated family practice physician could earn about $95,000 per year by coming to a designated underserved area. This was substantially lower than the $150,000 they could earn elsewhere. At Saguaro, however, the U.S. government would forgive the doctor's student loans up to $150,000 along with any taxes that would ordinarily be due on such a gift, if they would serve in a 'frontier' area for three years. Few docs stayed beyond the minimum required to pay off their student loans. Saguaro was isolated, patients were non-compliant, and the young docs were pretty much on their own, thus bearing more life and death responsibility than they would in a larger hospital setting. Some of the docs appeared earnest and caring, some less so. Sadly, too large a portion shared a work ethic comparable to the worst motor vehicle departments in the country. At a time when primary care physicians in most rural communities would see 25-35 patients per day, the Saguaro docs would see 8-10 and vigorously resisted any efforts to change. This puzzle had to be solved for any of the other pieces to be relevant. Joe focused his efforts working with Edward to manage this part of the turnaround plan using the age-old strategy of divide and conquer, culling the weakest performers and rewarding those willing to make things better.

The board reluctantly agreed to some personnel reductions and other elements of the survival plan. Interestingly, the board was most concerned about the impact of a recommendation to eliminate free food in the cafeteria for all employees, so this piece was dropped. Jim was successful in negotiating additional funds from the NAIHS for ongoing operations, and, along with some other successes, forestalled bankruptcy for the foreseeable future. We were also successful in locating a potential financing source for the much needed replacement hospital.

But there was no warmth with the board. The clan system is a powerful dynamic, and the board members felt their greatest duty was to their clan, and this was compromised by the layoffs that had occurred. We didn't yet know it, but we were all doomed. From our perspective we were saving the hospital and positioning it for a better future. From theirs we were unwanted interlopers interfering with their institution.

If things weren't sufficiently troublesome, soon after settling in as the interim CFO, Jim became increasingly suspicious of Edward's spending habits. During the first few months of our work together Edward acted in a careful and cautious manner. Once our collective efforts had steered the hospital away from imminent death, he changed. He apparently possessed a self-destruct button that periodically needed to be pushed. Most egregiously Edward hired his girlfriend, Marguerite*, to prepare a strategic plan and to convert the legal status of the hospital. Marguerite was a Navajo woman who had finished law school, but had not passed the bar and possessed little experience or knowledge pertinent to her assignment. Her hostile personality grated on virtually everyone with whom she came in contact.

Within a few weeks after getting settled, Jim reviewed an invoice from Marguerite for several tens of thousands of dollars. He asked Edward about it and received an answer that immediately sounded an alarm, "Don't worry about it, she's doing some work for me." Jim pressed for more detail, but was unsuccessful, so he told Edward, "I'll sign off on it when I see her work product." Shortly after this encounter, Marguerite stormed into Jim's office and screamed at him in front of four other Navajo women. She called him a racist and chauvinist for calling the legitimacy of her work into question and for failing to approve payment of her invoices. Later, the ladies in the accounting office who witnessed Marguerite's paroxysm, supported Jim fully, and told him to ignore Marguerite's explosion as, "She was not acting Navajo."

Marguerite was the first to go, and this was the start of an intensifying war between Jim and Edward. A few weeks later Jim called Edward with a list of questions about some travel expenses, and it wasn't long before Edward would once again seal his fate with bad choices. Within six weeks after taking over as interim CFO, Jim confronted Edward with a long list of questionable personal expenses and cozy vendor deals like the one with Marguerite. Edward then tried to fire Jim, but he didn't have sufficient power, as the board had warmed to their ponytailed CFO and correctly perceived him as the guy doing the heavy lifting. Edward negotiated a small buyout, packed up, and left. In his eyes the very people he brought in to help him had betrayed him, leading to his dismissal.

It was also the beginning of the end for all of us. Jim concluded his interim assignment after three months and was replaced by a capable permanent CFO. The losses had been stemmed, cash reserves had been increased by many millions of dollars, and in the short term, the turnaround was a success. The one unattended major problem was there was still no pathway to financing the much needed replacement hospital. The director of the fundraising operation, an attractive and likable Navajo lady was named permanent CEO. Her first official act was to terminate the use of all outside Anglo advisers. Joe, Jim, and I faded into the woodwork and are now long forgotten.

POSTSCRIPT

Saguaro continues to survive. There has been a revolving door of CEO's, with a new one coming on board each year. Currently, a Navajo man, with no previous healthcare experience, is serving as the CEO. They have continued to receive waivers from the State from the mandate that they either replace or close their facility.

Joe later told me that Edward subsequently began a prison term for defalcations incurred while running the nursing home in South Dakota.

The Navajo nation finally succumbed to the seduction of presumed riches to be derived from Casinos.

CHAPTER 9

David E. Martin

Edgar Martin grew under modest circumstances in Ardmore, Oklahoma. His father was the town's pharmacist, and his mother was the first woman in Ardmore to have ever graduated from college, although this did little to enhance her prospects in the dust-bowl state during the depression. Edgar received a scholarship to attend Drury College in Springfield, Missouri where he studied diligently while also working several part time jobs. He distinguished himself by scoring the last touchdown in Drury football history, as the school abandoned the sport the year Edgar graduated in 1932. He further distinguished himself by working his way up from the position of field geologist to become president of Standard Oil of Iran. Edgar married Ola, and they brought three sons and a daughter into this world, David being the third born. Edgar's career moves took the family from Texas to Oklahoma to Mexico City to Buenos Aires to NYC and eventually to Tehran.

David picks up the story from there:

"I was 16 when our family moved to Tehran in 1961. We lived in a mansion several blocks from the Shah's Palace, and he was often a guest in our home. My Mom once made him a pecan pie, using walnuts as pecans were not then available in Iran, and the Shah enjoyed it and later commented on her wonderful baking skills. He was a really nice man.

"Somehow my Mom had the idea that I should attend college in Beirut at American University. During the first weeks of my freshman year, it was common to hear gunshots being fired sporadically from a nearby neighborhood and then later reading about the ensuing carnage. The various factions were indiscernible, but equally vicious and indiscriminant in their terror. At that time the Israelis followed the doctrine: 'We reserve the right to hit you anytime, anyplace, if we consider you a threat.'

"One afternoon, I was standing on the balcony of my dorm room, and I observed a squadron of Israeli fighter jets diving straight down at the offending neighborhood, dropping their arsenal of weaponry, heading back over the Mediterranean, and voila no more gunfire from the vexatious quarter. I called my Dad to inform him of the situation. He overruled my Mom's sense of adventure on my behalf, and I caught the last flight out of Beirut to Tehran. He then made inquiries of his alma mater, Drury College, where he then served on the board of trustees, and acquired a conditional admission for me in the freshman class that started about a month earlier. The 'conditional' part of that still causes me some anguish. I did speak Farsi, Arabic, and Spanish, all with a Texas accent, but apparently that counted for little.

"After a ten-legged flight that took me from Tehran to Istanbul to Rome to NYC to St. Louis and Columbia, Missouri, I finally arrived in Springfield. I encountered green grass, trees with leaves, beautiful women who bathed, and other unimaginable luxuries. The first night's dinner at the Drury Commons featured duck and was memorably tasty. I thought to myself, 'I'm going to weigh 430 lbs by the time the year is out.' In Beirut our normal dormitory fare was a bowl of rice with five green peas on top. On weekends a smattering of chicken broth was dabbed on the peas for an added luxury.

"And thus began my return to America and the American way of life."

David was tall, handsome, and wiry, but he was also hugely self-deprecating. He married Jeanne, a beautiful woman both inside and out, earned his living as a general practice attorney, but mostly applied his abundant talents and energies to a plethora of unheralded hobbies. He lived every moment as though he were in a race. He built two houses, mastered bulldozer mechanics, introduced friends to the joys of hot tubbing, built a man-sized-walking gorilla out of a dozen erector sets and a handful of electric motors, raised horses and cattle, opened a hardware store, worked as a hospice volunteer, and became an alcoholic.

Our little nuclear family loved nothing more than to spend a day at David and Jeanne's farm featuring horseback riding, ponds for fishing, an Olympic-sized pool, a barn full of kittens, go-carts, a driving range aimed at a field of cattle, and a never ending array of amusements for young and old.

David had a heart of gold. He regularly visited shut-ins at nearby nursing homes, took on Quixotic lost causes as an attorney, and gave his time and treasure away heedlessly and generously. He once bragged that he never lost a jury trial. Old ladies in particular loved David owing to his abundant charm. He would do absolutely anything for a friend, but he was also the most mercurial man to have ever lived. We were pledge brothers and remained close throughout young adulthood, then became estranged over a perceived slight. He didn't speak to me for the next 30 years.

Then one day, out of the blue, he called to invite me to lunch, during which he told me the story recited above about how he came to Drury. He was a prideful man, so he concealed any hint of the 'riches to rags' saga through which he lived during the past few decades. He had been divorced twice and was currently married to a woman who cared little for him. He had lost most of the money he had earned and inherited, and he was well on his way to alcohol-dissipation oft noting in a W.C. Fields-like voice, "The first beer of the day is the best beer of the day." But David still retained his finest quality. He was wickedly funny.

At lunch he greeted me by saying, "You know I loved Judy (my wife, also a Drury graduate) well before you even met her. The only thing standing between Judy and me and perpetual joy is you." He came back from a trip to the restroom saying, "It said gentlemen, but I went in anyway."

A few weeks before the first of three increasingly incapacitating strokes David shared a piece of his recent correspondence:

Ladies and Gentlemen:

By way of introduction, I am David E. Martin, a Texan, a resident of Kansas City, Missouri, and a licensed attorney in Missouri and Texas. I have an issue of grave importance to us all, which must be addressed by the Council.

In 1940, my parents lived in Gilmer (Texas), and my late mother entered my older brother James P. Martin in Gilmer's Beautiful Baby contest. He placed thirty-first out of thirty-one babies. We have long been suspicious of bias on the part of the judges, even possible pay-offs.

We are requesting – actually demanding – an in-depth investigation into this sham/fraud and correction of the record. I recognize that some of these "judges" may need to be contacted by long-distance, but steps must be taken to eradicate this smirch on my family. My mother died four years ago, never having forgiven this abject corruption.

Although the Kansas City Star and the New York Times are eager to get this story, I do not wish to try this case in the newspapers. And while the hurt and humiliation can never be rectified, we are amenable to a cash settlement.

> *Yours very truly,*
> *David E. Martin, Attorney*

A few days later David received a somber call from the Gilmer City Attorney. David had to explain that the missive was an attempt at humor, apparently lost on the caller. At a minimum, one would think a statute of limitations had expired on a 75-year-old smirching.

POSTSCRIPT

I sent a copy of this story to David's younger brother, Mark, a retired physician who once used his considerable intellect to memorize the words to every dirty limerick known to man. He would be worthy of his own chapter were this not a PG rated book. He now serves as David's guardian, and he offered the following commentary:

"David is the biggest f___ing liar you'll ever meet. The Shah never once set foot in our house. It is true that we lived in the same neighborhood as the Shah's summer palace that was situated in the cool foothills outside of Tehran. He was a benevolent dictator, so there was never a hint of criticism about him. Whenever his entourage would drive by our house, all the servants were required to go outside and applaud. If our school bus happened to be in the vicinity, we were instructed to get out to wave and applaud. The Shah would wave back to us in a friendly manner. Our Mom did make pecan pie out of walnuts for the some of the oil ministers that worked for the Shah.

"David was in Beirut in 1964. At that time the city was known as the Paris of the Middle East, and it was as safe as Ardmore. It wasn't until 1967 that Beirut became a war zone and Israeli jets started their bombing raids. Beirut is nearly 1,000 miles from Tehran, but Dad would travel there often to make phone calls, fearing ours were bugged. He would fly over Iraq and Syria and back just to make a 10-minute call, and David and I would tag along.

"David once told a woman he was dating that our parents owned a vineyard in the south of France. She asked me if that was true, and I told her Edgar and Ola were teetotalers and devout Southern Baptists. They would no more own a winery than they would worship the devil and howl naked at the moon.

"And most assuredly, no one has ever eaten duck at Drury. The only thing David told you that is remotely true is the letter to the Gilmore City attorney."

CHAPTER 10

Albert A. Armstrong

1932 - 2006

Early on, I learned to avoid mentioning I was a CPA in a social setting. It was akin to exhaling visible leper vapors. Some people couldn't get away from you more quickly. Others would ask you a tax question. Both were undesirable outcomes. Perhaps many CPA's are deserving of the unwanted stereotyping of droll blandness, but not all.

I met Al when I was 30 years old. He was 13 years my senior and he quickly became my mentor, my champion, and my friend. He possessed the most high-powered, raw intellect of anyone I had ever met. This gift was enhanced by his remarkably intense intellectual curiosity. I can't imagine a time when Al was ever bored or idle. His mind and body were always racing at warp speed.

If one asked Al a question on Friday afternoon, he could expect a thoroughly researched treatise by Monday morning, even if the question was merely to inquire of the time.

Al had been a Navy pilot as a young man, loved flying and avionics, and embraced all new technologies. Al was on the leading edge of sophisticated computer modeling and applied statistical analyses long before these tools were commonly used. In the late 1970's when the first personal computers were introduced, Al went to the Zenith store, bought the parts and started building his own computers and helping those less capable build theirs as well. He knew more about Box Jenkins statistical analysis than anyone alive and even discovered a commercial application for this esoteric tool.

Al loved solving problems, the more technical the better. When pondering a complex matter, he liked to work his way around the puzzle by thinking out loud. Like many brilliant people, he possessed a few eccentricities. Most memorably, Al needed an audience for his best work to come forth. He would amble around his office, often using the standing position as an excuse to straighten his nuts. While strolling he would periodically let out a not so silent fart and then put all of his weight on one foot and lift the other just slightly off the ground straight-legged as though shaking the gaseous surprise down his pants leg. He apparently deduced that a malodorous, lighter than air fart could be shaken down one's pants leg thus a) lessening the likelihood of being detected or b) achieving some beneficial filtering effect should the fart leave his pants at ankle level rather than seep through his trousers at the point of impact. The presence of ladies did not alter Al's behavior and provided much merriment as the younger staffers would futilely attempt to stifle their chuckles during one of these performances.

I didn't always love listening to Al pontificate, but it was a rare occasion when I didn't come away with new knowledge. Al's genius level intellect wasn't totally devoted to math and statistics. He loved poetry and could recite dozens of poems verbatim with little prompting, his favorite being Rudyard Kipling's If. His formidable intellect knew no bounds, and he frequently surprised me with his knowledge of a wide range of topics.

Al was also a superb athlete. He played quarterback for Southwest High School, then the premier institution in Kansas City. He briefly played running back at the University of Kansas. After first seeing him play softball, I remember thinking, "This guy is really fast for an old guy." And he was uber-competitive. At age 64, Al participated in a corporate challenge track meet in the over-age-60 100-yard dash. At the sound of the gun, he sprinted to a 30-yard lead in the first 60 yards of the race then pulled up lame with an injured hamstring. Rather than pack it in, Al hopped on his remaining good leg for the final 40 yards and still finished 15 yards ahead of the second place finisher.

Al was intensely loyal. Early in our association, we were playing on the company softball team. I was playing first base, fielded a grounder, and ran to the inside of the bag to make the putout when the runner, a 225 lb. hard belly, ten years my junior, crossed the base on the inside, knocking me into foul territory. I was injured by this obviously dirty play. Al, who was sitting on the bench at the time, raced out of the dugout with a bat in his hand to challenge the offender who had the audacity to harm his charge. Envision the film clip of George Brett's rage as he ran out of the dugout during the 1983 pine tar incident, ratchet it up a few degrees, and you'll get a visual image of Al at that moment. He was 50 years old, and the object of his ire was half his age. Fortunately calmer heads prevailed, saving the young man from ruination. If you were Al's friend, you could always count on him being there for you. I don't doubt for a minute he would have taken a bullet for a friend. If there were ever a man with whom one would chose to share a foxhole, it would be Albert.

Another, almost scary incident, displayed Al's steadfast fidelity to a friend. Someone at the firm made the indescribably bad decision to hire a local comedian to perform at the annual Christmas party held at the University Club in downtown Kansas City. Virtually no one was entertained, and his appearance was mostly an irritant that interrupted an otherwise convivial evening. If entertainers ever sit around and compare audiences, I'm certain CPA's would rank among the most difficult. This particular comic made a bad situation worse by electing to mock his audience. He unwisely chose a recently retired partner as the foil for his attempted humor. The elderly gentleman was conservatively attired, and to the unknowing, might have appeared the archetypal meek accountant. The comic couldn't have known that the man from whom he tried to elicit cheap laughs had been a young infantry lieutenant in the Battle of the Bulge where he was wounded, captured, and made a prisoner of war. He survived the endless winter marches through Poland and eastern Germany as the POW camps were emptied in advance of the Russian armies. He had also suffered a disproportionate share of personal tragedy losing both his wife and a child. His sister had once been the governor of a large state. He carried himself with a quiet dignity and maintained a legion of loyal clients. And he was Al's close friend. It remains unfathomable how anyone might use this fine gentleman as a target for mockery. The onlookers reacted with predictable contempt. I'm certain the comedian had no idea how close he came to harm, as Al had to be physically restrained from ripping into the clueless comic.

The last time I saw Al was at my Mom's funeral in August 2006. We had both long since been retired from the firm, and I hadn't seen him for over a year. He didn't mention anything about his illness. He just gave me a hug and told me he loved me, and I told him I loved him, and we teared up. He died two months later, a victim of lung cancer, presumably acquired from chauffeuring his cigar-smoking father to work for ten years. He never smoked a day in his life. Al was a wonderful man, a genuine character, and a dear friend.

At his funeral his son Bob recited from memory Al's favorite poem as a departing gift.

IF by Rudyard Kipling

If you can keep your head when all about you
Are losing theirs and blaming it on you
If you can trust yourself when all men doubt you,
But make allowance for their doubting too;
If you can wait and not be tired by waiting,
Or being lied about, don't deal in lies,
Or being hated, don't give way to hating,
And yet don't look too good, nor talk too wise:

If you can dream—and not make dreams your master;
If you can think—and not make thoughts your aim;
If you can meet with Triumph and Disaster
And treat those two impostors just the same;
If you can bear to hear the truth you've spoken
Twisted by knaves to make a trap for fools,
Or watch the things you gave your life to, broken,
And stoop and build 'em up with worn-out tools:

If you can make one heap of all your winnings
And risk it on one turn of pitch-and-toss,
And lose, and start again at your beginnings
And never breathe a word about your loss;
If you can force your heart and nerve and sinew
To serve your turn long after they are gone,
And so hold on when there is nothing in you
Except the Will which says to them: 'Hold on!'

If you can talk with crowds and keep your virtue,
Or walk with Kings—nor lose the common touch,
If neither foes nor loving friends can hurt you,
If all men count with you, but none too much;
If you can fill the unforgiving minute
With sixty seconds' worth of distance run,
Yours is the Earth and everything that's in it,
And—which is more—you'll be a Man, my son!

CHAPTER 11

Bowling in Brooklyn with Ben

THANKSGIVING 2013

Judy and I celebrated Ben's birthday dining at a delightful Brooklyn restaurant, Five Leaves, with Ben, his fiancé Deb, and several of his friends. Ben and I enjoyed the house burger special, a tasty concoction of a ground beef patty topped with pickled beets, a slice of fried pineapple, a fried egg, and tomato.

The evening was capped off bowling until 1:30 am, an unusually late hour. The 8-lane venue shared space with a bar and was nestled in an isolated, industrial neighborhood, presumably a former warehouse. The loaner balls were almost round featuring crevices into which one could secret a bag of corn nuts. I bowled badly and even managed to bugger up my most important banjo finger, but it was a frolicsome group, and a fun celebration.

Deb's family is from Burma, thus adding alliterative luster to the lead. One of the guests at Ben's Thanksgiving feast was an effervescent girl from Bulgaria, adding yet another B to the string. Maria came to the U.S. for college and ended up at Cottey College in Nevada, MO, surely a culture shock. Her family operates a dance troupe featuring classic Bulgarian folk routines, and they have performed all over Europe. I told her she was the first Bulgarian I had ever met. In her impeccable English, she said she was glad to help broaden my horizons. From her I learned a new word, which I like, concordantly. Ben can be counted upon to assemble interesting company.

The nicer neighborhoods of Brooklyn are mindful of 1950's small town America. We purchased our turkey at a small Italian butcher, went across the street to a wine store, dropped the heavier packages off at Ben's apartment, then back to a corner grocer for final provisioning and a stop at a small hardware store. We patronized a variety of nearby restaurants, all of the mom and pop variety, and all excellent. Even though it was a gray, rainy day, people were uncommonly friendly and in a festive spirit, presumably attendant to the upcoming Thanksgiving holiday.

Giant corporate enterprises are few and far between. It's difficult to imagine how the merchants prosper in their tiny spaces given the high rents and difficult logistics, but they do, and there are few empty storefronts.

The food, both from restaurants or local stores, is consistently outstanding in even the most nondescript places. Ben's friend, Peter, noted that the power of social media ensures that any business not providing a good value will die quickly.

Our stay was brief, four days, so we confined our travels to Brooklyn, which I find to be quite pleasing. We're becoming fairly familiar with Ben's Williamsburg neighborhood and have hiked to Prospect Park. We took the East River ferry down to Brooklyn Bridge Park, hiked through Brooklyn Heights, then to downtown Brooklyn, and stopped at the NY Transit Museum (a worthwhile destination). Brooklyn has a much larger population than Manhattan (2.5m v. 1.6m), but it is noticeably less congested, occupying triple the square miles (71 v. 23). The pedestrian and car traffic is intense, but rather mild compared to most Manhattan neighborhoods. Tourist sightings are negligible. I saw few children on our Brooklyn walkabout, but there was no dearth of dogs.

Interestingly, one encounters few overweight people. I presume this is attributable to the necessity of walking as a mode of transport. Even the subway requires navigating many levels of stairs. Upon leaving Brooklyn we flew to our southern WHQ in Sanibel, Florida. We stopped at an Olive Garden near the airport for dinner and were comforted once again by the presence of large numbers of large people. Cracker Barrel would have been even more comforting I'm sure.

Ben lives in a neighborhood inhabited by hipsters. I know this owing to the ubiquity of porkpie hats and black, tight, high water jeans worn by men. There is a noticeable lack of color adorning the citizens. Occasionally you'll see a dash of gray, brown, or dark green sprinkled amidst the dominant black attire. It was quite cold, so I wore a day-glo stocking cap that I thought might add a bit of cheeriness. It did insure that I was not mistaken for a deer, but otherwise this micro-act of fashion rebelliousness went unnoticed. People walk fast and with their heads down, seemingly impervious to their surroundings. It's mindful of an Orwellian streetscape.

If one is not already sufficiently aware of their insignificance in the grand scheme of things, a trip to a large city will put you in the right frame of mind.

It's a miracle that more people don't die riding in cabs here. Our visit started off, as it almost always does, with a harrowing cab ride from LaGuardia. Our driver was either from India or from the Land of Stans. I can't be certain. The only understandable English words he used in my presence were, "Where to."

I told him, "Take the BQE to the Metropolitan exit, and I will guide you from there."

He offered no acknowledgement whether he heard or understood this response. He just took off, and we buckled up. We successfully got on the BQE going the right direction, so things were semi-okay save for the speed at which we were traveling. It was dark, raining heavily, and the traffic was predictably severe. Our driver was taking up two lanes engendering honks, and presumably unmentionable mutterings, from the proximate gasoline trucks, semis, and cement mixers.

Then our driver started chanting and gesticulating wildly whilst driving. At first I thought he was speaking to Judy and me, but then I surmised he was listening to something on an earbud. I'll never know the true source of his agitation, but I leaned forward to remind him that the Metropolitan exit was nearing. He was still in an interior lane, then swerved to the right through two lanes of traffic to exit on Meeker Street shouting something like, "Metropolitan! No good!" This was not pleasing, but we were still alive and blessedly now forced to go more slowly. With the aid of Google maps, I guided the cabbie to Ben's address, ending the turbulent trip. Ben was quickly at curbside with an umbrella. What a good lad. My terror of NYC cabs may be a function of advanced age, but I don't think I'm alone.

Real estate in Brooklyn has been on a tear lately with the highest values placed on locations closest to subway stations, particularly those with the fewest stops to nearby Manhattan. One might classify Ben's Williamsburg neighborhood as a middle class enclave based on outward appearances, but certainly not on price. Ben lives one half a block away from a subway station that is two stops from Manhattan, making it a highly desirable location. Most of the buildings are three stories with each story serving as a condo or apartment. Usually the buildings stand shoulder to shoulder with shared walls, but occasionally, there is a walkway between structures leading to tiny backyards.

On street parking is reasonably available, but it is still quite a hassle to own a car. Many of the buildings are newly renovated and quite handsome, some are rundown, but all are expensive. Ben showed us a small two-story building that is uninhabitable with an asking price of $800k. Decent residential space in his neighborhood goes for $800-$1,000+ per square foot and rents run in the range of $3-4,500 per month, but walking around you don't get the feeling you're surrounded by prosperous people. Ben explained, "Looks are deceiving."

The sidewalks and streets are not particularly tidy. What passes for a front yard, features an iron fence and gate surrounding a 6'-8' enclosure between the sidewalk and the house. This space is typically filled with garbage cans and bikes chained to the fence.

Ben lives on the third floor of a 150+ year-old house that was built as a three story flat. The stairway leading to his top floor unit is steep and narrow (30") giving one a sense of wonderment how the furnishings arrived. The handsome banister and wide board flooring in the common areas are similar to the apartment in the French Quarter that serves as our Mardi Gras WHQ.

In contrast, the interiors of the buildings are remarkably nice, if Ben's building is any indicator. His sunny place features a modern kitchen and bathrooms, attractive flooring, brick walls, and skylights. Ben's street is lined with large London Planes, close cousin to the Sycamore. They provide a welcome sense of hominess to visiting Midwesterners. Ben has taken up his Mom's passion for gardening and he keeps an abundance of well-tended plants including a 5' ficus tree growing in his dining room. He also has a tiny backyard that is home to a variety of interesting flora.

I was waiting on the stoop outside of Ben's home, and I finished leaving a phone message while watching two young men get out of a nearby parked car, a silver Hyundai. They were both heavily muscled, handsome, with military style haircuts. The one nearest to me pulled something heavy out of the backseat and tossed it to his comrade. They proceeded to put on bulletproof vests that covered their torsos well below the belt line. They slipped on unremarkable shirts, left them un-tucked, boldly surveyed their surroundings, and walked into the building directly across the street. I'm thinking, "Pulp Fiction?"

When Ben and Judy came down, and I described the scene that had just unfolded. I asked Ben, "What do you think that was all about." His uninterested reply, "I have no idea."

On Wednesday we dined at Roberta's, a five-stop subway ride into the bowels of Brooklyn. It is noteworthy for their tasty pizza and a prominent sign one might expect in a less urbane setting, "Farts are just the ghosts of dinners past." Ben shared that on an earlier visit to Roberta's, the lead singer of the Grizzly Bears was dining at a nearby table. Seminal events such as this make life worth living.

The subways on which we rode were all shiny and clean, unmarred by the ugly graffiti that used to be commonplace in NYC subways. Kudos go to the Giuliani and Bloomberg eras.

Did you know that a license for a single cab in NYC currently goes for $1.2 million?

In the 1880's the new minor league baseball team was named the Brooklyn Trolley Dodgers, a pejorative term hipper Manhattanites used in describing the conveyance avoidance habits of their cross-river neighbors. This was later shortened to the moniker now more familiar to fans in Los Angeles.

I sat next to a lady about my age while waiting for our flight out of LaGuardia. She asked if there were a banjo in my case. I replied affirmatively, and the conversation went thusly:

"Is it a four-string or six-string banjo?"

"Five."

"My Dad used to play banjo. He was born in 1903, and he was really good. I still have his old banjo. Do you think it would be worth much?"

"Depends. If it's a Gibson, it could be quite valuable."

"I don't know about that, but it did have two light bulbs inside it."

CHAPTER 12

The Pickle Factory

I joined an army reserve unit in New York City shortly before graduating from Harvard Business School. This was somewhat disruptive of the normal post-graduate plans, as six months active duty awaited me at a time to be chosen by Uncle Sam. I noticed a small advertisement in the placement office, "Seeking HBS graduate to run a pickle factory in Springfield, Missouri." I responded and talked to Gordon Beaham, the president of Faultless Starch Company in Kansas City. He was an HBS grad, had an option to buy the pickle operation, and needed 'his guy' to learn the business and run it for him. He said, "Fly to KC, let's meet, and we'll see if you're a good fit." I informed Gordon of my eminent six-month absence to fulfill my active duty obligation. He brushed it aside as a minor inconvenience. I was hired and headed back to Springfield where I had attended college. Perfect. My lifelong dream of becoming a pickle magnate was within grasp.

Shortly after graduation I showed up at the northeast Springfield location of the pickle factory for the first time and met Dick DeGraffenreid, the president of DeGraffenreid Pickle Company. Dick was a wiry man about 45 years old. He'd be the kind of guy you'd describe as having ants in his pants. He was in constant motion, smart, practical, and shrewd. I would learn to admire him greatly. His wife worked as a telephone operator for Southwestern Bell, but otherwise everyone remotely related to the DeGraffenreid clan worked at the pickle plant.

My first introduction to the business was with Tony, who ran the trucking operation. He asked if I'd every driven an eighteen wheeler, and suggested I might try backing a truck loaded with cucumbers into a dock. I didn't take that course in school, but I slowly and haltingly figured it out. Later, I went with him on a trip to southwest Colorado where he introduced me to the farmers who grew the cucumbers for the DeGraffenreid's. On route Tony gave me a tutorial on the mechanics of futures contracts for cucumbers and shared a little history on the clan.

The family was from nearby Walnut Grove, MO and made a little money hauling freight for various enterprises in the Ozarks. During WWII, Dick's father obtained a contract to haul building materials to Fort Leonard Wood, about 85 miles northeast of Springfield, then being built as a basic training site to handle tens of thousands of troops for the war. Tony continued, "Old man DeGraffenreid was a pretty shrewd character, and he made good money in everything he did. The Army had him hauling cucumbers to the Fort from farms near Pueblo, CO, where he made the contacts that ultimately led to the founding of the Pickle Company."

By the time I arrived on the scene, Mr. DeGraffenreid (Ole man DeGraffenreid to everyone else), was in his 80's, and spent a good bit of his time on a cot in the main office of the factory. It was equipped with a spittoon, which he used with minimal efficiency, and a set of old time ledgers, which he used with maximum efficiency. Upon entering the drab offices one might notice a dusty display of the Company's various pickle and relish products, mustards, vinegars, and brines that were sold at both the wholesale and retail level. They had small trucks delivering retail-sized pickle jars to area grocery stores, and long haul trucks carrying 5 and 10-gallon pickle containers to the newly emerging fast food franchises. McDonalds was not a household name in 1969, but it was clear to even the dimmest that pickle consuming burger joints had a future.

One of my close friends from high school told the life changing story about how his Dad, a lifelong purchasing agent working for TWA, had an encounter with an ex-milk shake machine vendor by the name of Ray Kroc, who told him to invest in one of his McDonald's restaurants. Instead he bought a Dairy King (not Queen) franchise, which went bust shortly thereafter, leaving my friend in the not unenviable spot of fending for himself.

I warmed up to Dick DeGraffenreid quickly. He said, "If you don't mind working, I will teach you as much as I can about this business as quickly as possible. Be on time, do what I tell you, and this will work out fine. If I was you, and I thought some day I might be responsible for this operation, I think I would want to know how every single job is done. So that's what we're going to do." I would arrive every day at 6 am, and he had the day planned.

A pickle plant is a relatively simple operation. Cucumbers are hauled in from Colorado and stored in giant, wooden slatted, vats, each about the size of a small town water tower. They cure in a dill flavored, briny solution for several months before being dipped onto a slicing/packaging line. The cucumber, now pickle, was fed onto a conveyer belt that runs through a slicing machine. Envision four blades encircled by a steel wheel, like a child's toy helicopter blade, with varying gaps between the slicers determining the thickness of the pickle. Once sliced, the pickles flowed on a belt past a team of inspectors and then into a packaging machine, past a labeler, then manually placed in boxes, stacked on pallets, and stored in the warehouse. The packaging varied from small, retailed sized jars to 10-gallon aluminum and plastic containers. The principal customers were food wholesalers operating within a 300-mile radius of Springfield. Special care was taken for making sweet pickles, bread and butter pickles, and relish, all of which required massive amounts of sugar.

The strong salty, dill smell was overwhelming, but it was also quite pleasing. The essence of dill accompanied me home from work every day.

The company operated a dozen over the road tractors and trailers, and a handful of smaller vans that were used to deliver pickle products to area grocery stores. It was a sufficiently large fleet to warrant a full time diesel mechanic. I never had the nerve to ask him, but I would guess that Humphrey weighed well over 500 pounds. He always wore denim overalls and an XXXXL tee shirt. There was an overhead hoist in the shop that ordinarily would have been used to lift an engine out of a tractor, but Humphrey had constructed a special harness for himself, would hold the power controls in one hand, and maneuver his hulking carcass over whatever part of the engine needed attention. No one seemed to think this was out of the ordinary, but I can't say I'd seen anything quite like this. While chatting with Humphrey one day I learned that he ate two boxes of Post Toasties and a dozen eggs every morning for breakfast.

Most of the unskilled workers in the plant hailed from Walnut Grove, located 22 miles north of Springfield, just north of nearby Bois D'Arc (pronounced Bodark). These men lived for coon hunting, and during breaks would talk about their coon dogs and the hunt from the night before. I unwisely turned down an invitation to join them one evening and was never offered a second chance.

One of the key barriers to entry to the pickle business was access to the cucumber contracts with the Colorado farmers. The DeGraffenreids controlled long term contracts to buy set amounts of cucumbers providing a stable supply of product for the buyer and price stability to the sellers. Dick meticulously educated me on the mechanics of these contracts and made introductions to the key people and emphasized that this was one of the most critical success factors.

After a couple of months working on the line, mixing ingredients, stacking boxes, driving the fork lift, loading trucks, running the retail delivery routes, and other assorted tasks, I went into the office for the first time. Dick's sister basically ran the office, preparing invoices, collecting receivables, paying bills and payroll, and maintaining the books. Everything was done manually on paper ledgers save for one mechanical adding machine. In contrast to the owners' modest lifestyles, I quickly learned that the business was growing and extremely profitable. My employer had an option to buy the business for a scant four times cash flow.

MILITARY COMPLICATIONS

While still in school in Boston, I joined an army reserve unit in New York City, on 10th avenue and 47th street to be precise. The classmate who introduced me to the opening also signed up, but he failed the physical, and I was on my own. I was slated to be a truck mechanic in a transportation unit, and I journeyed to NYC once a month, first from Boston, later from Springfield. Kind college friends who were junior investment bankers put me up in their one bedroom apartment on the Upper East Side. I would catch the subway to Times Square and walk westward five blocks to my meetings. Young men in military uniform were not treated well anywhere in civilian America in the summer of 1969, but few places could have been less hospitable than Times Square. The film *Midnight Cowboy* starring Jon Voight and Dustin Hoffman accurately portrayed the neighborhood through which I journeyed during my monthly visits.

In mid-summer 1969, Ted Kennedy made headlines by escaping a pond in Chappaquiddick, Massachusetts unscathed leaving his companion, Mary Jo Kopechne, to drown. A few days later Neil Armstrong and Buzz Aldrin became the first men to walk on the moon. Of lesser note, I received orders from the U.S. Army by certified mail to report to Fort Dix, New Jersey for basic training.

I followed the instructions given to me, which involved submitting forms regarding transportation to Fort Dix that revealed my new

Missouri address. Shortly, thereafter I received another certified letter (always a heart-stopping occurrence) from the U.S. Army informing me that I had been discharged from my unit 'for the convenience of the army'. At first glance, one might think this was good news, but it was not. A carbon copy of the letter also went to my draft board, along with the explicit warning that I could soon expect a draft notice. For those unfamiliar with the times, a draft notice meant the recipient would owe Uncle Sam two years of active duty, with a high probability of becoming cannon fodder in Viet Nam.

This series of events caused me to search for another reserve unit, where one could expect six months of active duty and six years of monthly meetings and summer camps. Many reserve units were, in fact, called up during the war, but these units offered better odds than serving as a draftee. I first tried to enlist in the Marine Corps Reserves, but they turned me down. I was told by the recruiter, "You're too old (24), you're married, and you're too educated. You're not a good fit for us." Rejected, I had a contact from a college friend whose Dad was a dentist and an Army colonel who headed up the dental detachment in the 325th General Hospital Unit. I was accepted, and thus began my career as a fighting dental assistant, but this also reset the clock on my six-year obligation and restarted the wait for orders for active duty. (I would become one of the few reservists who served 7 years during war-time, getting no closer to danger than when handling an overheated dental drill.)

A few weeks later I received a call from my employer in KC. He asked me to come to KC for a chat, and I did. He told me that his circumstances had changed, and he would not be buying the pickle factory. I asked him if I would be free to pursue the transaction on my own. He gave me a month's severance pay, wished me well, and that was that.

I had been given an insider's education to a superb business opportunity. I trusted the sellers implicitly to not conceal bad news, and the sellers liked and trusted me. There were, however, a few obstacles. I had a negative net worth, owing to student loans, I would be called to active duty anytime, I knew no one with money, and I lacked funds on which to live while trying to put a deal together.

I knew banks would loan against the assets covering a portion of the purchase price, but I needed an equity investor that would be willing to leave me with a meaningful percentage of the ownership. I approached a high school friend's father, who owned a small business. I perceived that he was well-to-do, but when I presented him with the opportunity to invest in my deal, he laughed me out of his house. I then contacted an HBS classmate who came from a wealthy family. Dick later informed me, "One of your buddies approached me about buying the company, but he was leaving you out." Great friend! After a fruitless search for the millions of dollars needed, I abandoned the chase, and entered the more conventional corporate world, dreams of pickle greatness squashed.

CHAPTER 13

Banjo People

PAUL HOPKINS

I knew I would be driving through middle Tennessee near the hometown of the company that built my second favorite banjo, of the two I own. I had not bonded with this particular instrument, so I called the number on their website and told the owner of my concerns, making it clear I was a tyro player.

"Everything sounds too tinny and bright."

The banjo maker, who I would later learn had been a first rate performer in the 1960's and 1970's, told me, "Yes, I've had arch tops, and I'd love them for a period of time, and then I'd prefer something a little softer. However, six months later I'd want to return to that harder sound. I have a conversion tone ring on order that will change an arch top to a flat top. But, I'll forewarn you there will come a time when you'll want to return to the arch top sound." I told him that I was interested in the conversion kit and when I might be traveling his way.

A few days later, I received a package in the mail with a CD featuring my new acquaintance, two hats with his company's logo, a new set of strings, and a bridge that would lower the action (the space between the finger board and the strings) on my not-so-beloved banjo.

Before heading through Tennessee, I called again and inquired of the status of the conversion kit and confirmed the date of our rendezvous. He told me of his difficulties getting the needed parts from the machinists and chrome plating operations on which he depends, but said, "I'll have something for you when you arrive."

I called the morning of our appointment to say, "I'm here." The man with whom I had now spoken on three occasions said, "I'm glad to hear from you because I've got all the pieces to convert your banjo. I hope you've set aside some time, because I have prepared to spend the day with you." He gave me directions, along with a warning about a speed trap along the way.

I was halfway expecting to meet a geezer in overalls with a chaw of tobacco wearing a moonshiner hat. But it wasn't to be. Instead, I arrived at a 500-acre estate nestled in the heart of walking horse country, accented by a federal style home overlooking immaculately groomed grounds. I was directed to two outbuildings on the property comprising the banjo manufacturing operation.

I was greeted warmly, introduced to some other guests who quickly departed, and then received the full attention of my host. I spent the next seven hours with a man who knew nothing of me other than I had purchased, used, one of his banjos, and that I had only been playing three years.

My host was a chatty fellow, but in a good way. While it is my nature to want to get on with things quickly, I was sufficiently intrigued to recognize that this was a time to 'just go with it.'

He said, "Did you get a chance to walk through the barns?" Then he took me on a tour of his farming operation including a building housing dozens of immaculately restored trucks and cars, most impressively featuring two 1948 International Harvester coal trucks, one red the other green. His array of large and small tractors, dozers, backhoes, and assorted other machines was sufficient to give me a major dose of farm equipment envy.

I said, "You've got a lot of toys."

To which he replied, "Yes, I do."

Then it was off to the banjo operation that was surprisingly small, consisting of two buildings, one the size of a mobile home and the second the size of a double wide. They contained an immaculate woodworking and machine shop, a ventilated paint/varnish room, assembly area and storage. He walked me through the entire process of building a quality banjo including how he shapes the necks, sets the pearl inlays on the fingerboards, builds the resonators, etc.

He demonstrated the nuances in sound between walnut, mahogany, and maple necks and trim and chrome, gold and nickel-plated tone rings. Walnut/chrome creates a bright, bold sound. Maple/gold plated is softer and more melodic. The tone ring, the metal piece that clamps the drum-head on the frame of the banjo, is the most critical piece of the puzzle. He said, "When I started to make banjos in the early 1970's I focused my attention on the tone ring. I would start with a relatively heavy casting, assemble the banjo, play it, shave 1/10 of an ounce off, re-assemble, and play again. I'd do that until I thought I hit the sweet spot, note the weight, and then keep going."

I said, "Are you self taught at building banjos?"

He expounded, "Yes and no. I knew a lot, but I didn't know how much I didn't know until I hired a genius from Gibson. He had learned from the masters who built the Gibson banjos in the 1930's and helped me take our craftsmanship to a higher level."

He said, "I'm sure glad you showed up, because I made two extra trips to Nashville to get these castings machined and chromed for you. Let's take a look at your banjo."

He picked it up and started playing. In his hands my banjo sounded like the most perfect instrument ever created. He said good-naturedly but sternly, "It would be a crime to convert this banjo to a flat top. This is one of the best sounding arch tops I've ever made. Are you sure you want to change it?" Until this point in time, I had little appreciation for the distinction in tone created by one skilled v. one less so. I gave pause, and he added, "You will be a much better banjo player if you learn on an arch top. It will force you to play more crisply. You'll hear every mistake you make."

"And that is a good thing?"

"Yes."

It was noonish, and he said, "I'll call my wife, and we'll take you to lunch." She drove down from their home, and we were introduced while he went off to give some instructions to a part-time farm mechanic.

We drove along a winding country road to nearby Bell Buckle, Tennessee. During the course of our trip we chatted amiably. They mentioned that they were both from the coal country of southwestern Virginia near the Tennessee/Kentucky border and were married at age 19. I mentioned my basic training tussle with a redheaded 'Deliverance-like' boy from the hills of eastern Tennessee. My host's wife commented, without a molecule of mirth, "You are very lucky to be alive to tell the tale." She went on to say, "Growing up in that region, you learned early to stay way from those folks. They are born with a rifle in their hands, and they'll use it."

Bell Buckle is an old railroad village of preserved and restored Victorian homes and churches. The Bell Buckle Cafe features a giant display of Moon Pies for $.91 and terrific food. I enjoyed a tasty lunch of chicken fried steak, pickled beets, black eyed peas, oatmeal cake, and coffee. The place was packed and for good reason.

I offered to pick up the tab for our lunch, but my hosts would not hear of that. "You may not pass this way again, so I've set aside the day to show you around my shop, introduce you to my collection, and I'll give you a lesson while we're at it." And he proceeded to do all of the above. And this man did not know me from Adam.

He started playing banjo at age 5. I asked him how he got interested in banjo at such a young age. "My uncle was a serious player, and he left his banjo around and encouraged me to play around with it if I wanted to. And I did." I told him of one of my grandson's interests in sitting in my lap and strumming along, and he said, "Just leave a banjo near him and let him know he's welcome to pick it up. The worst he can do is break a few strings." (I didn't argue the point, but three days after this conversation I was attending my twin grandson's 4th birthday party, where I was to provide the accompaniment for a game of musical chairs. I left my banjo in its case in the presence of a few small boys and later observed one of them trying to ride it like a rocking horse.)

I mentioned an article I read in the *WSJ* stating it takes about 10,000 hours to become accomplished with an instrument. He responded with the following anecdote. "A fellow once encountered Chet Atkins, possibly the best guitar player ever, and said, 'I'd give anything to play as well at you.' And Chet responded, 'Would you give your life?'"

In 1969, Earl Scruggs and Lester Flatt split up their band, the Foggy Mountain Boys. Lester needed a banjo player to replace Earl, and he offered Paul the job. He declined, and I inquired, "Why?"

He said, "Lester offered me $200 a week, but I was making more than that with my coal mine. In addition to being a banjo maker and performer, I would learn that I was dining with a tycoon with a degree in electrical engineering. He and his wife have owned coal mines, apple orchids, radio stations, and cell phone towers, all dwarfing the banjo business in dollars, if not in passion.

After lunch, we took a tour of his mountain on which one of his cell towers stands. He told me of the necessity of getting a DC law firm specializing in FCC matters when negotiating with Verizon or ATT. If one were to judge this man by his dress or dialect, he would severely underestimate the level of his sophistication.

After the mountain tour we went to his studio situated above his four-car garage. Four banjos were on stands in the middle of the room along with two guitars, a piano, and a standup bass. Two of the banjos were 1934 and 1935 Gibson's, gold-plated and engraved, possibly the most valuable banjos that exist. One of them was previously owned by Earl Scruggs and was used in the recording of his Foggy Mountain Breakdown album. The two guitars were pre-WWII Martins. A nearby closet contained about 50 pre-WWII banjos of varying makes including a Gibson Florentine and several Degas. I noticed a photo dating back to the 1960's of my host jamming with Jerry Garcia, John McKuen, and Steve Martin. I was duly impressed.

He played a few tunes for me and rhapsodized about times past performing in the 60's. He picked a catchy version of *Puff the Magic Dragon*, first on one of the Martin guitars and then on the 1934 Gibson banjo and said, "I would introduce this song by saying, 'now we're going to play some hard core bluegrass.' Folks loved it. We'd get our biggest applause of the evening."

Then he said, "Okay, it's time for a lesson. Get out your banjo." He listened and watched me play a few tunes. He winced slightly when I mentioned the beginning instructional books I'd been using. Then he had me mimic a few rolls he played, each a little more complicated than before, and then he declared, "You have what it takes to become a banjo player."

We went into his recording studio, and he put an Earl Scruggs record on a turntable. He slowed it down, and played along, then speeded it up. Then he put on one of his records and did the same thing. "See how crisp that sounds, at both slow speeds and fast? Spend time trying to play these songs in time with the record. Start real slow, and then get up to speed."

He gave me some helpful tips, showed me how to replace broken strings rapidly, as if one were on stage, but mostly he encouraged me in my quest.

Although he had incurred a significant expenditure of time and money getting a conversion kit ready for me, I decided to follow his advice and leave my Walnut Deluxe arch top unaltered. I offered to compensate him, but he declined. "I'll be able to sell those kits to someone else."

As I was leaving, his wife came out of their house to bid farewell. They gave me directions to the interstate. I left in a state of bewilderment with my arch top in tact.

POSTSCRIPT

I sent a copy of this story to my host, along with a copy of my book and a thank you note and received the following in reply:
"When you travel through Tennessee again, please stop, and we might talk about some others who've dropped by; Warren Buffet and Armand Hammer."

MARK JOHNSON

Four years ago I purchased an introductory book for 5-string bluegrass (aka three finger or Scruggs style) banjo and diligently worked my way through the basics of learning how to read tablature (aka musical nomenclature for dummies on stringed instruments), forward rolls, backward rolls, and simple chords. These modest tools eventually built my skill level to a point where I could produce sounds remotely resembling music.

Three months after first picking up the instrument I attended the Suwannee Banjo Camp. The experience was helpful, inspiring, and intimidating. I owned the distinction of being the worst player among the 120 participants, but one has to start somewhere, and I could begin to envision what might be possible.

At that time I was introduced to nuances in the banjo world that were previously unknown to me, most notably the existence of a style called 'old time' or 'clawhammer' banjo. The first time I heard the 'old time' style played, I loved the sound and the foot-stomping beat, but I was put off, because it appeared too difficult.

Bluegrass style is probably more familiar to non-enthusiasts and was made popular in the 1970's by the likes of Lester Flatt and Earl Scruggs. An old friend and excellent guitar picker once explained his disparaging view of banjo players, "It's an easy instrument. You only have to know four songs and people will think you know what you're doing: *Foggy Mountain Breakdown*, *The Theme from Deliverance*, *Cripple Creek*, and *The Ballad of Jed Clampett*."

One year later I again attended the camp and decided I wanted to learn 'old style'. But it meant starting over, not unlike switching to oboe. With clawhammer, one strikes the strings with the thumb and fingernail of one finger, middle in my case. The four fingers of the right hand are held in a claw-like fashion, thus the name, and to the casual observer not much is happening, but, in fact, all is quite busy featuring fun-sounding embellishments like double drop thumbing.

I didn't give up on bluegrass style, but I spent the next year focused on the basic elements of clawhammer. I bought the beginner books and worked through the drills learning the fundamentals from which one can eventually construct a song.

I've now attended four banjo camps, most recently at Live Oak, FL. I've advanced somewhat from novice to the intermediate level, and I have been introduced to new nuances that have greatly piqued my interest. One session in particular, Round Peak style clawhammer, really called out to me. The origins are distinctly Scotch Irish, but the toe-tap-defying tunes and the picking style took on an American flavor from denizens of the Appalachian hollows of northwest North

Carolina and SE Virginia in the late 1800's.

These distinctions are meaningful to no more than a few hundred people on the planet earth, but I've now discovered, I am one of them. I was contemplating taking up poisonous snake collecting, but I think this will be a better fit for me.

For those who enjoy acoustic music, the faculty concerts at the Suwannee Banjo Camp are worth the price of admission. My two favorite performers are Adam Hurt and Mark Johnson. Virtually unknown to the broader world, they are remarkable musicians, capable teachers, and nice people willing to share some of their knowledge with those less gifted.

I had a helpful class with Mark one morning, and as I was packing up my banjo case, he said, "Come to my afternoon class, I think you'll enjoy it." I told him it was listed as 'advanced', and beyond my ability, but he said, "Come anyway." He's a big, handsome man with a commanding presence, and I told him I would.

Typically 6-7 students show up for each session, but it turned out I was the only one to show up for 'clawhammer: advanced techniques', resulting in a one-on-one lesson. I knew of Mark from an earlier camp, at which time I purchased two of his CD's, and I listen to his music often. In the micro world of banjo enthusiasts, he's a big honking deal. He produces unique tones on his specially crafted Deering instrument in a style he created called clawgrass, eponymously blending elements of bluegrass and clawhammer. And he has a pleasing voice.

We chatted a bit, and I asked him about his background, how long he's been playing, what it's like to be an accomplished, but unheralded musician. He's been playing since 13, he's now 59, and he plays and writes music, because that's who and what he is. In 2012 he won the third 'Steve Martin Banjo Player of the Year Award' that yielded a $50,000 prize and an appearance on the David Letterman Show. His music is played regularly on the Sirius bluegrass radio channel, and he recently completed a 6-week performance tour in Europe. But he also has a day job as the director of the emergency agency of a coastal county in northern Florida.

Then he said something that's both odd and rare for one who has earned a semblance of modest fame, "Enough about me, tell me about yourself and your banjo journey."

He listened politely to a brief recitation of my humdrum existence, and he said, "Play your best stuff for me. Maybe I can offer a few helpful hints."

I tuned to double C and started with, *The Great Remember (For Nancy)* one of my favorite clawhammer tunes written by Steve Martin. He listened patiently and quietly as I played. Half way through he started playing harmony and counter-melodies, delicately compensating for my many deficiencies, blending some pleasing sounds heard only by the two of us. When we finished, he said, "Can I tell you a story about that song?" And I replied, "I'm all ears."

"For several years, I have been giving lessons to Steve Martin. He once invited me to his home in NYC for dinner and a jam session. I brought a gift of special Florida orange marmalade as a hostess gift for his lovely wife and arrived at the appointed hour at his upper Westside apartment. I told the doorman that I was a guest of Mr. Martin. He motioned to some security type folks near a bank of elevators. They made a call and then gave the sign to allow me to proceed. He told me to go to the 11th floor, and I asked 'What apartment number?' and he shook his head in disbelief. He said, 'Just go to the 11th floor, you'll figure it out.'

"The elevator opened into one of the most elegant dwellings I'd seen, featuring panoramic views of the New York City skyline rising above Central Park. Steve and his wife could not have been more gracious hosts. Shortly after I arrived, his aging dog Wally ambled in, and he introduced me to the dog. Then he got down flat on the floor to chat with Wally. He's a playful and nice man, it's not just an act.

"We had an exquisite dinner, and afterwards played banjo for four hours. When it was time to leave he volunteered to walk me to my hotel. I was scheduled to return the next evening to perform for some of his friends at a dinner party they were hosting. He stopped and put his face about a foot from mine, eyeballed me, and said, 'There will be celebrities present tomorrow evening. Will that be a problem?' I assured him it would not. People are people, no big deal.

"When I arrived the next evening I learned the celebrities included: Meryl Streep, Paul Simon, Lorne Michaels, Kevin Kline, and many others. My partner, (Emory Lester, who plays guitar and fiddle) arrived from Toronto for the event, and we played a one-hour set. Afterwards, a stunningly beautiful blond woman came up to me and said, 'That was truly wonderful! I had no idea a banjo could produce such delightful music. I'd like to introduce you to my husband and some of our friends.' Nancy took me over to meet her husband Martin Short. They were generous with kind words, and said they'd hope to have me come perform at an event they host at their home in Canada."

"Six months passed, and I never heard a word from them. No big deal, I figured, stuff happens. Later during a session with Steve he introduced me to one of his new songs, *The Great Remember (For Nancy)*, and he told me that it was written in memory of his friend, Nancy Short, who passed away several months after the dinner party."

CHAPTER 14

Leroy

The nickname Leroy was a juvenile attempt at antonymic irony as we thought this label conveyed an image of an ignorant, redneck, hillbilly. The real Leroy was the antithesis of this goofy moniker. He was tall, handsome, and carried himself with a gracefulness that belied his rural Ozarks upbringing. His father was a lumberman in a small town in southeast Missouri that presumably accounted for his relative affluence among our social circle at Drury.

We became friends early our freshman year living near each other in the dorm, and then both pledging Lambda Chi. Our senior year we shared a room in the fraternity house. Leroy was a calming influence amongst the zanier boys in the house and one of the coolest guys in the entire school. He drove a red Thunderbird convertible, always dressed well in the fashions of the day, dated the prettiest girls, earned good grades, exhibited a wicked dry wit, and was an interesting and delightful individual. In the fall of 1963 he handed me a copy of the Beatles first album, and said, "Play this, I think you'll like it." We were comfortable friends, and he later served as a groomsman in my wedding.

It was only after college that our relationship developed to another level. While I went off to graduate school, the army, and corporate life in succession, Leroy went to New York City to a more glamorous lifestyle. Within a few years after graduation, he had become the assistant fashion editor of *Playboy Magazine*, had come out of the closet, and adopted an openly gay lifestyle. My gaydar failed me early and often, as I had no idea my roommate was gay, but then I really didn't have an iota of awareness of the existence of homosexuality. But it mattered not. Friends are friends. For several years after graduation we would see each other at Christmas gatherings, as many college friends would congregate in Springfield for the holidays. Each year his costumes became more outrageous, culminating with one featuring a short-waisted, tan, leather Eisenhower jacket covering a white silk tunic, bloused trousers, and jodhpur boots with half chaps. He stood out in staid Springfield. My contrasting attire consisted of khaki pants and an oxford cloth button down blue shirt. We were on different life trajectories, but we remained friends.

Shortly after Lucy was born in 1975, we reconnected at a Springfield holiday affair. We exchanged pleasantries and a brief update on the different worlds we inhabited, and Leroy suggested we should begin a meaningful correspondence. What a great idea I thought, and for a while we exchanged letters. Being a chatty-Cathy sort of chap I wrote about my pedestrian life as a new Dad and the amazing transformation associated with parenthood. Leroy wrote of the artistic world of which he was a part. After several such exchanges, he sent a letter basically saying, "This isn't exactly what I had intended. Perhaps this wasn't such a good idea at all." For some reason, he mistakenly thought I might fit into his world of arts and letters in a manner reminiscent of Gertrude Stein or Virginia Woolf. My musings were lamentably more fitting to a saloon than a salon. In spite of this rebuke we stayed on friendly terms, although distant, throughout the subsequent decades.

In the summer of 2009 Judy and I were in Springfield and encountered a mutual friend who said, "Leroy is back in Springfield and is confined to a nursing home. He is not doing well and would love to see you if you've got time to stop by." We did and had a conversation that bridged the chasm of 40 years. He knew he was dying, a consequence of complications from his long standing HIV, but spoke calmly and with great empathy. He inquired about my wellbeing and my family. He remembered my father kindly as Dad had extended many courtesies to him during his stays at our home and when my parents visited Drury. We then talked about all the things that remained unspoken between us since graduating in 1967. When did you know you were gay? How did you feel about the charade that you had to play all those years? Did you ever nail that Pi Phi you were dating? How did you feel about your straight friends? Did I ever do anything to grievously offend you? If so, is it too late to apologize?

He told of being part of the Stonewall riots in 1969 where gays stood up to the constant harassment of the police against their brethren at the Stonewall Inn in the Village, resulting in nearly 2,000 gay men standing against the New York City police force and inaugurating the gay pride movement in that city. He told of his life in the New York gay community in the 1970's and 80's and the intensity of the sex, drugs, and rock n' roll. He told of the arrival of the AIDS pandemic in the mid 1980's and the hopelessness and helplessness he felt as he attended hundreds of funerals of friends and lovers who had died quick but agonizing deaths from the disease. He told of contracting the HIV virus and of his unwise decision in spending all of his savings and cashing in his life insurance policy to fund a pre-death binge intended to dull the pain associated with his imminent demise. Instead, new drug cocktails were discovered and administered, sparing him from an early grave but leaving him an impoverished alcoholic. Eventually, he reconstructed his life, started a new career, but nothing again ever resembled the halcyon days of New York in the 70's. He also told of being estranged from his parents, not because they had abandoned him, but he had chosen a self imposed exile from them as he wanted to spare them the ridicule he envisaged would come their way if their queer son were to ever return to their provincial town.

Shortly before returning to Springfield, he contracted chronic obstructive pulmonary disease, a progressive disease that makes it difficult to breathe. He was living on the third floor of a three-story walkup in New York, had no support system, and was encouraged by his sister to return to Springfield. He did, and rented a modest two-bedroom apartment, with luxuries unimaginable from his NYC experience such as a washer/dryer, a garbage disposal, and a garage all for a tiny fraction of his earlier rent payments. Sadly, within months of moving into his new apartment, the disease forced his admission into a nursing home. After our visit, we vowed to stay in touch. I sent Leroy a box of books, but they never reached him. He died two days later.

CHAPTER 15

Tom Ward

Tom and his younger brother Steve both served as helicopter pilots during the Vietnam War era. Tom flew a Sikorsky H-19 for the Oklahoma National Guard. Of the 40,000 pilots trained during that era, 2,200 were killed in combat along with the thousands of passengers they carried when they crashed. It was a dangerous business, but fortunately, all of Tom's flying occurred in Oklahoma. Old-time comedian George Gobel once spoke of being a fighter pilot in WWII on the Johnny Carson Show. When asked where he served, he told the audience, "Oklahoma," and added, "You laugh, but I want you to know that no Japanese planes ever got past Tulsa." Steve flew a Cobra gunship, one of the fiercest weapons used in the war, and survived two years of close combat. He would speak little of his war experiences to others, but he once told his brother, "I never felt more alive than when I was in a shit-storm in that gunship."

Tom returned from the war and eventually became the CEO of a large trucking company. Steve returned from the war suffering the classic symptoms of post-traumatic stress syndrome, alcoholism and withdrawal from society. Steve's life ended tragically driving his car through a farm field, hitting a stump, and drowning in a pond.

Tom really missed his calling and might have been a gifted pastor. He is thoughtful, kind, and caring. He will listen patiently to anyone for as long as they might drone on. He can even elicit truthful information from snarly teenagers in the presence of their parents. He possesses the unique gift of being able to persuade people to challenge, and even change, some of their most closely held prejudices.

Most of all, he is a passionate patriot. A giant McMansion was built in Tom's neighborhood replacing a smaller cottage-like structure. Once completed, the owner placed a pathetically small flagpole in his front yard. After a few weeks of cogitating, Tom knocked on the door and spoke to the lady of the house. He politely pointed out the incongruity of having a grand house but only a Lilliputian pole. A week later a flag flew that would have done justice to a Perkin's Pancake House.

The Ward boys grew up in the small northwest Missouri town of Craig. Tom invited me to tag along for the day as he checked on the harvest at the farm that has been in family hands since the late 1800's. Tom knows virtually everyone in the county, everyone knows Tom, and he is one of the most gregarious people on the planet. Traveling with Tom entails a great deal of social interaction, as he loves to chat people up.

It was election day, and Tom would ask everyone he encountered, "Did you vote today?" followed quickly by, "Are you one of those people who doesn't mind saying how they voted?" During the course of the day, Tom surveyed 17 people resulting in 16 for McCain and 1 for Obama. His sample included a county sheriff, conservation agent, county assessor, two assessor clerks, farmers, grain elevator employees, restaurant employees, passersby on the street, and a real estate broker and his son. Needless to say, this unscientific exit poll of rural Missourians didn't accurately predict the outcome.

It was a sunny, warm November day, and Tom provided a grand tour of Holt County, located in the northwest corner of the state. Our first stop was to visit the county sheriff in Oregon, the county seat. Kirby Felumb (as in "feel 'em"), a long time friend of Tom's and the tenant of a house they still own, unfortunately lost his bid for re-election and would soon be seeking other opportunities. We received a brief primer on the sheriff's duties and weaponry, learned that female inmates of the jail are much more trouble than males. Kirby complained to anyone who would listen, "They're always whining about the food or the temperature", and he pointed towards the meat loaf cooking in the nearby kitchen for today's jail lunch. Fortunately, there is not a lot of crime in Holt County, just the occasional cattle rustling and domestic disturbances. The meth epidemic hitting much of rural Missouri hadn't yet travelled north. The building housing the entire operation is small, about the size of a two-chair barbershop. We then walked over to the county courthouse so Tom could say hi to Billy Paul Sharp, the county assessor and some other public servants.

From Oregon we made our way to Craig, Tom's boyhood home. Craig lies at the eastern edge of the Missouri River bottomlands, about 10 miles distant from the river. The Ward's home is located on the first high ground just east of Craig. It's a handsome old house surrounded by walnut trees, numerous outbuildings including a chicken house, barn, storm cellar, and a two-seater outhouse. The pleasing property features a perpetually running spring coming out of the glacial loess providing a constant water supply for the house and cattle. In days gone by, stagecoaches used to stop by the Ward place for the water. It is a beautiful setting save for the fact the house now sits within 100 yards of Interstate 29 that has bisected the Ward family farm since its construction in 1957. The house and yard are in good shape and still full of family mementos. Most impressive was Tom's 1932 Chevrolet sedan that is stored in the garage. It's still in working order, and with a little dusting could be ready for a parade.

From the house we drove up a steep incline to rolling fields overlooking the Missouri River valley and a 300-acre field of soybeans being harvested by Tom's farming partners, the Drewes's (pronounced dray vis), the Dad, age 71, and two sons. The Drewes's farm about 3,000 acres, but they have equipment sufficient to farm 4,000, and they are looking to expand. They own two combines, including a new

S-series John Deere with a list price in the low $400k range. Tom drove into the field and hailed Robert, who was driving one of these beauties. He stopped, and I was invited on board.

The cab seats two comfortably with A/C and stereo. More impressive was the array of electronics and five computer screens providing constant information regarding the moisture content of the grain, bushels per acre, GPS, engine settings, and an entertainment center. The machine was set up with a 30' fold-and-go floating header that cuts a few inches above ground. Scissor-like devices cut the stalk at the base, then a rotating rake bends the plant into an augur, feeding the processing core of the combine where the soybean is separated from the stalk and shell, blowing the bean into a storage bin behind the driver's compartment, and discharging the waste out the back. Sensors on each end of the 30' cutting head adapt to the terrain automatically. When the combine's load of grain nears capacity (300 bushels / 18,000 lbs.), Robert would call his son to bring a grain-hauling wagon alongside. The combine operator swings a giant arm out over the wagon, switches on the high-speed augur, offloads the 300 bushels in about one minute, and continues uninterrupted harvesting. The grain wagon then offloads to a large grain truck with its built-in augur, which when full is driven to either the grain elevator in Craig or St. Joseph, or is transferred to the Drewes' own grain storage bins. The landowner receives a third, and the Drewes get two thirds for providing seed, fertilizer, labor and equipment. After all the risk and expense associated with getting a crop in the bin, it is clear why everyone is so upbeat during the harvest season.

It wasn't exactly exhausting sitting in the comfortable combine, but afterwards we headed to downtown Craig for lunch at the only restaurant in town, the Duck Inn. A middle-aged lady behind the counter greeted us, "Hi Tom, do you remember me?" Tom said warmly, "Sure I do. How are you?" She said, "My Dad used to work with your Dad at the bank." We dined on the special of the day and the only item on the menu, ghoulash, green beans, beets, and apple pie. It was remarkably tasty, and I commend the restaurant to anyone who happens to be in Craig at noon. Tom then commenced with his political surveying with the cook and dishwasher who were also standing behind the counter. The dishwasher took a break from his duties, pulled up a chair, ate a piece of pie and shared a thoughtful 30-minute discourse on the state of the world.

As we were leaving the restaurant a man approached Tom to inquire if he could store an old airplane in a shed (a former airplane hangar) the Ward family owns. Tom said he needed to check and would get back to him. Tom's Dad had been a pilot for TWA, as well as a farmer and banker, and they used to have a grass airstrip in the middle of one of their farm fields. They plowed the airstrip, for fear of liability but retained an old airplane hangar, and we later checked it out to see if it was empty and habitable. While flying for TWA, Tom's Dad, Tom, Sr., devised the system currently used for transcontinental flight, figuring that an Arctic route was the shortest route between the U.S. and northern Europe.

Craig has seen better days. A goodly number of the houses in town appear to be unoccupied and falling down. The hamlet does boast an ethanol plant, a sizable grain elevator, one gas station, a hardware store, and restaurant, but that's about it. There is a major rail line running through town, but it's been at least 50 years since it last stopped in Craig. Any town can have a bad century now and again.

The next stop on our grand tour was the Craig grain elevator. Tom needed to settle the corn contracts he sold last winter. While there, we observed a steady stream of grain trucks coming by to have their grain weighed and tested before dumping their loads and heading back to their fields for more. A grain truck drives on the scale adjacent to the office, the elevator operator sticks a five foot hollow brass tube into the grain, twists the top of the pole opening up slits at various lengths to capture samples of grain from various depths of the load, twists it closed, and then dumps the contents into a container. He then weighs the sample and places the grain in a sifter which separates any dirt or debris from the beans and weighs the debris, which if over 1% the owner gets docked. Then the grain sample is run through a machine to test moisture content. Moisture over 13% for soybeans results in further dockage. Grain payments for soy beans are based on a 60 lb. bushel, and the grain buyer doesn't want to pay for dirt or water. He then takes the weight of the load, less the weight of the truck, adjusts for debris and moisture, and credits the farmer's account. It's amazingly simple, yet sophisticated.

Next Tom drove me to see Drewes's chicken operation. Robert Drewes told me they were raising "Smart" chickens. Apparently "Smart" chickens are raised and processed in a more costly manner to avoid any potential of salmonella poisoning. When I said how many, I was thinking they had a few in a coop outside their house. He said "We raise 120,000 chickens every two months." Each of their four buildings house 30,000 chicks. They start with hatchlings, feed them for 5-6 weeks, and sell them. While impressive in scale, this is not a pleasant smelling operation.

We toured a few more fields that are part of the Ward family farm including 40 acres that has been in the family since 1865. Family legend has it that Tom's great grandfather, a Confederate soldier, walked every step of the way back to Craig after the war and being released from a Union prison camp in Georgia. He married a Craig girl, and her Father gave the couple the 40 acres as a wedding present. For the remainder of his life, this ex-rebel soldier would never allow anyone in his family to wear blue. We made a quick visit to a pine shaded, cemetery overlooking the Missouri River valley where many generations of the Ward clan are planted.

Next we headed to neighboring Mound City, MO to see a real estate agent who is trying to sell 80 acres of duck hunting land for Tom. The real reason that we went to Mound City is that, like Tom, the real estate guy is an avid helicopter pilot, and they enjoyed swapping yarns. Tom was pointing out the photo of a crashed helicopter that looked like a giant ball of twine, as his friend walked up and said, "You know, there are only two types of helicopter pilots, those who have crashed, and those who soon will." He then took us for a ride in his new helicopter.

And we returned home.

CHAPTER 16

Charles Orr

1922 - 2012

*"Among the men who fought on Iwo Jima,
uncommon valor was a common virtue."*

Admiral Charles W. Nimitz

Charles P. Orr passed away on March 18, 2012 at the age of 89. He was a kind and gentle man. He had reason to be proud of each of his children and grandchildren, all of whom are interesting people and productive citizens that you'd be honored to have as friends. He had a successful business career, was a loving husband, and a superb bridge player and cook. If you met him, you would think to yourself, "What a nice man." But there is so much more.

Shortly after graduating from high school in Ash Grove, Missouri, Charles enlisted in the navy. He was trained as a medical corpsman and was assigned to the Fourth Marine Division. He received Bronze Stars on two separate occasions and a Purple Heart for repeatedly entering 'no man's' land during the Marine Corps landings on Saipan and Tinian risking life and limb to assist men he did not know. It's not well remembered, but medics had the second highest fatality rate of all military occupations in the battle for the Pacific, trailing only flamethrower operators. The Japanese took special pains to target the corpsmen who were often vulnerable in the hottest spots.

Charles later earned the Silver Star for uncommon valor on Iwo Jima. He was nominated for the Navy Cross, second only to the Congressional Medal of Honor in terms of valor, but the award was later downgraded by the Force Awards Board to Silver Star. He ran through a field of enemy fire and approached a burning tank to tend to an injured Marine. He ultimately had to amputate the man's leg with bandage shears as it was pinned under the overturned hulk. He then carried the man, again through enemy fire, to an aid station and returned to the battlefield to tend to more wounded Marines. Charles went on to live an unheralded, but substantive life. A few months before his death he was able to join other, now elderly, veterans on a special flight from Springfield to see the WWII Memorial in Washington DC.

He rarely spoke of his military experiences. My cousin, and Charles' stepson, Bob Foltyn (Colonel USMC Retired), only learned of Charles' distinguished combat record by reviewing old family scrapbooks. Bob is an avid student of the War in the Pacific, and he located several documents related to Charles' service during the Pacific campaign that tells more of his story.

BRONZE STAR CITATION - SAIPAN

Citation

"For heroic achievement while serving with a rifle company in action against the enemy of SAIPAN ISLAND, MARIANAS GROUP, on 9 July 1944. Pharmacist's Mate Second Class Orr was working with his company as an aid man when the unit on the right was hit by heavy

enemy fire. Obtaining permission to leave his company, and with complete disregard for his own safety, he volunteered his services to the adjacent unit. He moved over difficult terrain constantly under enemy fire to administer first aid to wounded men. His courageous action was an inspiration to all and was in keeping with the highest traditions of the United States Naval Service."

> H.M. Smith
> Lieutenant General
> U.S. Marine Corps

IWO JIMA ARTICLE

Staff Sergeant J.B.T. Campbell, Jr., a Marine Corps Combat Correspondent

Somewhere in the Pacific. An Ash Grove, MO doctor's son, whose hopes for a medical career were dimmed by the war, has been awarded a Silver Star Medal for performing a difficult amputation while under fire on D-day at Iwo Jima.

He is Navy Pharmacist's Mate First Class Charles P. Orr, 23-year-old son of Dr. and Mrs. Charles H. Orr of Ash Grove.

A medical corpsman attached to the 23rd Marine Regiment on D-day at Iwo Jima, in the words of the citation accompanying the Silver Star:

".....went to the rescue of a wounded man who had both legs pinned under an overturned tank located in a minefield on an open air strip under enemy observation and intense machine gun and mortar fire. He remained with this man for over one hour, relieving his pain and treating him for shock with serum albumen until he was able to extricate one leg. When all other methods failed, he forced his arms and shoulders under the precariously jacked-up tank and amputated the other trapped leg, freeing the man and safely evacuating him."

The man had been so pinned for nearly seven hours when Orr came to help him. Other members of the tank crew had been making pitiful efforts to dig him out with canteen cups - the biggest implements they could employ in the cramped space they had in which to work. Orr accomplished the amputation with a pair of bandage shears. He did not have to cut the bone, which had already been shattered.

Orr had never performed an operation before, but said that the injured Marine's strength was going down so rapidly that it was a case of having nothing to lose.

"The necessity was so clear to me at the time", says Orr, "that I did what had to be done almost automatically, without worrying about the responsibility I was assuming."

He also has the Bronze Star and a Letter of Commendation and a meritorious promotion for treating wounded men under fire at Saipan and Tinian.

Graduating from Ash Grove High School in 1941, Orr began premedical studies and then quit to enlist in the Navy in June 1943. He has been overseas with Fourth Marine Division since March 1944

Orr says he would like to study medicine after his discharge from the service, but fears he may be too old.

FROM AN EYEWITNESS ACCOUNT

Colonel Foltyn located a book titled Tanks on the Beaches containing the following of Charles' Silver Star actions:

"Captain Robert Nieman commanded "C" Company, 4th Tank Battalion in its assault across Motoyama Airfield #1 on February 20, 1945. He witnessed Sgt. Joe Bruno's (1st tank platoon) tank strike an IED made from an aerial torpedo or bomb. The tank exploded, with its turret separating and the hull overturning. The crew of five was assumed dead but hours later, Bruno was found alive and evacuated.

His gunner was also found wounded with a leg pinned under the turret. After initially failing to extricate the Marine, Lieutenant Joe Dever led a daring rescue patrol across no-man's land, which included the battalion surgeon and a corpsman, Charles Orr. The doctor was too fat to enter the turret and conversed with Charles though a firing port. Unfortunately, the Japs spotted the rescue team and took them under fire. Both Dever and the doctor were wounded in the barrage and evacuated.

"Charles completed the gunner's amputation, extrication and evacuation. The gunner, name unknown, survived the war and first learned details of the rescue at a post war reunion. Robert Neiman wrote of the gunner 'He became an ordained minister, raised a family and sent all of his children to college'. Neiman also nominated Charles, Lieutenant Dever and the 'fat' surgeon for the Silver Star."

Lieutenant Joseph Dever on the far left. 1943 New Caledonia

"Charles' personal account verified the details in the news release and Silver Star citation. An M4 Sherman tank struck an IED/mine, made either from an aerial bomb or more likely a torpedo. The explosive force was tremendous, mangling and overturning the 30-ton vehicle.

"The incident occurred at an open area at the edge of Motoyama Airfield #1, and it is key to understanding this story to note that the tank lay between the opposing forces. The Marines had fallen back to whatever cover they could find. The tank and approaches to it were in a minefield and continuously swept by enemy machine gun, mortar and artillery fire. The Japanese were firing from dozens of well-camouflaged and fortified positions.

"As noted in the citation, Charles and the medical officer had been summoned to attempt the rescue after the other survivors. It was no small task to simply make it to the site. Once there, the hull of the tank provided some protection to the would-be rescue team.

"But as the battle continued around them, the unnerving sound of bullets and fragments hitting the armor plate added a personal touch to the ferocious, nonstop din of exploding artillery and mortar rounds. The front lines moved back and forth regularly, as would be the case for the entire 36-day fight for Iwo Jima. For these reasons, an exposed, disabled vehicle was not a comfortable place to pause. The medical officer concluded that there was little that he could do and left Charles alone with the wounded Marine. Charles spent several hours alone with the wounded Marine, both attempting the extraction and providing blood plasma, morphine, comfort and protection.

"The decision point came as darkness approached and the tank still remained between the lines. It would be extremely unsafe to remain forward of friendly lines. Japanese tactics included regular nighttime counter assaults and infiltration of sapper teams. The sappers would stealthily probe the Marines' lines with the intent of killing and capturing, usually with knives, bayonets and swords.

"Charles reported being present for nightly infiltrations, many of which ended in Marine fighting holes with hand-to-hand combat. With these perils in mind he made one last ditch attempt to dig his patient out and then performed the amputation. Under fire, Charles carried the Marine to the aid station.

"To my way of thinking, there would've been sufficient time spent in close proximity for a personal relationship to develop. Anyway, I asked Charles if he had stayed in touch with this fortunate Marine. At a minimum, I would've expected some form of gratitude to be expressed. Charles reflected only briefly and then responded, 'You know, I never caught the fella's name, but I think he was from Chicago.' Charles ensured that the Marine from Chicago was promptly transported to the beachhead for evacuation to one of many LSTs being used as a hospital ship.

"Although Charles would check later to see that the man had survived his wounds and emergency amputation, his immediate focus shifted back to matters at hand, the wounded. He recounted, with intensity, his frustration in getting other corpsman to make rescues that evening. After taking a few minutes to resupply his medical kit and fill his canteens, he returned to his duties. Triage. First aid. Comfort. Protect. Extract. Save.

"It is not lost on me how likely it is that Charles may well have performed even greater acts of valor that were not recorded and equally downplayed. The Silver Star event was most likely recorded because of the presence of the medical officer. Of the 65,000 Marines landed on Iwo Jima, more than 22,000 were wounded. 6,821 were killed in action, one third of USMC KIA for World War II.

"Corpsmen were central figures throughout the battle. From the first day on Yellow Beach, across the airfields, through the bitter fighting in the 'Amphitheater' and for 'Turkey Knob', Charles and his

Battalion were at the center of the fight. All witnessed the carnage. But the corpsmen shared it intimately.

"By all accounts, Charles was the 'go to' corpsman for his Battalion and those adjacent. His previous experience on Saipan and Tinian, rank and age (24) would have made him one of the more senior men. Reading between the lines of our conversations I can easily see Charles making 'saves'. By his own description he was initially overwhelmed with fear during his first hours of combat on Saipan. But in the crucible of battle Charles proved himself to be a man of valor driven by a sense of duty and with a brave and compassionate heart. It may never be known how many survived to foster future generations as a direct result of his intervention. Also lost in history is the undeniable contribution that individual acts of selflessness and heroism make in inspiring others to perform similarly.

"I asked Charles if he was armed while in battle. He looked at me with a rare show of emotion, that being pity for asking such a stupid question. 'In every action, I carried an M-1 Garand Rifle, a M1911A .45 caliber pistol, and strapped as many grenades on my body as I could carry. Everyone was armed to the teeth.' And this was in addition to the 40-60 lb. medical kit he carried.

"Charles was awarded a Purple Heart on Iwo Jima after receiving a shrapnel wound to his arm. Charles downplayed the matter. He refused evacuation and stayed on the line. After treating and seeing hundreds of dead, dying, disemboweled or traumatically wounded, the puncture by a single fragment may have seemed relatively insignificant.

"It is also unusual for a Marine to be given multiple awards for a single battle even if there were multiple acts of heroism. Landings on Saipan, Tinian and Guam were part of the July 1944 operation to capture the Marianas Islands. To those involved, the landings and battles were separate and distinct, but not to the commanding staff to whom the islands were successive objectives in the Marianas Campaign for their subordinate divisions.

"Charles was reluctant to discuss his combat experiences. Like most veterans, he would never accept the title 'hero', reserving that exclusively for the fallen. I believe that Charles would simply prefer to be recalled as a man who answered God's call to duty. One of many who served with distinction."

EXCERPTED FROM AFTER ACTION REPORT OF CHARLES' UNIT, REGIMENTAL COMBAT TEAM 23 IN IWO JIMA

"Seventy years ago Charles P. Orr landed on Yellow Beach as part of a 75,000-man assault on the Japanese held island of Iwo Jima.

"Charles was assigned to the Third Battalion of the 23rd Marine Regiment. He boarded the landing craft about the time that the first waves were landing on the morning of February 19, 1945, but his Battalion was held in reserve. They circled in their boats offshore until needed. After three waves of marines landed under heavy opposition and devastating enemy fire, the 23rd Regiment was called in at 1655. By 1800 he and his comrades were ashore and had relieved another Battalion where it had been stalled by decimating casualties at the edge of Motoyama Airfield #1.

"Thousands of dead Marines, human remains, blood, the twisted hulks of vehicles and boats, tatters of clothing/equipment, and scattered supplies littered the bomb craters. Tons of this matter had been atomized and mixed with black sand and was continually sprayed through the air from the explosive force of a heavy artillery/mortar barrage. 250-pound projectiles rained down on the dug-in Marines. One dared not look too long lest he be eviscerated by a chunk of white hot shrapnel or one of thousands of bullets snapping overhead. Besides, there was work to do, the mission.

"Charles' Regiment moved 200 yards inland by jumping from shell hole to shell hole. There they stopped for a sleepless night awaiting a Japanese counterattack. All would endure and some would survive the uninterrupted close combat for the next month. No breaks, no shelter, and no quiet time. They covered approximately 2 1/2 miles at a rate of 100 to 1,000 yards per day, always under continuous fire and observation from camouflaged, enemy fortifications.

"On D+4 news reached the 23rd Marines that Old Glory had been raised on Mount Suribachi following its capture by the 28th Marines. No one knew then, not even the men who had raised it, what an historic moment it was to become. That discovery was to be made in the photographic dark room on Guam, where Associated Press photographer Joe Rosenthal's famous picture first saw light. But it made Marines feel proud to know that after four days their flag flew at the island's highest point. More importantly, there was comfort in knowing that the enemy could no longer look down their backs. When asked, Pharmacist Mate Charles Orr seemed moderately irritated about this subject. After shaking his head and thinking a moment he responded politely 'We were too busy to look or think about it.' More than a month of intense fighting remained before the island was declared secure.

"Charles' unit had just taken Airfield # 1, but the 23rd Marines and its parent 4th Division had no time to rest. The costliness of fighting on the open terrain left no one in the mood for celebration. In four days the division suffered 25% casualties that included most of its officers and one third of its corpsman.

"On February 23, the battle was begun for Airfield #2 and 'Charlie-Dog Ridge'. The fighting between the two airfields was among the bitterest on Iwo. Probably no other section of the island of equal size boasted such an elaborate system of defense. The wild terrain featured hundreds of bomb craters, resembling the surface of the moon. The ash was ankle deep, and when the wind blew, it pelted the men's faces like buckshot.

"In addition to other hazards, the heat from volcanic activity beneath the surface made life miserable for those sheltering in the shell craters. The defenders converted every dune into a bunker from which the muzzles of machine guns and anti-tank weapons jutted defiantly. Many men, taking cover from the unrelenting fire overhead, suffered incapacitating burns from contact with the ground underneath.

"The attack was made following a heavy artillery bombardment. When the infantry charged they found enemy all around them. Captain LaVerne W. Wagner, commander of an assault company in the Twenty-third, reported that more hand-to-hand fighting took place in the two-day battle than in any engagement he had ever seen. 'The lines literally melted away,' he said. 'We were chasing the Japs down trenches, and they were chasing us. Grenade duels took place everywhere. More often than not, we found ourselves in the rear of Jap pillboxes which were still doing business on the other side.'

"When the initial battle was over, 40% of the comrades with whom Charles came ashore were dead, wounded or crazy. After 36 days on Iwo Jima, covered with dirt, blood, and human remains, Charles boarded a landing craft and returned to the safety of a navy transport. There he enjoyed a warm meal, a shower, and a replacement uniform. Then the remnants of his unit returned to Camp Maui where they would prepare for the next battle (the assault on mainland Japan).

An Iwo Jima veteran, Robert Ganon, wrote of the experience:

Monuments and Memories (for those who never came home)
Some people say I should not waste the hours of my life
On monuments and memories recalling times of strife.
They seem to think it only is a name upon a stone,
While I reflect that easily that name could be my own.
Should I forget those men I knew who stood and fell by me?
Should I forget those torrid isles upon that sultry sea?
Should I forget that smiling lad from Arizona's plain,

Who fought alongside me though wounded and in pain?
Or should I just forget about that corpsman standing fast,
Who put his body over mine and took that mortar blast
Should I forget those countless men who waded into shore
And gave their lives defending my country and my Corps?
I can't forget one single name; those men are with me still.
If I don't remember them I ask you then, who will?

"I hope that you will join me in remembering Charles and the tens of thousands of young Marines who faithfully performed their duty during this perilous time."
Semper Fidelis,
Bob Foltyn, Colonel USMC Retired

LETTER HOME

While in Camp Maui awaiting the final assault on mainland Japan, Charles wrote this poignant letter to his parents.

Dr. Charles H. Orr
Ash Grove, MO
July 14, 1945

Dear Mom and Dad,

The day after your birthday Mom, and a special day it is. I sure hope it was a nice day for you, and I was thinking about how much I would liked to have been there.

Maybe you should have someone dig me a foxhole when I come home for I won't be able to sleep in a bed. Things are going well here, but I've had some experiences that I don't want to live over.

No, Mom, I haven't had an answer to John's letter but will send you the letter if I do. You might cable me if John does get home for I sure am anxious about him. Write airmail, and I will when I can.

Love,

C.P.

POSTSCRIPT

Though Charles was awarded a Silver Star for his exceptional bravery under fire on Iwo Jima, he never received the actual medal, a consequence of a bureaucratic SNAFU. Charles miraculously survived landings on Saipan, Tinian, and Iwo Jima, over a nine-month period and was training for the assault on the home islands of Japan. After the war, Charles went on with his life, giving little thought to the missing medal. When Colonel Foltyn learned of Charles' heroics with the 23rd Marines, he set about righting this wrong. In the summer of 2005 a Marine Corps company assembled at Richards' Gebaur Air Force Base in Kansas City, MO to recognize Charles' exemplary service. The commanding officer read the citation written 60 years earlier and pinned the Silver Star on Charles' lapel in front of an assembly of family and friends. Afterwards the company of sturdy young Marines filed by to shake his hand and as one cheered, "You Rock, Sir!"

Charles receiving the Silver Star. Colonel Foltyn is to Charles' right.

Colonel Robert 'Carrot' Foltyn is a graduate of the U.S. Naval Academy. He became a Marine Corps aviator flying jet fighters with hundreds of carrier landings to his credit, 60% at night. He was a Top Gun pilot and later an instructor for that elite group at the Naval Air Station in Miramar. He once took us on a tour of the decommissioned carrier USS Midway. He explained that every pilot is rated for each landing. The highest of five possible ratings is 'ok'. The lowest is 'NAFOD', no apparent fear of death. Receipt of the latter shortens one's flying career, one way or another. Regrettably his career in his beloved Corps was cut short by the onset of Parkinson's disease. He is now a dedicated scholar of the Marine Corps' role in WWII in the Pacific.

CHAPTER 17

Frank Priest

PROLOGUE

My daughter, Lucy, and I went to visit her husband's grandmother in the hospital. Jane had just turned 91, and she was sharp as a tack, but her health was failing. We caught her on a good day when we entered her room, she recognized us quickly, and inquired, "How's that book of yours coming?" Then she added, "I've got a good story for you." And she began the story that follows about her father. Sadly, she passed away two days later before she could fully expand on that which follows:

In 1908 a ten-year-old boy arrived alone by train in Wichita, KS having traveled from Chicago with his name, Frank Priest, penned to his jacket. He had recently been orphaned, and authorities discovered the boy had a distant aunt living in Wichita. They contacted the lady and sent him on his way.

The aunt was not a kindly woman, and she ungraciously accepted the unwanted boy. One of Frank's most vivid memories was of asking his aunt for a nickel to buy candy. She begrudgingly acceded to this modest request, and then held it over his head, like a delinquent mortgage, for the remainder of her pathetic life.

Frank was a good student, made friends easily, and found his salvation in the Boy Scouts. In 1917, the U.S. entered the War to End All Wars, and Frank was the first boy from Wichita to enlist. He tested highly in mathematics and was assigned duties as an artilleryman serving in Battery D, 129th Field Artillery Unit alongside another young officer by the name of Harry S Truman. Frank also befriended Jim Pendergast, nephew of Tom, the all-powerful Democratic boss of Kansas City. Jim would introduce Truman to his uncle after the war, but that is another story. In March of 1918 their unit was shipped to France. Frank rose from the rank of lieutenant to captain by the end of the war.

This excerpt from D. M. Giangreco's, "The Soldier from Independence: Harry S. Truman and the Great War" hints of Frank's experience:

"Truman's battery was frequently employed well forward. He was detailed to provide fire support for George S. Patton's tank brigade during the Meuse-Argonne offensive, engaged German field guns and was credited with either wiping out or forcing the permanent abandonment of two complete batteries. When firing on these and other targets, he disobeyed orders and fired "out of sector" against threats to his division's open flank. Truman's 35th Division, a National Guard formation made up of units from Missouri and Kansas, suffered grievously in that battle, and the battery was sited approximately 150 yards forward of where Patton was wounded in an area referred to by one artilleryman as "a cemetery of unburied dead."

"The 27,000-man division lost nearly 7,300 men during six days of fighting. A total of 1,126 killed or died of wounds; 4,877 severely

wounded. The casualties suffered on these few days represent the highest loss rate for any U.S. division during the war – virtually all occurring within two to three miles of Truman's artillery battery as it moved forward through the battlefield and went about its deadly work."

Like Truman, combat in WWI had a profound impact on Frank. He returned to Wichita, started work as a clerk in an insurance business, married, and started a family. He also remained close to friends from Battery D, including the man who would become the 33rd president of the United States.

He eventually became a partner in his insurance company, was active in numerous civic functions, but his passion was in helping boys grow into men. He was known for his frequent encounters with 'young ruffians down by the river' and successfully enlisting them in his Boy Scout troop.

In later life he besieged Truman with letters admonishing the president to grant a fourth star for another of his Great War comrade in arms, General George Patton.

When Frank died in 1971 the entire Wichita police force lined the path of his funeral cortege to honor the man who did so much for the youth of their town.

Jane shared a portion of her Dad's remarkable correspondence:

October 30, 1961

FRANK T. PRIEST

G. S. Patton, Major, Armor
Armed Forces Staff College
Norfolk, Virginia.

DEAR MAJOR PATTON:

Mine is quite a long story. As I indicated to you on Saturday last I was a First Lieutenant in Field Artillery, as was Harry Truman when we went over seas together to go to a Second Corp Artillery School. Our regiment - the 130th Field Artillery, ended up with six inch Howitzers, Truman ended up with three inch French guns, but I knew him very well. We were both promoted in France to Captains and I have seen him off and on as the years went on, while he was a Senator, then later as President.

At any rate in late March of 1945 I was concerned about your dad that we all loved so much, we knew he was a terrific soldier, so I wrote to Mr. Truman, as Vice-President, to Senator Clyde Reed from Kansas, Senator Chandler of Kentucky and Representative Andrew May (I believe he was at that time Chairman of the Military Affairs Committee).

Here are the original letters received from Mr. Truman and Senator Chandler - perhaps you would like them for your memoirs.

When Mr. Truman signed this letter of April 10th, he was Vice-President. When he wrote the note at the bottom in pen as he did, and knowing Truman as I did, I knew he thought as much of General Patton as I did. About the time I received this letter Truman had suddenly been made President of the United States, I think the record will show that some ten days later he nominated General George S. Patton, Jr. to be promoted to the Rank of 4-Star General. I think the facts will bear this out.

I am delighted I found your name and address in time this last week, also after considerable search I found my letters having to do with your father. They are very interesting to me. You may keep them all.

Sincerely,

250

N W. BARKLEY, KY.
, KEELY, W. VA.
IR T. BONE, WASH.
GRASSY, Orio
MAN MINTON, IND.
T S. TRUMAN, MO.
LEX O. ANDREWS, FLA.
N C. JOHNSON, COLO.
T H. SCHWARTZ, WYO.
R HILL, ALA.
ST LUNDEEN, MINN.
STEWART, TENN.

HENRIK SHIPSTEAD, MINN.
CHARLES W. TOBEY, N. H.
CLYDE M. REED. KANS.
CHAN GURNEY, S. DAK.

M. W. MITCHELL, CLERK

United States Senate

COMMITTEE ON INTERSTATE COMMERCE

Kansas City, Missouri.
August 27th 1943.

Hon Frank T Priest,
Dulaney, Johnston & Priest,
200 Central Building,
Wichita, Kansas.

Dear Frank:

I certainly appreciate your good letter of
August 23rd and also appreciate your thought-
fulness in sending me the 1884 dollar.

I am going to put it in my Beech Good Luck
cover.

I am glad you had a successful trip to Colorado
and I'll bet that boy was glad to see his mother.
Please remember me to that good Pi-Phi daughter
of yours. I sincerely hope that she and my
daughter may become good friends.

I know that the Rawdon T-1 airplane will work
our alright.

I haven't seen Jim, but the first time I do I
will tell him he is indebted to you for a letter.

Sincerely yours,

Harry S. Truman, U.S.S.

HST:VC

Letter from Harry S. Truman to Bess W. Truman, August 8, 1943. Truman Papers - Family, Business, and Personal Affairs Papers.

Emporia, Kansas. August 8, 1943

Dear Bess:

It was good to talk to you a little while ago. I hated to hang up until you said it was time and then I still hated to. They really gave me a go around in Wichita. Lowell Dyer and Frank Priest entertained me for fair. Jim Pendergast was in Priest's battery after he received his second commission at the Doniphan School. Dyer & Priest took me to dinner after the luncheon at noon, took me breakfast yesterday and after taking me out to inspect a new light plane, in which I took a pleasant ride, they took me to lunch and saw that I made the train.

Priest has a lovely 19-year-old daughter named Jane who is a Pi Phi at K.U. She was extremely nice to me when I called attention to her arrow and told her that my beautiful daughter wore one. He took Dyer and me by his beautiful home on the way to the soldier dinner. Mrs. Priest was making chili sauce in kitchen and Miss Jane acted as hostess.

Just had a telegram from Bill that Mr. Halstead is taken care of in the Solid Fuels Dept of Ickes set up.

Well I went to church this morning to hear Dr. Judd preach a sermon. It was a Methodist Church and the roof didn't cave in. It was pretty well built.

Had breakfast with Congressman Ben Reese of this place. I told Mrs. Reese to get some ration tickets from you when you get back to Washington. They have a nice 15-year-old boy.

We speak tonight and they say it will be a big crowd. Judd preached a good sermon so I'll I've to try myself for Bill White's edification.

Love to you. Harry.

CHAPTER 18

Micro Stories

PATRICK VAN HOOREBEEK

We shared five meals together during Patrick's recent visit to Kansas City. He wore five different outfits. He favors pastel sport coats and suits, always accented with a colorful boutonneire. The most striking outfit featured a canary yellow linen suit with a purple corsage and handkerchief perfectly tucked in the breast pocket. For a more casual lunch, he wore a lime green, cotton sport coat with leather pants, and cowboy boots. Had it not been summertime, I'm certain he would have selected darker colors.

And he's not gay. He's a self-declared bon vivant.

Patrick was raised in a small village in Belgium, and he explained in his heavily accented English. "I knew I was a bon vivant when I was five. Mothers would take their children to the beach and organize games. The little girls would make paper flowers with materials provided for that purpose. They would build sand castles and stick the flowers in the ramparts. The little boys would then bring seashells to the little girls. The exchange rate was five shells for one paper flower. But I was not interested in the paper flowers. I filled my bucket with shells and approached the prettiest girl and offered the entire contents of my bucket in exchange for a walk on the beach. That's when I knew I was a bon vivant."

Patrick first gained local notoriety while working as the maitre d' at the Bistro at Maison de ville, a small restaurant in the French Quarter. There his bon vivant-ism blossomed, as he entertained legions of locals and broadened his network. Sixteen years ago Patrick gained a modicum of fame when he founded, and became the King For Life, of the Krewe of Cork, a New Orleans parading society comprised of people who enjoy wine and fine dining, many of whom work in the hospitality industry.

After Katrina, the Bistro changed hands, and Patrick moved to The Rib Room, an elegant French Quarter restaurant situated in the Royal Orleans Hotel. On a busy Mardi Gras evening the Rib Room dining room might contain more than 100 people. All of them would know Patrick, and he, in turn, would know all but the tourists by name. During a recent Mardi Gras, Patrick joined our small group for dinner. He wore a black top hat with a dark pink velvet sport coat. Several members of the staff stopped by our table to greet Patrick formally using the honorific, "Good evening King! I hope you are well!"

One of our favorite French Quarter haunts was a local bar, nestled off the interior courtyard of a small hotel. One would not accidentally stumble in. It no longer exists, but many years ago it was owned by an irascible, but attractive, woman. One evening after dining at a nearby restaurant, we listened as she lamented the constant sorrows attendant to her love life and the troubles she was having with her, then, boyfriend. We nodded absent mindedly and sympathetically that the man was undoubtedly a reprobate. 'How could anyone mistreat one so lovely?' The alleged lout was none other than Patrick, and after being introduced, would become our friend, and the lady bar owner disappeared from our lives.

When Patrick was eleven, his father abandoned his family in Belgium. He worked in the beer business, and he eventually relocated to New Orleans. Patrick followed in his father's footsteps, also working in the beer business, but staying in Brussels. When he was 35, Patrick received a call from his father, the first contact in over two decades. He invited Patrick to come spend a year in the U.S. "Come see if you like it here. You'll learn a lot in a year, even if you return to Belgium." Patrick spoke several languages at the time, but English wasn't among them. But he came to New Orleans and immediately knew he would stay, and now rightfully boasts of his recently acquired U.S. citizenship and his successful eponymous French Quarter wine bar, Patrick's Bar Vin.

PRAIRIE VILLAGE STANDARD

October 1, 2010 was a sad day in the life of anyone who has ever lived in our little suburban community. The Prairie Village Standard station closed for good. Presumably this venerable institution will now become the site of a branch bank. The owner explained that the bank offered him a sum for a 99-year land lease that was far greater than his potential earnings from operations. It was one of the last of a dying breed of gas stations where the operative word was 'service'. Attendants cleaned windshields and checked your oil and tire pressure while pumping gas. They maintained a full repair shop with capable on-site mechanics, sold tires, batteries, and accessories, operated a tow truck service and car wash, and offered free compressed air. More importantly, it provided practical schooling to several generations of boys and young men.

Buford Roney was a young man himself in 1947 when he opened his gas station at Mission Road and Tomahawk in the newly constructed Prairie Village Shopping Center. His new business accompanied a drug store, bank, grocery store, ice cream parlor, and a small assortment of other shops comprising one square block in the new city being carved out of the farm fields southwest of Kansas City.

One of the many reasons I loved the PV Standard was they featured a picture of me in their small, untidy office. Buford sponsored the little league team in 1955 on which I played. For reasons I can't explain, that photo was one of several that offered a glimpse of life in Prairie Village in the mid 1950's. So there I was with Dohn Kennyhurtz, Kip

Niven, Charlie Shoemaker, and a dozen other 10-year-old boys. I'd walk in their small office to visit with Buford's son Johnny, who had taken over the operation of the station, and say to whoever would listen, "Hey, that's a picture of me." The uninterested victims would yawn politely with nary a glance at the photo.

Buford knew his customers and could be counted on to look after them. One winter's morning at 6:00 am Buford called our home to say that Casey, our yellow Labrador retriever, must have gotten out of our gate, and said he'd keep him at the station until we came down to retrieve him.

Five years ago the Prairie Village Standard station became the Prairie Village Phillips 66 station. Johnny told me that the Standard people would require him to stay open 24/7 in order to keep the brand. He said they were not moved by his arguments that little happens in our quiet little town between the hours of 9 pm and 6 am, far removed from any major thoroughfare, so he switched to Phillips. The familiar Standard Oil emblem was removed, but the name stayed the same to knowing patrons.

Ben worked for Buford throughout his high school years. In addition to learning some useful mechanical skills in the garage, Buford would coach the young workers in the art of working for a living. He'd offer instruction on 'talking the customer up' and on the importance of hustling in one's work and showing up on time. Buford came from the old school where the highest praise came in the form of the absence of a kick in the ass. He was a great influence on both the privileged and not-so-privileged boys with whom he came in contact.

An additional benefit to Ben of working part-time for the PV Standard was in meeting the interesting characters that would have made the perfect cast for a reality television show. Foremost among these was Earl*, a middle-aged, muscular African-American man who was the lead mechanic and tow truck operator. He took Ben under his wing and showed him how to change and repair tires, change oil, and perform minor mechanical repairs. Earl was a handsome man and had a body that appeared to have been chiseled out of granite. He could have been a model for Michelangelo.

Ben was sufficiently observant to notice that Earl seemed miscast in his role as service station employee. He was smart, witty, and hardworking so Ben broached the topic of his employment delicately, and Earl told him the following story: "When I was in my late teens I was riding with some older guys who stopped the car, got out, and said, 'We'll be back in a minute.' They then robbed a bank, got back in the car, and we were later all arrested. I spent the next 17 years in an Indiana prison, and this is the kind of work that I can get." He told the story without bitterness and outwardly appears to go through life with a light heart.

Ben's been long gone from PV Standard, but virtually every time I see Earl he would shout out at me "Hey, how's Ben Hurr?" When Ben's in town, he would stop by and could always expect a big hug from Earl. He is a good man.

Robert usually manned the full service pumps. Driving by the station in warmer weather, one could observe Robert leaning against a pump reading a book awaiting the next customer. He walked with a pronounced limp, always wore a tan leather cowboy hat, and would inquire about Ben whenever I came to the station. He was a surprisingly erudite man. He was well read and would often suggest books I might like, would inquire about the latest developments in the bond markets, enjoyed discussing politics, but most often speculated glowingly on Ben's future. "That boy's going to make his mark." He was particularly pleased that Ben had learned Chinese. Robert said he had a degree in chemical engineering from Texas A&M, had worked in the nuclear power industry for a period of time, yet never quite explained how this path had led him to the PV Standard. He was a friendly, but mysterious, man.

It is now be too late to learn more about the people that made the PV Standard Station special, as this eclectic cast of characters has drifted off to other callings. I mourn the passing of this magical enterprise.

MARSHA

Years ago I had a lunch with a new client, soon to be friend. We dined at a restaurant called the Monastery, featuring wait staff wearing coarse, brown monk robes with pointed hoodies. Even better, they chanted while shuffling from table to table carrying flagons of wine and, when necessary, wiped their greasy hands on the fur of a big dog lying by the fire.

My guest was the CEO of a mid-sized, but complex, enterprise, and I found her to be enjoyable company and a person of great substance. We engaged in the time honored social lubricant of inquiring about one another's background. This quickly morphed into a mild form of one-ups-man-ship wherein one seeks to add a few molecules of luster to the modesty of their achievements by emphasizing the humbleness of their origins.

I may have exaggerated a bit, prattling on about being raised by literate, but kind, wolves in northeast Missouri.

Then she began her story somberly, "We were the only Jewish family in our town and county. Let me tell you, it was not easy growing up as an overweight, Jewish girl in Toadsuck, Arkansas."

"You win!"

And the story reminded me of one of my favorite songs:

THEM TOAD SUCKERS
(Mason Williams)
"Look at them toad suckers. Ain't they snappy?
Suckin' them bog-frogs sure makes 'em happy.
Them huggermugger toad suckers, way down south,

Stickin' them sucky toads in they mouth!
How to be a toad sucker? No way to duck it.
Gittchyseff a toad, rare back and suck it!"

VERNOLA

Recent travels took me to Homewood, Alabama. I checked Yelp to find a suitable establishment for breakfast and found a 4.5 star rating for Salem's Diner located nearby. We arrived and discovered a modest strip mall with a tiny restaurant. It featured a 7-seat counter facing the cook's grill and four small, yellow plastic booths. The place was packed, so our foursome was seated at the counter. The decor featured early Alabama football memorabilia.

We inquired about the various photos c. 1950, and the owner, standing proudly behind the counter, informed us his father had recently been inducted into the University of Alabama football hall of fame. In Alabama, this makes Wayne Salem pretty darn close to royalty. We were greeted warmly with a query, "You boys must not be from around these parts", and we recited our origins: Kansas, New York, Tennessee, and Iowa. My brother, the Tennessean, then received some good-natured ribbing about the recent gridiron dominance of the Tide over the Vols.

Our waitress, Vernola, approached bringing hot coffee and ice water and took our orders. We were told we must try their homemade spicy sausage patties and Wayne's Mom's special marmalade, and we complied as instructed. Vernola was a bit on the wiry side, probably mid-to-late-40's with short dishwater hair, and spoke with more than a hint of a southern accent. What she lacked in babaliciousness, she made up with the purposeful application of her womanly wiles.

I was sitting at the counter adjacent to the cash register. Every time Vernola came near, she found a reason to rub her boob on my shoulder or arm. Her coffee refills were mindful of the lap-dances I've heard the more randy boys speak of. Breakfast would turn out to be one of the more tactile dining experiences I've had.

When we returned to the car, I asked if Vernola had shared her attentions with the others. I was mildly disappointed to learn that I had not been singled out. All agreed that the exaggerated display of her feminine charms favorably impacted her gratuity, sort of a 'Mardi Gras-like-variation' of tits for tips.

Everyone in the restaurant was friendly and offered recommendations on what we should do and see in the area. The eggs were prepared perfectly, the sausage was terrific, and all was good. Wayne said, "You boys come back, you hear."

And so we came back the following morning before our golf outing. Once again Vernola was our server, but unfortunately we were seated in a booth. Any forthcoming boob rubs would have required a pratfall. She was not in great spirits this particular morning, and we inquired why. "I spilled hot coffee on my hand, then I dropped a plate of food. It's not been a good day." Then she dropped a spoon on the floor. A wiseacre in our group comforted her, "Don't worry, the help will be along later to pick that up." She failed to see the humor.

Vernola was absent on our fourth and final visit to the diner. We were seated and greeted by Becky. She introduced herself graciously, "Hi, I'm Becky. What can I get for you boys?" She spoke in the softest of voices and spurned the customary two-syllable pronunciation of her name. Instead we heard a version where the "eck" reverberated pleasantly for several seconds. Becky informed us it was Vernola's day off. Her service was equally exemplary, although less touching.

MIKE WILLIAMS

I was introduced to Mike earlier that morning, as he was a fellow guest in a golf foursome in Vail Valley. I was told he was quite a character, lives in Mississippi, formerly owned a carnival business, and is an avid bow hunter. He is a fit, handsome, and friendly fellow.

After thirteen holes, a siren blasted a warning of a coming thunderstorm and lightning. We hightailed it to a nearby shelter and waited for the storm to pass. Once there, Mike encountered a fellow hunter, and the chance meeting prompted him to tell the following story:

"When I was 41, I was bow-hunting for polar bear in the Arctic region of Greenland, 8-days in by dogsled from Baffin Bay. I was accompanied by two Inuit, one of whom spoke English and one who did not. We stopped and set up camp because of a whiteout. The dogs were going crazy because one of the bitches was in heat. The next morning we awoke and noticed that six of our thirteen dogs were missing, as they had bitten through their leather bindings.

"The English speaking Inuit told me, 'We have to find those dogs. We'll take the snow mobile and look for them. You stay here.' It was -30 degrees, but I was bored and decided to take a walk around. It was still in slight whiteout conditions, so I made sure to stay within eyesight of our tent. I was several hundred yards into my walk, when I heard the sound of breaking ice, and I fell into freezing waters up to my chin. The shock of cold almost stopped my heart. Fortunately, I spread my arms out and caught the lip of the break keeping my head from going under. I immediately started a furious backstroke pushing through the softer ice until I reached a hard edge. I then kicked up with my legs and was able to get a heel on the surface. Then I rolled out of the water and ran back to the tent.

"My clothing was frozen almost solid by the time I got in the shelter. I stripped everything off and was able to get one of our two miniature stoves going. I was shaking and freezing but alive.

"Several hours later one of the Inuit threw open the tent flap, presumably thinking he would encounter a dead man having seen my frozen clothing outside. He gave me some Caribou garments, and I warmed up quickly. In fact, I was soon overheated."

The two hunters exchanged anecdotes on the merits of Caribou clothing. Then Mike started telling of the time he acquired 170,000 acres in Botswana for use as a hunting reserve, but was interrupted by the 'all clear' alarm, and we returned to golf.

JUDY'S GARDEN

Judy combined two passions, gardening and defending underdogs, when she started a community garden in an empty lot near our church, St. Paul's Episcopal located at 40th and Main in Kansas City. It was once a very nice neighborhood, but by the 1990's it had declined. An eighth grade graduation ceremony held on the church lawn was interrupted by gunfire resulting in the murder of a young man within earshot of the assembled celebrants.

The idea originated in 1992 when Judy was working at the church's food pantry. A neighborhood woman walked in with a nasty black eye. She explained that a man approached her as she was entering her apartment building, hit her in the face, and stole her purse. The community garden would be Judy's first of several for actions to improve the neighborhood.

It was a long and narrow lot bordered by side streets on the north and west, abutting the side of a derelict three-story occupied apartment buildings on the east and the side of a smaller building on the south. Judy hired a man to plow the ground. She laid out several dozen individual plots in a checkerboard pattern, each about the size of a twin bed and bordered by mulched paths.

The church provided water, seeds, and tools. Judy and a random gathering of neighborhood volunteers provided advice and labor to help people get started. Judy kept a regular schedule on the premises and would chat up anyone walking by and encourage them to start a garden. She wore a large wooden cross and bedraggled work clothes both for her personal safety and so she wouldn't be confused with the prostitutes who worked the area. Some residents asked if she were a nun.

Some grew vegetables and some grew flowers, but it was a colorful and vibrant scene in a tiny corner of the city that was formerly home only to broken glass, weeds, trash, and a worn dirt path leading to a first floor apartment window that served as a 'walk-by' drug emporium.

But serious problems remained. Residents and passersby would regularly approach Judy with tips about drug dealing in the neighborhood. Judy would call them in to the police and quickly became acquainted with the beat cops and, more ominously, known to the druggies. Over the years, two men showed up regularly to serve as her self-assigned protectors, and they worked along side her on the garden.

A first floor resident of the adjacent apartment building was a drug dealer. He frequently conducted his business out of his window that was located on the inside corner of the garden. One day Judy was working nearby when she heard a commotion at the drug dealer's apartment. A concerned resident tried to stop the transaction in progress. The good guy pulled a knife on the bad guy. The latter fled, and the former gave chase. Interestingly, both the pursuer and the pursued meticulously respected the integrity of the garden by following the zigzag pattern of the mulched paths.

It's one thing to flee for your life from a knife-wielding assailant, but you just don't mess with Judy's garden.

STEVE LACEY

"When a civilized nation goes to war, any hint of civilization goes out the door.' Some old guy said that to me before I left for Vietnam, and I just blew it off, but within days of my arrival, I knew he was right. Absolutely nothing mattered except 'my family' of fellow soldiers. We viewed the enemy as dog-meat. They wanted to kill me and my friends and would unless we killed them first."

Steve was 18-years-old when he was drafted by the U.S. Army in 1967. He was 5' 8" and weighed 120 pounds and had traveled little outside of his home in Kansas City. Fortunately, he was given the option of enlisting for two years versus being drafted for two years. The distinction of being an enlistee vs. a draftee was subtle but substantive, particularly if one didn't have to give up an additional year of service. Steve was designated RA (regular army, volunteer enlisted) affording higher status than US (draftee) and was given more latitude in choosing a career path. A high percentage of draftees would become 11B (infantryman) and 11C (indirect fire infantry aka mortar man). Steve was asked what he would like to do. He said, "Surveyor", and he was assigned to be a gunner in an artillery battery. Close enough.

One year after graduating from high school, Steve arrived in Viet Nam. "They first put us through an in-country orientation program. Most memorably they had all of us stand in a field and wait. Then machine gun fire erupted out of nowhere. We all hit the deck and tried to bury ourselves in the dirt. The firing stopped, and the orientation guy came out and told us that was a test and the guns were firing blanks. Then he said, 'Each one of you just dug in the dirt. What you should have done was run towards the machine gun. If you don't take it out, they will pick you off at their leisure. It's counter-intuitive, but it's what it takes to survive.' I'm thinking to myself, 'that is insane.' "

Steve was assigned to a battery consisting of six 105mm Howitzers. "We were dropped onto a mountain top that gave a good vantage point to support the infantry operations in our vicinity. If we were lucky, a Chinook helicopter would bring in a dozer, and the engineers would clear a space about the size of half a football field. If not, we had to clear and burn the area by hand. Each team of six guys would then prepare the parapet for their artillery piece. Then helicopters would bring in the howitzers. The top of the mountain also housed a large bunker buried under sand bags used to store the powder and shells. We'd build our hooches in the ring below the top, basically digging caves into the side of the mountain fortified with sand bags and furnished using wood from empty shell crates. Below our hooches we built eight defensive bunkers. Then we'd lay a circle of razor wire behind which we'd set Claymore mines (a defensive device that would spray hundreds of deadly ball bearings with a killing range of 50 meters). We'd dig in, set up, and begin operations."

"They'd keep us busy 24/7 either firing, pulling guard duty, or moving dirt from one spot to another. At the time it didn't make any sense. We were a crew of forty-five 18-19 year olds, and our boss was a 21-year-old second lieutenant. The constant labor helped keep our minds busy.

"A 105mm howitzer fires a forty pound shell about 3.5' long and about 4" in diameter. Behind the shell the loaders place 1-4 bags of powder, depending on the distance. All the calculations for targeting were done by the second looey and were done manually, factoring the coordinates, the type of ordnance being used, altitude of the firing position, etc. We'd calculate and set the fuse depending on whether you wanted an airburst, bunker buster, or whatever. We wouldn't use airbursts if there were any friendlies in the area. They were wicked destructive. When possible we'd fire a smoke round to see if we were on target. Many times, the calls for support would come in from the infantry unit to 'fire for effect' meaning, 'we're in deep shit, fire the real stuff now!' Our battery could cover an area with a 7-mile radius.

"Each gun had a crew of six to operate, but often times you'd make do with 4-5 guys. There were two loaders, a gunner, an assistant gunner, and two powder men. When I first arrived, my job was to keep a constant flow of 100 pound crates from the ammo hooch to our parapet. Eventually, I worked my way to loader and gunner. We were there to protect our guys, and we took the job seriously. When there was a fire mission, often at night, we could aim and fire up to 6 rounds per minute, and the barrage might last 10-15 minutes.

"We had two M55 Quad 50 caliber machine guns to protect our battery from direct enemy attacks. Each had four barrels, situated in a square, capable of rapid firing bullets the size of a fat man's fingers. One of those guns could chop down a forest. I'd never seen anything like it.

"For artillery units, the most dangerous situations were being situated in valleys. Most of the batteries that were overrun during the war occurred in the lowlands. Mountaintops were safer, but certainly not safe. Virtually all attacks occurred at night.

"On occasion our battery would be mixed in with those firing larger artillery pieces. One night we were in our hooches when the 8" guns started firing over us towards the enemy position. The walls shook, dirt fell, and the roar was deafening. I can't even imagine being on the receiving end of one of those shells. One of the guns had a 35' foot barrel with a range of 35 miles. Our 105's were like peashooters in contrast."

"I don't recall ever seeing anyone using earplugs or anything. It's amazing we can still hear. You just became immune to the noise, the bugs, the heat, and being tired."

"I arrived in Vietnam in the fall of 1968, several months after the Tet offensive. Shortly thereafter, a proclamation came down from headquarters instructing all troops, 'There will be no more taking of ears as souvenirs.' I couldn't imagine anyone doing that, but there had to be some reason for the order.

"I came in direct contact with the enemy on only one occasion. Every day, six guys were assigned to patrol the area around our defensive perimeter. We'd go out about 1-2 kilometers. Over time we became increasingly complacent, as we didn't expect to see anyone.

One day we came upon two Viet Cong soldiers swimming in the river. They appeared as shocked to see us as we were. They grabbed their clothes and ran into the nearby tree line. We never got a shot off, but we called our artillery and gave them the coordinates of the direction they were heading. Our guys fired off about 200 rounds. We definitely wanted to discourage anyone from getting near us.

"I've never been so cold as I was in Vietnam. People think it was hot, and it was, but it was also cold. We'd get soaked to the bone out on patrol, and we were in the mountains. I thought I'd never warm up.

"I was with a group of newbies on patrol one day. We were at the border of some grasslands and a forest and thought we heard something. We stopped to listen, and it continued. We decided to throw grenades towards the sound, which was really stupid. Several bounced off trees back at us. We retreated quickly, and miraculously no one was hurt. We used to open the back of Claymore mines to borrow some of the C4 explosive for cooking purposes. It was the texture of Play-Doh, and you could light a small portion of it to heat up a cup of water. Once I kicked some of it, only later realizing how dangerous that was. But we were only 18.

"It was a culture shock returning home. There was a big difference in how I was treated (in civilian America) when I returned in the summer of 1969 vs. when I left in 1968. But I was home and in one piece, and I had the GI Bill and was headed to college and the hope of normalcy."

RANDY MILLER

I hosted former KC shock jock Randy Miller and his producer Michael Seward for lunch as a 'thank you' for their having me as a guest on one of their podcasts.

Randy was a big-time morning show host in Kansas City radio starting in the mid-1980's. He now runs an ad agency and hosts a daily on-line show. He's a personable, funny, and likeable fellow.

During the course of conversation, he shared some of the stunts that gained him some notoriety. On one occasion he sent his sidekick and an Egyptian intern out on a prank. He dressed them in orange prison jumpsuits and handcuffed them together. Randy instructed them to go to a wealthy neighborhood south of I-435 on State Line (the road separating Missouri and Kansas) at 8 am. They were to knock on doors and politely ask if they could borrow a hacksaw. He told them, "Make sure you are in Kansas (where suburban police deal with lesser miscreants than do their Missouri counterparts). And make sure you are excessively polite."

Unfortunately, the two young goofballs found themselves on the Missouri side of the line. Predictably, a handful of concerned citizens alerted the authorities, and the two were quickly apprehended. Randy was on the air when he received a pleading phone call from his intern, "Tell the cops that this is just a stunt. I'm lying facedown with a shotgun pointed at my head." And Randy's initial reply was, "Who is this?"

Later all was straightened out. The penalty required Randy to spend 40 hours of community service writing comedy ads for the KCPD.

Randy explained that once upon a time outrageousness was acceptable and profitable. The antic that would get you fired at station A would get you hired at a higher salary at station B. Accordingly, he moved around going from KC to Chicago to San Diego to KC to San Francisco et al. When he first arrived in San Diego, a mini-storm of protest was underway aimed at a veteran radio host in the area. For ten years, this particular host used a character with a comical Asian dialect as a foil for many jokes. The Asian Anti-Defamation League was in an uproar over the matter.

Randy defended the guy, even though he didn't know him, and

the wrath of the AADL was quickly redirected at the newcomer. In response, Randy devoted a show where listeners would call in with their favorite Asian joke. When he went off the air, his boss awaited, "Are you crazy? These people want you roasted on a spit. You will have to give a big-time apology, or you're gone."

Randy calmed him down, and said, "Don't worry, I'll apologize on the air this coming Friday at 8:30 am." The date came and the studio was crammed with television news crews, representatives of the AADL, newspaper reporters, and the station executives.

At the appointed hour, Randy explained to a record-breaking listening audience the circumstance leading up to this hour, and he began, "I am velly, velly, solly." And he was fired on the spot.

Author's note: You can listen to Randy at his podcast www.RandyMillerRadio.com. Check out episode 55.

BOB FAY

I received a call from a friend and former client I hadn't seen for many years. Someone had given him a copy of my book, and he called to say that he enjoyed it. Later, he stopped by, and we had a visit during which he shared a story of his own.

"Your basic training story, particularly your experience of speaking up during the character guidance session, reminded me of my own experience during the Korean War. After two years attending MU, I was drafted. After completing basic training several officers took me aside and asked me to sign up for officer training. I declined, but then, in an offhand manner, I expressed concerns about the war. They apparently didn't care for my political views, and several weeks later I was on a troop ship bound for Korea.

"By December of 1952 the war had reached a stalemate. U.S.

forces had ceased offensive operations, but the Chinese were still going full force. We were positioned on a series of hills on one side of the valley that later became the 38th parallel (now separating North and South Korea), and the Chinese were on the mountain range on the opposite side."

"My platoon was positioned in the 'point' bunker, aka the closest to the enemy and furthest from friendlies. Every night the Chinese would probe our defenses, and we were engaged in constant skirmishes. I was one of only 25 in our company (out of approx. 200 men) who came home unscathed.

"General Maxwell Taylor (then head of all forces in Korea) decided to take a tour of the front lines, and I was chosen to be his guide. After he learned I played bridge, I was invited to complete a foursome with three senior officers. Bridge gave me several days respite from the front lines, perhaps saving my life."

"We once went 45 days without eating a hot meal. I went nine consecutive months without eating at a table, so I constantly dreamed of a home-cooked meal sitting in our family dining room. When I returned home, my Mom announced she was having a picnic in our backyard with friends and family to celebrate my safe return. She noted my disappointment, and I explained. She then moved the picnic inside."

WAVERLY

This last story was told to me by a little girl named Waverly.

Once upon a time, two little boys were visiting Useppa Island with their Mom and Dad. After lunch, the boys ran down to a sandy playground that was situated near the beach. The first little boy ran to the swing set and started to swing as high as he could. The second little boy sat down on the grass to take off his shoes.

The boy on the swing was swinging higher and higher until he flew off and landed in a heap in the sand and immediately yelled to whomever might listen, "I'm all right!"

The boy in the grass started dancing in a frenzy and tore at his clothes. It turned out he sat on an anthill, and the biting wee beasties covered him in an instant.

Nearby, the little Magic Mermaid Princess was flying overhead and heard their cries for help.

On most days she's a normal little girl, but with a wriggle of her nose she becomes the Magic Mermaid Princess. She can fly like an eagle and swim like a tuna. She also has unusually keen hearing, and she is very strong. She flew to the sounds of distress.

So she swooped down upon the boy on the anthill. Was he ever surprised!

She picked him up and set him down gently in the nearby surf. The ants floated away, and his bites were soothed by the salty sea.

Then she flew over to the little boy who landed in a pile of sand, and she picked him up and set him down by his brother.

The boys looked at each other and then back at the Magic Mermaid Princess. She gave each boy a butterfly kiss and then swam off into the ocean. And Finn said, "Charlie, was that a tiny flying mermaid?"

THE END

ABOUT THE AUTHOR

Charles (Chuck) Wells worked as a financial and strategic adviser to community hospitals. He was born in West Plains, Missouri and raised in Bowling Green, Missouri, and Prairie Village, Kansas. He received a BA from Drury University and an MBA from Harvard Business School. He is now a collector of stories, writer, banjo aspirant, climber of 14ers, farmer, husband to Judy, Dad to Lucy and Ben, and Papa to Waverly, Finn, and Charlie. He lives in Mission Hill, Kansas and Sanibel, Florida.

Chuck and nephew Wylie on Salt Spring Island, British Columbia

You may connect with the author on line:
    Email: cbjwells@sprynet.com
    Blog: http://OrdinaryPeopleWhoAren't.blogspot.com